# HEALTHY COOKING FOR TWO

## REVISED AND UPDATED

# HEALTHY COOKING FOR TWO

Brenda Shriver, Author
of No Red Meat,
and Angela Shriver, R.D.

**REVISED &
UPDATED**

THE SUMMIT GROUP
Fort Worth, Texas

The Summit Group

1227 West Magnolia, Suite 500, Fort Worth, Texas 76104

10   9   8   7   6   5   4   3   2   1

Library of Congress Cataloging-in-Publication Data

**Shriver, Brenda, 1941-**
  Healthy cooking for two/Brenda Shriver and Angela
Shriver.—Rev. ed.
    p. cm.
    Includes index.
    ISBN 1-56530-179-X

    1. Low-fat diet—Recipes. 2. Low-cholesterol diet—Recipes
I. Shriver, Angela. II. Title.
RM237.7.S556  1996
641.5'638—dc20                                      94-48783
                                                    CIP

*Book design by Sean Walker.*
*Cover photograph by Truitt Photography.*
*Dinnerware compliments of Plate & Platter, Fort Worth, Texas.*

# Nutrient Analysis Data Source

Nutrient composition of all recipes was
calculated by a registered dietitian using the
Computrition software program.
Nutritional data on some specialty items was
provided by the producer.

*In memory of my mom, Oma J. Day*

# Contents

Foreword ................................................ xi

Acknowledgments ............................... xiii

Preface ................................................ xv

Introduction ........................................ xvii

Food Guide Pyramid ........................... xix

Your Total Fat Allowance ..................... xxv

Ways to Reduce Your Fat Intake ................. xxvi

Appetizers ............................................ 1

   Dips ................................................ 3

   Meats .............................................. 14

   Snacks ............................................ 16

Soups ................................................ 25

Breads ................................................ 61

Salads ................................................ 93

   Salad Dressings ................................. 129

Main Dishes:

Meats ................................................ 141

   Poultry ............................................ 143

      Baked ........................................ 145

      Grilled ....................................... 162

      Italian ........................................ 168

      Mexican ..................................... 176

      Various ....................................... 185

   Seafood .......................................... 207

   Red Meat ........................................ 241

Meatless .............................................. 253

Vegetables ........................................... 275

Desserts .............................................. 319

Sauces ................................................ 363

Appendix:

   Herbs .............................................. 381

   Spices ............................................. 387

   Measurement Equivalents
      and Substitutions ....................... 389

   Healthy Menus for Any Occasion ...... 395

   Index .............................................. 407

# F o r e w o r d

Welcome to the heart-healthy kitchen of Brenda Shriver!

Brenda has done it again...provided her reader with delicious heart-healthy "down-home-cooking" recipes, but with a new twist: *Healthy Cooking for Two* (easily adaptable for the single...just freeze for later or refrigerate for a fast meal the next day). As usual, she includes an accurate analysis of the calories, protein, fat, carbohydrate, fiber, cholesterol and sodium, those concerns and "bugaboos" of modern living. She even provides the reader with sample menus to make planning and shopping just that much easier for a time- and nutrition-conscious couple / single.

Brenda's daughter-in-law, Angie, a well-qualified registered dietitian, has written additional material that will give interesting and useful information for most readers. Angie's explanation of the food pyramid and how to use it effectively should be most valuable.

Many cooks feel intimidated by large, family-size recipes. They hate to waste food, don't have extra freezer space, and are fearful of failure when trying to reduce the yield of a recipe, let alone reducing the fat content of the recipe by major proportions. Brenda has done it for them! Her recipes are a compilation of family favorites and favorite recipes of friends which she has adapted to small-size, low-fat healthy eating. Her recipes range from appetizers to desserts with everything else in between. In fact, this is the only cookbook a nutrition-conscious cook will need.

*Ann M. Tinsley, Ph.D., R.D.*
*Associate Professor,*
*Department of Nutritional Sciences,*
*University of Arizona*
*Tucson, Arizona*

# Acknowledgments

I have been blessed by God in so many ways and with so many gifts, with my family being my most precious gift. But, he has also blessed me with a love of cooking and a curiosity to experiment in the kitchen. Therefore, my first acknowledgment of thanks and gratitude is to God, for giving me this gift and making it possible for me to pursue this dream.

A special thank you to Angela Shriver, R.D., my daughter-in-law and my coauthor, for providing nutritional information and a helpful explanation of the Food Guide Pyramid, for the many recipes she tested, all the questions she helped me find the answers to, and for her patience.

To Ann Tinsley, Ph.D., R.D., for providing such a glowing foreword for this book and for her encouragement and faith in what I was doing. To John Fry, my "help-desk," who kept my computer in order and spent endless hours try-ing to help me understand the complexities of this wonderful machine.

A big thank-you and hugs to my daughter, Audrey Scalzo, who has a B.A. degree in home economics, for her faith in me and for testing recipes.

To my son, John, III, for his support and pa-tience while helping me with the computer and his support to Angela.

And finally to my husband, John, my most vocal critic and my strongest supporter. John, for all the "different" foods I tested on you, for your patience, and most of all for your faith in me.

# Preface

In 1982 we became aware that my husband, John, had coronary artery disease. John's cardiologist mandated that he change his eating habits and continue a vigorous exercise program. I was willing to change my method of cooking but needed some guidance. Finding the recipes in "heart cookbooks" unsatisfactory, I began to experiment with my own recipes and to create new ones. The result was my first cookbook, *No Red Meat*, published in 1989.

Upon reflection, it seems I have been involved in food preparation and/or food handling most of my life. I grew up assisting in a family-owned restaurant and during three summer vacations I worked in different restaurants and learned various aspects of food preparation and handling. After we were married and started our family, I was very happy to be in my own kitchen and apply the different aspects of food preparation I had been taught over the years. As our children went off to school I became involved in various volunteer activities, many of which were food related. I enjoy working with food and find a special challenge in creating nutritious, attractive, and economical meals.

When we moved to Texas in 1988, we came without children or extended family. After the moving boxes were cleared away and we were beginning to feel more settled, I stopped to consider our position and realized we had come full circle. We started as a couple, adding children, then extended family and friends, now we were back to two people again. Which also meant I had gone from cooking for any number of people back to cooking for two. I could relate with people whom in the past I have heard comment, "I can't cook for just two people" or "It's not worth the effort to cook just for the two of us." From this realization came the idea for a

new cookbook, which is presented here as *Healthy Cooking for Two*.

Many households consist of career couples or newlyweds, as well as the "Baby Boomer" generation—who are now becoming "Empty Nesters"—and the elderly. I think we must recognize the many subdivisions that coexist in this group and the fact that each subgroup has its own specific health and nutritional challenges. I think there is a need for this cookbook to serve the needs of these people.

*Healthy Cooking for Two* meets the needs of people in their search for nutritional recipes for two servings. Included here is very basic information about the new Food Guide Pyramid, developed by the U.S. Department of Agriculture. I suggest you study this guide closely and try to plan your daily intake of foods within these guidelines.

This book has a wide variety of nutritious, low-fat, low-cholesterol, and economical recipes, which are mostly for two servings. I have also included a few basic recipes which have more than two servings for those occasions when you might be entertaining. Also, some of the recipes freeze well and can be prepared ahead of time for those busy days. The recipes are short, simple to create, and call for common ingredients readily found in the neighborhood grocery.

It is my hope that through this book, I will be able to share my love of healthy cooking with other people, and encourage them by making this style of eating a little easier and more appealing. Whether on medically restricted diets or just health conscious, hopefully these recipes will help you in maintaining a healthy, good-tasting, low-fat, low-cholesterol diet.

*Brenda Shriver*

HEALTHY COOKING FOR TWO

# Introduction

The Food Guide Pyramid was developed by the United States Department of Agriculture to help you make healthier food choices. It is based on the "Dietary Guidelines for Americans," which is nutritional advice for healthy individuals two years of age or older. The Food Guide Pyramid is composed of four levels. At the base of the Pyramid, or first level, is the bread, cereal, rice, and pasta group. The foods in this group supply energy from carbohydrates and provide vitamins, minerals, and some fiber. You need the most servings from this group. The second level contains the vegetable and fruit groups which also supply vitamins, minerals, and fiber. The third level contains two food groups primarily of animal origin: dairy products and meat/meat alternatives. These are important sources of protein, calcium, iron, and zinc. The tip of the pyramid is the fourth and smallest level. It contains fats, oils, and sweets. These provide few nutrients, are high in calories, and should be used sparingly.

The Food Guide Pyramid shows a range of servings from each group to help you choose a variety of foods and eat the right amount of calories to maintain a healthy weight. The number of servings right for you depends on your calorie needs. The National Academy of Sciences suggests the following daily calorie levels:

| |
|---|
| 1,600 calories for sedentary women and some older adults. |
| 2,200 calories for most children, teenage girls, active women, and many sedentary men. |
| Pregnant or breastfeeding women may need somewhat more calories. |
| 2,800 calories for teenage boys, many active men, and some very active women. |

And the table below tells you approximately how many servings to choose from each food group to meet your calorie needs.

| | Many women, older adults | Children, teen girls, active women, most men | Teen boys, active men |
|---|---|---|---|
| Calorie Needs | about 1,600 | about 2,200 | about 2,800 |
| Bread Group Servings | 6 | 9 | 11 |
| Vegetable Group Servings | 3 | 4 | 5 |
| Fruit Group Servings | 2 | 3 | 4 |
| Milk Group Servings | 2-3** | 2-3** | 2-3** |
| Meat Group Servings | 2, for a total of 5 ounces | 2, for a total of 6 ounces | 2-3, for a total of 7 ounces |

*\*Women who are pregnant or breastfeeding, teenagers, and young adults to age twenty-four need three servings. Many authorities suggest that all adult women could benefit from three servings per day as milk is our best source of calcium, and women are most at risk for osteoporosis.*

# Food Guide Pyramid

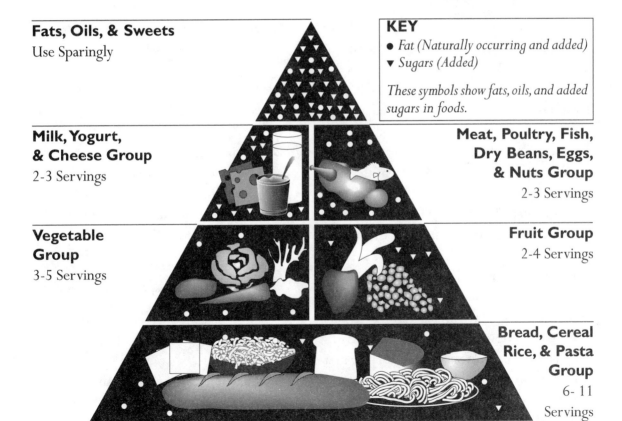

**Fats, Oils, & Sweets**
Use Sparingly

**KEY**
● *Fat (Naturally occurring and added)*
▼ *Sugars (Added)*

*These symbols show fats, oils, and added sugars in foods.*

**Milk, Yogurt,
& Cheese Group**
2-3 Servings

**Meat, Poultry, Fish,
Dry Beans, Eggs,
& Nuts Group**
2-3 Servings

**Vegetable
Group**
3-5 Servings

**Fruit Group**
2-4 Servings

**Bread, Cereal
Rice, & Pasta
Group**
6- 11
Servings

The Food Guide Pyramid shows the relative amounts of fat (naturally occurring and added) and sugars (added) in each food group. As you can see, the highest concentration is in the fats, oils, and sweets group. But fat and added sugars can also be found in other foods such as cheese or ice cream from the milk group and French fries or fried zucchini from the vegetable group.

The Food Guide Pyramid focuses on fat because the typical American diet is too high in fat. A high-fat diet increases your risk for cardiovascular disease and some types of cancers, such as breast and colon cancer. It has also been associated with obesity, diabetes, and hypertension. Diets low in fat may reduce these risks and can help control your weight. So, your best step toward disease prevention and better health is to reduce the total amount of fat in your diet.

## What Counts As a Serving?

### Milk Group
*1 cup milk or yogurt
*1½ ounces natural cheese
*2 ounces processed cheese

### Meat Group
*2-3 ounces cooked lean meat, poultry, or fish
*½ cup cooked dry beans, 1 egg, or 2 tablespoons peanut butter count as 1 ounce lean meat

### Vegetable Group
*1 cup raw, leafy vegetables
*½ cup other vegetables, cooked or chopped raw
*¾ cup vegetable juice

### Fruit Group
*1 medium apple, banana, or orange
*½ cup chopped cooked or canned fruit
*¾ cup fruit juice

*Bread Group*
\*1 slice bread
\*1 ounce ready-to-eat cereal
\*½ cup cooked cereal, rice, or pasta
\*½ bagel or hamburger bun

What about cholesterol? Cholesterol, a fat-like substance, can also increase your risk for cardiovascular disease by raising the blood cholesterol level. Dietary cholesterol is found only in foods of animal origin: meat, poultry, fish, milk and milk products, and egg yolks. The National Cholesterol Education Program and the American Heart Association recommend limiting cholesterol intake to three hundred milligrams or less per day. To control your intake of cholesterol, follow the Food Guide Pyramid, keeping your total fat to the amount that's right for you.

You do not need to completely eliminate all foods high in cholesterol. You can include three to four egg yolks a week, including those used in cooking. Use lower-fat dairy products and occasionally substitute vegetable proteins, such as dry beans and peas, for animal proteins. In addition to dietary cholesterol, you should also limit saturated fat intake, which has an even greater impact on raising the blood cholesterol level. Saturated fats are found in animal products, such as meat, poultry, fish, eggs, and dairy, as well as in tropical oils such as palm, palm kernel, and coconut oils.

The American Heart Association recommends limiting saturated fat to less than 10 percent of calories (one-third of total fat intake). To accomplish this, keep total fat intake within recommended levels and choose fat mostly from foods higher in polyunsaturated

fats, such as sunflower, corn, safflower, soybean, and cottonseed oils, or monounsaturated fats, found in olive, canola, and peanut oils.

What about trans-fatty acids? What are they, and what is their relationship to cholesterol? A 1992 U.S. Department of Agriculture study showed that trans-fatty acids raise cholesterol as much as saturated fats. Trans-fatty acids are found in margarine and shortening, cookies, cakes, pies, frostings, chips, crackers, and many other commercially packaged foods. Trans-fatty acids are formed when food manufacturers hydrogenate (or partially saturate) a liquid oil to make it more solid. This process keeps fats from becoming rancid. It makes margarine spread more easily, and it makes baked goods more tender and flaky.

Does this mean you should switch from margarine back to butter? No. Butter is still the worst choice and margarine-butter blends aren't much better. Choose a margarine spread that is very low-fat or one that is whipped with water (a "light" or "diet" margarine). Unfortunately, the amount of "trans" fat is not listed on food labels. If a label lists both the monounsaturated and polyunsaturated fats, you can estimate the amount of "trans" fat in the food by subtracting the saturated, mono-, and polyunsaturated fats from the total fat. Here are a few ways to avoid "trans" fat:

- *Use canola, olive oil, or another liquid vegetable oil instead of butter, margarine, or shortening whenever possible.*

- *Choose foods that are labeled "saturated-fat-free." These are also low in "trans" fat.*

- *Avoid deep-fried foods. Choose lower-fat processed foods such as reduced fat or nonfat crackers, cookies, chips, etc.*

There are many different types of fats in foods, each having some or no effect on blood cholesterol levels. Choosing foods with the right type of fat can be overwhelming. Just remember . . . the most crucial step you can make in reducing your risk from chronic disease is to simply reduce your total fat intake.

# Your Total Fat Allowance

How much dietary fat is right for you? The American Heart Association and other health authorities recommend that Americans, age two years or older, limit total fat intake to less than 30 percent of calories. So, if you take in 1,600 calories, that amounts to 53 grams of fat, 73 grams of fat in a 2,200-calorie diet, and 93 grams in a 2,800-calorie diet. A daily tally of your fat intake is not necessary, but you may want to do a fat checkup once in a while to make sure you're on the right track. If you find you are eating too much fat, choose lower-fat foods from all food groups more often and cut down on added fat such as margarine, gravy, and salad dressing. (There are many fat-free salad dressings now available. A recipe for fat-free gravy can be found in *No Red Meat* by Brenda Shriver and Ann Tinsley.)

# Ways To Reduce Your Fat Intake

One way you can help reduce the total fat and cholesterol content in your diet is by reading food labels. Reading food labels can tell you how much fat and cholesterol are in a product as well as type of fats found in an item.

By using a simple formula, you can compute the percentage of calories derived from fat in a particular food product:

$$\frac{\text{grams of fat/serving} \times 9 \times 100}{\text{total calories/serving}} = \%$$

*Note: There are 9 calories/gram of fat*

*Example: 8 oz. 1% milk*
*Calories:     100*
*Fat:          3 grams*

$$\frac{3\ g\ of\ fat \times 9\ calories/g\ fat \times 100}{100\ calories} = 27\%$$

*27% of total calories is derived from fat.*

(The new food label shows the number of calories from fat. This makes your work easier. Just divide this number by the total calories to get the percentage.) One-percent milk is a good food choice because its fat count is below the 30 percent of total calories recommended by the American Heart Association and other health authorities. Skim milk is also a good choice for your diet. Reading the ingredient list will tell you the type of fat in a product. Avoid products containing the following saturated fats high on the ingredient list:

- Lard or animal fat
- Coconut oil
- Palm or palm kernel oil
- Vegetable shortening, hydrogenated fat or oil
- Whole milk solids
- Cream
- Butter

Low-fat cooking techniques and modifying recipes with low-fat substitutions are other ways you can reduce your total fat and cholesterol intake.

When preparing your meals, reduce fat intake by using the following cooking tips:

- *Sauté or stir-fry vegetables with very little fat (one teaspoon vegetable oil) or simply use water, wine, or broth.*

- *Use nonstick pans and spray with vegetable spray.*

- *Put olive oil, or any polyunsaturated oil, in a small spray bottle and use lightly as a spray.*

- *To make thick sauces or gravies without fat, mix the thickening agent (cornstarch or flour) with a small amount of cold liquid, then stir this mixture slowly into the hot liquid you want to thicken and bring back to a boil.*

- *Chill soups, stews, and gravies, and skim off fat before reheating.*

- *Use lean cuts of meat (flank steak, round steak or roasts, sirloin or tenderloin, loin pork chops, extra lean ground beef), and cut off all visible fat before cooking. Include fish and poultry more often. Remove the skin from poultry.*

- *Bake, broil, grill, poach, or microwave instead of frying.*

- *Use herbs and seasonings in combination with lemon juice or vinegar instead of added fat.*

Try reducing fat by one-quarter to one-third in baked goods. This works well in quick breads, cookies, and muffins, but may not work well for cakes. When substituting liquid oil for solid fats, use ¼ less than the recipe calls for. For cakes or pie crusts, use a recipe that already calls for oil. If a cake calls for extra oil for a "richer" recipe, try it without.

Simple recipe substitutions can turn a high-fat dish into a healthy one. You can control the amount and type of fat and cholesterol in recipes by making the following substitutions:

| Instead of | Use |
| --- | --- |
| 1 whole egg | 2 egg whites or ¼ cup egg substitute |
| butter or hydrogenated shortening (i.e., Crisco) | margarine (where liquid vegetable oil is listed as the first ingredient) or vegetable oil |

| Instead of | Use |
| --- | --- |
| sour cream | fat-free or light sour cream, plain low-fat or nonfat yogurt, buttermilk, or blended low-fat cottage cheese (If yogurt is to be heated, add 1 tbsp. cornstarch to 1 cup of yogurt to prevent separation.) |
| 1 cup heavy cream | 1 cup evaporated skimmed milk or ¾ cup buttermilk and ¼ cup oil or Cool Whip Light |
| whole milk | skim, 1 percent milk, or evaporated skimmed milk |

| Instead of | Use |
|---|---|
| hard cheese | low-fat (less than 5 grams/serving) or fat-free cheese, or simply reduce the amount of hard cheese called for |
| bacon | Smoked turkey breast, Canadian bacon, imitation bacon bits, lean ham |
| 1 oz. (1 square) baking chocolate | 3 tbsp. powdered cocoa + 1 tsp. oil |

| Instead of | Use |
|---|---|
| canned condensed soup: | |
| cream of celery | 1 cup white sauce* + 2 tbsp. finely chopped sautéed celery and ½ tsp. celery salt |
| cream of chicken | 1¼ cups white sauce + 1 tsp. chicken bouillon granules |
| cream of mushroom | 1 cup white sauce + ½ cup chopped sautéed mushrooms |

*White Sauce Recipe

In this cookbook, Brenda incorporates low-fat cooking techniques, and recipe modifications have already been done for you. Each recipe lists the amounts of calories, fat, and cholesterol per serving to help you stay within your daily allowance.

Use this cookbook along with the Food Guide Pyramid to make healthier food choices and reduce your total fat intake. Eat a variety of foods from the five food groups. Choose more breads, cereals, pasta, and grains. Eat more fruits and vegetables. Choose low-fat foods from all food groups more often.

Use fats, oils and sweets in moderation. Include low-fat cooking when preparing meals, and try modifying your own favorite recipes. By making these changes gradually, you can develop healthier eating habits and reduce your risk from chronic disease.

*Angela Shriver, R.D.*

*Angela Shriver, R.D., received her bachelor's degree from the University of Arizona and served her dietetic internship at United Health Services Hospitals, Inc., in Johnson City, New York.*

# APPETIZERS

I try to keep my appetizers as simple as possible and also to keep them at a minimum. I don't want to stuff my guests with appetizers and spoil their appetite for the main course. However, I do make an extra effort to have an attractive presentation (on the next page are some suggestions).

When using fresh vegetables, keep them refrigerated and crisp until serving time. A nice variety of colors and textures adds appeal; whether using vegetables or fruits, be sure to use only the freshest fruits and vegetables available to you. There is a wide variety of low-fat or nonfat products on the market today. The nonfat or low-fat cheeses, sour cream, cream cheese, and mayonnaise make it possible to enjoy a wide variety of foods.

You will also find chips and crackers which have been baked, not fried, with or without salt added, to accompany dips and spreads or to eat alone as a snack.

This is an opportunity to include fruits or vegetables in your diet as suggested in the Food Guide Pyramid. Following are some simple favorites I use to start a meal.

# Making an Attractive Presentation

When using red or green peppers, cut in half, either vertically or horizontally. Remove the seeds and membrane and fill with your favorite dip.

Start with a small colorful head of green, red, or purple cabbage, and cut a thin slice off the bottom end so it will stand alone. Cut a hollow bowl in the top of the cabbage (save cabbage you cut out for another dish), and fill with your favorite dip. *This requires at least one cup of dip to make an attractive presentation.

For an unusual container, use fresh pineapple, cantaloupe, or honeydew shells as containers for a fresh fruit salad, dips, or spreads.

Instead of breaking cauliflower and broccoli into flowerettes, slice vertically into thin slices.

Using a round loaf of pumpernickel, rye, French, or any type of course bread, cut the very top portion off and hollow out the center, leaving about a one-inch shell. Use the bread you removed from the loaf as a dipper for the dip. Fill the hollow bread with your favorite dip. *This requires one to two cups of dip to make an attractive presentation, depending on the size of the loaf.

To give cucumber slices an attractive appearance, pull a fork down the length of cucumber to score the skin, then cut into slices.

Citrus fruits, especially oranges, lemons, and limes, are a natural for garnish. Slice them crosswise into thin slices for a nice garnish which can also be easily eaten.

I use fresh herbs as a garnish in almost every meal. This is such a simple touch, yet it adds color, fragrance, and appeal to the dish.

DIPS

# Betty's Crabmeat Dip

*To economize use imitation crab.*

1 (6 oz.) can white crabmeat (or imitation)

2 tablespoons fat-free sour cream

1 tablespoon fat-free mayonnaise

1 tablespoon minced onion

2 teaspoons minced red or green pepper

½ teaspoon Beau Monde seasoning

½ teaspoon dry mustard (or more to taste)

3 tablespoons seafood sauce (optional)

In a small bowl, combine crabmeat, sour cream, mayonnaise, onion, pepper, and seasonings; stir until well blended. Cover and chill for at least 30 minutes. Serve with fresh veggies or fat-free crackers.

Yield: 1 cup or 4 (¼ cup) servings

1 serving contains:

| Cal | Prot | Fat | Carb | Fiber | Chol | Sodium |
|------|------|-----|------|-------|------|--------|
| 62kc | 5g | 1g | 2g | 0g | 41mg | 175mg |

DIPS

# Sassy Clam Dip

*Colorful, easy, and good*

½ cup fat-free cottage cheese

2 tablespoons mild salsa

1 tablespoon thinly sliced green onion

1 tablespoon finely chopped red pepper

2 tablespoons minced clams, drained *

3 drops Louisiana Hot Sauce

In a small bowl, combine cottage cheese, salsa, onion, pepper, clams, and hot sauce. Chill for at least 30 minutes, serve with fresh raw veggies or fat-free crackers.

Yield: ¾ cup or 3 (2 tablespoons) servings

1 serving contains:

| Cal | Prot | Fat | Carb | Fiber | Chol | Sodium |
|-----|------|-----|------|-------|------|--------|
| 34kc | 6g | 0g | 2g | 0g | 6mg | 11mg |

*If you use a 6½ oz. can minced clams, save the remaining clams and juice; add a bottle of clam juice for making clam sauce to serve over pasta.*

DIPS

# Baked Crabmeat Dip

*Use as appetizer or serve with soup for supper.*

1 (6 oz.) can white crabmeat

½ cup fat-free sour cream

¼ cup fat-free mayonnaise

1 tablespoon fat-free Italian salad dressing

2 tablespoons minced onion

1 tablespoon white wine

1 teaspoon minced fresh dill

2 bakery-fresh hoagie buns or hard rolls

Preheat oven to 350 degrees. In a small bowl, combine crabmeat, sour cream, mayonnaise, Italian dressing, onion, wine, and dill. Carefully cut the very top ⅛-¼" off rolls, set aside. Hollow out the rolls leaving ¼" shell intact. Carefully spoon dip into roll shells, replace top on rolls, wrap in aluminum foil. Bake in 350-degree oven for 1 hour. Serve hot by dipping bread cubes into dip, also eating the roll itself.

Yield: 6 servings as appetizer

1 serving contains:

| Cal | Prot | Fat | Carb | Fiber | Chol | Sodium |
|------|------|-----|------|-------|------|--------|
| 88kc | 8g | 1g | 11g | 0g | 34mg | 255mg |

DIPS

# Creme de Cassis-Yogurt Dip

*An appealing dip for appetizer or dessert*

¼ cup fat-free vanilla yogurt, sweetened with
  artificial sweetener

½ banana, mashed fine

¼ teaspoon creme de cassis (black currant liquor)

lettuce leaf

1 cup fresh fruit (strawberries, pears, nectarines,
  bananas, etc.) treated with ascorbic acid or
  lemon juice

In a small bowl, combine yogurt, banana, and liquor, cover and refrigerate 10-20 minutes to allow flavors to blend. When ready to serve, place lettuce on a small serving dish, arrange fruit and bowl of yogurt on plate, or drizzle yogurt over fruit. Serve with wooden picks. Serve immediately.

Yield: 2 servings

1 serving contains:

| Cal | Prot | Fat | Carb | Fiber | Chol | Sodium |
|-----|------|-----|------|-------|------|--------|
| 71kc | 2g | 1g | 16g | 3g | 1mg | 23mg |

DIPS

# Creamy Vegetable Dip

*This is so simple, yet very tasty.*

1 tablespoon fat-free mayonnaise

½ cup fat-free sour cream

1 tablespoon chopped green onion

1 teaspoon parsley

½ teaspoon fresh dill

¼ teaspoon Beau Monde seasonings

In a small bowl, combine all ingredients. Cover and refrigerate 30 minutes to allow the flavors to blend. Serve with assorted fresh veggies.

Yield: 2 (3 tablespoons) servings

1 serving contains:

| Cal | Prot | Fat | Carb | Fiber | Chol | Sodium |
|-----|------|-----|------|-------|------|--------|
| 19kc | 2g | 0g | 3g | 0g | 25mg | 71mg |

D I P S

# Fiesta Dip

*Corn gives this color and a different texture.*

¼ cup fat-free cream cheese

2 tablespoons mild salsa

1 tablespoon chopped green chilies

1 tablespoon chopped red pepper

¼ cup frozen or canned corn, drained, thawed

In a small bowl, combine all ingredients, cover and refrigerate 30 minutes to let flavors blend. Serve with fresh veggies, crackers, or low-fat, baked tortilla chips.

Yield: 2 (¼ cup) servings

1 serving contains:

| Cal | Prot | Fat | Carb | Fiber | Chol | Sodium |
|-----|------|-----|------|-------|------|--------|
| 35kc | 3g | 1g | 7g | 0g | 31mg | 87mg |

D I P S

# Mock Guacamole

*It is hard to tell the difference between this and the real thing.*

1 (10½ oz.) can asparagus, drained very well

2 tablespoons chopped onion

½ cup chopped tomato

1 tablespoon lemon juice

1 clove garlic, minced

1 tablespoon fat-free mayonnaise

¼ teaspoon chili powder

⅛ teaspoon Louisiana Hot Sauce or as desired

Process drained asparagus in food processor until smooth; line strainer with paper towel and drain 20 minutes more. In a small mixing bowl, combine asparagus, onion, and tomato; add lemon juice, garlic, mayonnaise, chili powder, and hot sauce, stir to blend. Cover and refrigerate 20-30 minutes for flavors to blend.

Yield: 3 (⅓ cup) servings

1 serving contains:

| Cal | Prot | Fat | Carb | Fiber | Chol | Sodium |
|------|------|-----|------|-------|------|--------|
| 32kc | 2g | 0g | 6g | 1g | 0mg | 423mg |

DIPS

# Indian Dip

*Quick, easy, and great with fresh veggies*

½ cup fat-free cottage cheese

2 tablespoons low-fat mayonnaise

¼ teaspoon curry powder

2 teaspoons minced red pepper

2 teaspoons minced green pepper

In a small bowl, combine cottage cheese, mayonnaise, curry, and peppers; cover and chill for at least 30 minutes. Serve with fresh veggies.

Yield: 3 (3 tablespoons) servings

1 serving contains:

| Cal | Prot | Fat | Carb | Fiber | Chol | Sodium |
|------|------|-----|------|-------|------|--------|
| 48kc | 4g | 2g | 3g | 0g | 6mg | 142mg |

D I P S

# Salmon Dip

*An extra special treat*

½ cup fat-free plain yogurt

2 tablespoons minced, smoked salmon

2 tablespoons seeded, chopped cucumber

1 teaspoon finely chopped chives

pinch of fresh dill

In a small bowl, combine yogurt, salmon, cucumber, chives and dill; cover and chill for at least 1 hour. Serve with nonfat crackers or fresh veggies.

Yield: ¾ cup or 3 (4 tablespoons) servings

1 serving contains:

| Cal | Prot | Fat | Carb | Fiber | Chol | Sodium |
|------|------|-----|------|-------|------|--------|
| 39kc | 5g | 1g | 3g | 0g | 3mg | 137mg |

DIPS

# Shrimp Dip Olé

*Shrimp is always a favorite.*

4 oz. small shrimp, deveined, cooked and drained

1 tablespoon chopped green onion

1 tablespoon chopped red pepper

3 tablespoons salsa

2 tablespoons fat-free cream cheese, softened

1 tablespoon low-fat mayonnaise

Finely chop shrimp, leaving 3 whole for garnish. In a small mixing bowl, combine shrimp, onion, pepper, and salsa. In another small bowl, blend cream cheese and mayonnaise, add shrimp and vegetables, mix well. Cover and chill for at least 1 hour to let flavors blend. Serve with veggies or crackers.

Yield: 5 (2 tablespoons) servings

1 serving contains:

| Cal | Prot | Fat | Carb | Fiber | Chol | Sodium |
|-----|------|-----|------|-------|------|--------|
| 37kc | 5g | 1g | 1g | 0g | 52mg | 86mg |

DIPS

# Spicy Smoked Turkey Dip

*The salsa adds an extra zip to this dip.*

¼ cup fat-free cream cheese

¼ cup salsa

¼ cup finely chopped smoked turkey

1 tablespoon fresh chives

In a small mixing bowl, combine all ingredients. This can be served cold or hot. To heat: place in microwave-safe dish and heat on 50-percent power for 1 minute, stir and continue to heat for 1 minute more or until warm. Serve with fresh veggies.

Yield: 4 (3 tablespoons) servings

1 serving contains:

| Cal | Prot | Fat | Carb | Fiber | Chol | Sodium |
|------|------|-----|------|-------|------|--------|
| 24kc | 4g | 0g | 2g | 0g | 21mg | 226mg |

MEATS

# Lisa's Tortilla Rolls

*These make a nice appetizer for a Mexican dinner.*

2 tablespoons finely minced, cooked chicken breast

2 tablespoons fat-free cream cheese

2 teaspoons chopped black olives

2 teaspoons minced onion

2 fresh flour tortillas

½ cup salsa

In a small mixing bowl, combine chicken, cream cheese, olives, and onions. Divide the mixture between the 2 tortillas and spread, covering the top surface. Roll tortilla jelly-roll style, wrap in plastic wrap, refrigerate until ready to serve. When ready to serve, slice each roll into 8 slices, arrange on tray with salsa. Using toothpick, dip in salsa when ready to eat.

Yield: 4 (4 rolls each) servings

1 serving contains:

| Cal | Prot | Fat | Carb | Fiber | Chol | Sodium |
|-----|------|-----|------|-------|------|--------|
| 72kc | 5g | 2g | 7g | 1g | 17mg | 119mg |

MEATS

# Oriental Chicken Nibbles

*Spinach adds an exotic touch.*

1 boneless chicken breast half, skinned, cut into 1" cubes

¼ cup low-sodium teriyaki sauce

8-10 medium spinach leaves

1 teaspoon olive oil

2 teaspoons egg substitute

2 tablespoons fat-free sour cream

1½ teaspoons sugar

2 teaspoons rice vinegar

dash paprika

leaf lettuce (garnish)

4 cherry tomatoes (garnish)

Place the chicken cubes in a bowl, mix teriyaki sauce with chicken, cover and refrigerate for 30 minutes or longer. When ready to prepare: wash spinach, pour boiling water over it, drain well, set aside. Drain chicken. In a small nonstick skillet, heat olive oil on medium-high, add chicken and cook quickly until tender and no longer pink. Remove from skillet and let cool slightly. Place each chicken cube on the stem end of 1 spinach leaf, roll over once, folding leaf on both sides. Continue to roll, secure with wooden pick, and chill until ready to serve. In a bowl, combine egg substitute, sour cream, sugar, vinegar, and paprika. Cover and refrigerate until ready to serve. When ready to serve, arrange lettuce leaf on serving plate, place bowl with dip to one side of plate, arrange chicken nibbles and tomatoes on lettuce. Dip each cube into dip before eating.

Yield: 2 (4-5 cubes) servings

1 serving contains:

| Cal | Prot | Fat | Carb | Fiber | Chol | Sodium |
|------|------|-----|------|-------|------|--------|
| 113kc | 8g | 3g | 16g | 1g | 7mg | 771mg |

S N A C K S

# A p r i c o t - C h e e s e   S p r e a d

*Ginger adds interest to this delightfully easy spread.*

4 oz. fat-free cream cheese

1 tablespoon apricot preserves (all fruit, no sugar added)

3 dashes ground ginger (approx. $^1/_{16}$ tsp.)

In a small bowl, combine all ingredients; cover and refrigerate 30 minutes.

Yield: 5 (2 tablespoons) servings

1 serving contains:

| Cal | Prot | Fat | Carb | Fiber | Chol | Sodium |
|-----|------|-----|------|-------|------|--------|
| 31kc | 1g | 0g | 3g | 0g | 1mg | 34mg |

Serving Suggestion: Serve with tea breads or fat-free crackers.

Variations:

## Garlic-Herb Spread

*omit preserves and ginger, add:*

1 teaspoon minced onion

⅛ teaspoon garlic powder

⅛ teaspoon dried dill weed

½ teaspoon minced parsley

## Mexican Spread

*omit preserves and ginger, add:*

1-2 tablespoons salsa

S N A C K S

# Cucumber-Stuffed Tomatoes

*Very pretty and easy to serve*

*3 tablespoons shredded cucumber*

*3 tablespoons fat-free cream cheese*

*dash dill*

*dash garlic powder*

*2 teaspoons minced green onion, divided*

*8 cherry tomatoes*

Drain cucumber on paper towel. In a small bowl, combine cream cheese, dill, garlic powder, and 1 teaspoon onion; add cucumber. Cover and refrigerate for 20 minutes or more. Rinse and dry tomatoes, cut off tops, scoop out pulp (reserve for another use). Invert on paper towel to drain. Spoon cheese mixture into tomato shells, garnish with remaining onion.

Yield: 2 servings

1 serving contains:

| Cal | Prot | Fat | Carb | Fiber | Chol | Sodium |
|-----|------|-----|------|-------|------|--------|
| 22kc | 2g | 0g | 4g | 1g | 23mg | 68mg |

S N A C K S

# C u r r y - S t u f f e d   T o m a t o e s

*The curry enhances fresh tomatoes.*

*2 tablespoons fat-free cottage cheese*

*½ tablespoon fat-free mayonnaise*

*dash curry powder (or more)*

*1 teaspoon minced green onion*

*8 cherry tomatoes, rinsed and dried*

*1 teaspoon minced fresh parsley (optional)*

In a small bowl, combine cottage cheese, mayonnaise, curry, and green onion; cover and chill for at least 1 hour. Rinse and dry tomatoes, cut tops off, scoop out pulp (reserve for another use). Invert on paper towel to drain. Spoon curry dip into tomato shells, garnish with minced parsley.

Yield: 2 servings

1 serving contains:

| Cal | Prot | Fat | Carb | Fiber | Chol | Sodium |
|-----|------|-----|------|-------|------|--------|
| 23kc | 2g | 0g | 3g | 1g | 1mg | 26mg |

S N A C K S

# D e v i l e d   E g g s

*A delicious new way to have your eggs and eat them, too*

4 hard-boiled eggs

½ cup fat-free cottage cheese

2 tablespoons fat-free mayonnaise

1 teaspoon brown mustard

¼ teaspoon curry powder

¼ teaspoon turmeric

dash paprika

Peel eggs, cut in half top to bottom, discard yolks, set whites aside. In a small bowl, combine cottage cheese, mayonnaise, mustard, curry, and turmeric. Evenly divide the cheese mixture among the egg whites, place on serving dish and dust lightly with paprika.

Yield: 4 servings

1 serving contains:

| Cal | Prot | Fat | Carb | Fiber | Chol | Sodium |
|-----|------|-----|------|-------|------|--------|
| 35kc | 7g | 0g | 1g | 0g | 1mg | 104mg |

S N A C K S

# Marinated Mushrooms

*Eat alone or use to garnish a salad, delightfully simple.*

½ cup mushrooms, washed and stemmed

¼ cup fat-free oil Italian salad dressing

Place mushrooms in small bowl, pour dressing over them, cover and refrigerate for 8 hours or longer. Serve with toothpicks.

Yield: 2 servings

1 serving contains:

| Cal | Prot | Fat | Carb | Fiber | Chol | Sodium |
|------|------|-----|------|-------|------|--------|
| 13kc | 0g | 0g | 3g | 0g | 0mg | 283mg |

S N A C K S

# B a k e d   P o t a t o   S k i n s

*Serve with soup for a light supper.*

*2 small baking potatoes (approx. ½-¾ lb.)**

*1 teaspoon low-fat margarine*

*1 tablespoon chopped chives*

*1 teaspoon grated Parmesan cheese*

Preheat oven to 400 degrees. Scrub potatoes, pierce skins with fork, place in oven and bake about one hour or until tender and skins are crisp. When cool enough to handle, cut in half and scoop potato pulp out*, leaving about ⅓" of pulp in the shell. Return shells to oven, bake about 10 minutes; spread margarine around the insides of shells, sprinkle chives and cheese into shells. Return to oven and bake 5-10 minutes or until crisp. Serve immediately.

Yield: 2 servings

1 serving contains:

| Cal | Prot | Fat | Carb | Fiber | Chol | Sodium |
|-----|------|-----|------|-------|------|--------|
| 195kc | 7g | 4g | 34g | 4g | 7mg | 200mg |

*Use the pulp another day in an omelette or sauté with chopped onion in a skillet sprayed with vegetable spray.*

S N A C K S

# Smoked Salmon Cheese Spread

*This is great with fancy crackers.*

4 oz. fat-free cream cheese, softened

1 teaspoon fresh lemon juice

2 teaspoons minced onion

dash garlic powder

dash dill

¼ cup smoked salmon, chopped

In a small bowl, combine all ingredients. Shape into a ball, wrap in plastic wrap, and refrigerate several hours or until firm.

Yield: 4 (3 tablespoons) servings

1 serving contains:

| Cal | Prot | Fat | Carb | Fiber | Chol | Sodium |
|-----|------|-----|------|-------|------|--------|
| 36kc | 6g | 1g | 1g | 0g | 36mg | 250mg |

Serving Suggestion: Sprinkle with chopped parsley and serve with fat-free crackers or fresh veggies.

Variation: Substitute smoked turkey for smoked salmon.

S N A C K S

# T r a s h   N i b b l e r s

*This is a little of everything and so good for munching.*

1 tablespoon melted low-fat margarine

¼ teaspoon salt

½ teaspoon chili powder

¼ teaspoon garlic powder

¼ teaspoon onion powder

¼ teaspoon ground cumin

1 cup tiny fat-free pretzel sticks

1 cup O-shaped oat cereals

1 cup square, crispy corn cereal

3 cups popped corn (without salt or fat)

In a small bowl, combine margarine, salt, chili powder, garlic powder, onion powder, and cumin. In a large Ziploc plastic bag, combine pretzels, oat and corn cereals; carefully pour margarine mixture over all, close bag and shake well. Add popcorn, close bag and shake well again. Spread mixture evenly onto a large jelly roll pan. Bake at 275 degrees for 30 minutes, stirring twice. Cool completely. Store in an airtight container.

Yield: 5 (1 cup) servings

1 serving contains:

| Cal | Prot | Fat | Carb | Fiber | Chol | Sodium |
|-----|------|-----|------|-------|------|--------|
| 148kc | 4g | 3g | 28g | 1g | 0mg | 600mg |

# SOUPS

Homemade soups are one of my favorite foods; they are nutritious, easy, colorful, and a wonderful comfort food. Use low-fat, low-sodium products whenever possible for making soup. Simmer any type of stock for a period of time to reduce volume and therefore concentrate its flavor.

Herbs are a wonderful addition to soups. When possible I use fresh herbs; citrus juice or citrus zest will also add extra flavor to soup.

I prefer to make a large quantity of soup and either serve it a few days apart or freeze a portion of it. Most soups freeze wonderfully.

SOUPS

# Bonnie's Jambalaya

*A quick, nutritious, and tasty soup*

3 cloves garlic, minced

½ cup chopped onion

1 cup sliced celery

¼ cup water

2 cups low-fat, low-sodium chicken broth

1 (14 oz.) can seasoned, diced tomatoes (low-sodium)

1½ cups cubed smoked chicken or turkey

2 tablespoons Worcestershire sauce

1 teaspoon fine herbs* or fresh herbs of choice

dash Tabasco sauce

2 cups cooked white long grain rice (cooked without added fat or salt)

In a medium-sized kettle over medium-high heat, cook garlic, onion, and celery in ¼ cup water until tender. Add broth and tomatoes.

Cover, bring to a boil, reduce heat to low and simmer about 30 minutes. Add chicken, Worcestershire sauce, herbs, and Tabasco sauce, and continue to cook on low about 10-15 minutes. You can either add rice to jambalaya at this point, or when ready to serve, place rice in individual soup bowls and spoon jambalaya over rice.

Yield: 6 (1 cup) servings

1 serving contains:

| Cal | Prot | Fat | Carb | Fiber | Chol | Sodium |
|-----|------|-----|------|-------|------|--------|
| 147kc | 10g | 1g | 25g | 1g | 15mg | 230mg |

Serving Suggestion: Serve with a green salad and crusty French rolls.

*See Herb section

S O U P S

# B r u n s w i c k    S t e w

*A wonderful, hearty stew; it is even better the next day.*

*3 boneless chicken breast halves, skinned*

*2 stalks celery, cut into large chunks (approx. 1 cup)*

*½ cup onion, cut into large chunks*

*5 cups water*

*½ cup onion, chopped*

*1 (28 oz.) can tomato pieces*

*1 (8 oz.) can tomato sauce*

*1 (15 oz.) pkg. frozen baby lima beans*

*1 (10 oz.) pkg. frozen whole kernel corn*

*1 (16 oz.) can creamed corn*

*3 medium potatoes, cubed (approx. 1 ½ cups)*

*2 cubes Knorr chicken bouillon (each makes 2 cups)*

*1 teaspoon salt*

*⅛ teaspoon freshly ground black pepper*

*⅛ teaspoon red pepper, or to taste*

*4 drops Liquid Smoke*

*10 saltine crackers, crushed*

In a large soup kettle, combine chicken, celery, onion cubes, and water. Cover and bring to a boil over high heat. Reduce heat to low and simmer 45-50 minutes or until chicken is tender. Remove chicken from broth; cool, tear into bite-sized pieces, set aside. Remove celery and onion cubes from broth; discard. Add chopped onion, tomatoes, tomato sauce, and lima beans to broth. Using medium heat, bring to a boil. Reduce heat to low and simmer about 20 minutes. Add whole kernel corn, creamed corn, potatoes, bouillon, salt, peppers, Liquid Smoke, and chicken. Using medium heat, bring to a boil. Reduce heat to low and simmer for four hours, stirring occasionally. Add more water if needed, but this

should be fairly thick. Add cracker crumbs
and cook a few minutes more to soften.

Yield: 12 (1 cup) servings

1 serving contains:

| Cal | Prot | Fat | Carb | Fiber | Chol | Sodium |
|-----|------|-----|------|-------|------|--------|
| 184kc | 12g | 2g | 32g | 3g | 18mg | 696mg |

This is great to freeze.

To reduce the sodium content use salt-free
canned vegetables.

S O U P S

# C h i c k e n   V e g e t a b l e   S o u p

*A perfect meal to ward off winter chills*

1 boneless chicken breast half, skinned

½ onion, quartered (approx. ½ cup)

1 teaspoon thyme

1 clove garlic, minced

1 bay leaf

2 quarts water

1 cup stewed tomatoes

1 Knorr chicken bouillon cube (makes 2 cups)

½ cup carrots, cut into cubes

½ cup celery, chopped

½ cup fresh or frozen lima beans

½ cup coarsely chopped cabbage

½ cup potatoes, cut into cubes

½ cup fresh or frozen corn

½ cup fresh or frozen peas

1 tablespoon chopped fresh basil

In a medium soup kettle, combine chicken, ¼ cup of the onion, thyme, garlic, bay leaf, and water. Cover, bring to a boil over high heat, reduce heat to low and simmer until chicken is tender, about 45-50 minutes. Remove chicken from broth; cool, tear into bite-sized pieces. Remove onion pieces, discard. To the broth, add remaining onion, tomatoes, bouillon, carrots, celery, beans, and cabbage; cook for about 20 minutes. Add potatoes, corn, peas, and basil; cook for about 20 minutes more or until all the vegetables are tender.

Yield: 4 (1½ cups) servings

1 serving contains:

| Cal | Prot | Fat | Carb | Fiber | Chol | Sodium |
|------|------|-----|------|-------|------|--------|
| 165kc | 12g | 1g | 28g | 3g | 18mg | 400mg |

S O U P S

# C r e a m   o f   C o r n   S o u p

*Creamy, rich flavor*

¼ cup chopped onion

1 tablespoon water

1 cup fresh corn, cut from the cob *

1 ½ cups skim milk

½ cup evaporated skim milk

1 ½ tablespoons all-purpose flour

¼ teaspoon salt

1 teaspoon grated Parmesan cheese, made with
   skim milk

Place onion and water in medium saucepan and cook until tender. Add corn and 1 ½ cups skim milk, reduce heat to low, and continue to cook 10-15 minutes. *Do not let the milk boil.* In a jar with a lid, combine evaporated skim milk and flour; shake until flour is dissolved. Slowly add milk-flour mixture to the corn, stirring constantly until thickened. Add salt; stir. Ladle into individual soup bowls and sprinkle with Parmesan cheese.

Yield: 2 (1¼ cups) servings

1 serving contains:

| Cal | Prot | Fat | Carb | Fiber | Chol | Sodium |
|-----|------|-----|------|-------|------|--------|
| 231kc | 15g | 2g | 41g | 1g | 6mg | 298mg |

Serving suggestions: Garnish with chopped chives. Garnish with whole-grain croutons and chopped parsley.

*Canned cream-style corn can be substituted for fresh.*

S O U P S

# J u d y ' s   C h a l u p a   S o u p a

*A delightfully different soup and easy to prepare*

½ cup chopped green pepper

½ cup chopped onion

1 clove garlic, minced

1 (16 oz.) can vegetarian refried beans*

1 (14 oz.) can low-fat, low-sodium chicken broth

¼ cup minced mesquite-smoked turkey breast

½ teaspoon chili powder (or to taste)

dash freshly ground black pepper

dash Tabasco sauce

2 tablespoons shredded fat-free cheddar cheese

½ cup chopped fresh tomatoes

1 cup baked low-fat tortilla chips

In a medium soup kettle over medium heat, cook pepper, onion, and garlic in ¼ cup water, cooking until tender. Using medium heat, add beans; stir; add broth, turkey, chili powder, pepper, and Tabasco sauce; stir. Continue to cook until heated, stirring frequently. To serve: Ladle soup into individual bowls; sprinkle cheese and tomatoes over. Crumble 3-4 chips onto soup and serve the remaining chips with the soup.

Yield: 4 (1 cup) servings

1 serving contains:

| Cal | Prot | Fat | Carb | Fiber | Chol | Sodium |
|-----|------|-----|------|-------|------|--------|
| 247kc | 13g | 4g | 43g | 7g | 11mg | 642mg |

*To lower the sodium content, use 2 cups home-cooked, mashed, pinto beans.

SOUPS

# Ground Beef Stew

*Exceptionally easy and tasty stew*

½ lb. ground round of beef

½ cup chopped onion

2 carrots, sliced

1 stalk celery, sliced

2 peeled, chopped fresh tomatoes or 1 (16 oz.) can tomatoes

1 (10 oz.) pkg. frozen mixed vegetables

½ bay leaf

¼ teaspoon salt

dash black pepper

In a medium soup kettle, using medium-high heat, cook ground beef in a little water until it starts to lose pink color; add onion and cook until tender. In a small microwave-safe dish, precook carrots and celery for 3 minutes on high. Add tomatoes, carrots, celery, mixed vegetables, and bay leaf to meat. Adjust heat to medium-high, cover and bring to a boil, reduce heat to low and simmer 45 minutes or until vegetables are tender. Add salt and pepper.

Yield: 2 (1½ cups) servings

1 serving contains:

| Cal | Prot | Fat | Carb | Fiber | Chol | Sodium |
|-----|------|-----|------|-------|------|--------|
| 325kc | 35g | 8g | 39g | 7g | 82mg | 465mg |

SOUPS

# Hearty Lentil Soup

*Smoked turkey and root vegetables make this a full meal.*

1 cup lentils

6 cups water

2 Knorr chicken bouillon cubes (each makes two cups)

1 (8 oz.) can tomato sauce

2 cloves garlic, minced

1 teaspoon paprika

1 teaspoon Italian spices

¼ lb. smoked turkey, cut into 1" cubes

1 small celery root, cubed (approx. ½ lb.)

1 small onion, sliced (approx. ½ cup)

3 carrots, sliced ¼" (approx. ⅓ lb.)

2 cups sliced cabbage

½ teaspoon salt

⅛ teaspoon freshly ground black pepper

dash cayenne pepper

Sort and wash lentils; place in a kettle; cover with cold water and allow to soak for 2-3 hours. (Soaking is not essential, however, the lentils cook faster and are more tender if soaked.) Drain. In a medium soup kettle, combine lentils, water, bouillon, tomato sauce, garlic, paprika, and Italian spices. Cover. Using medium-high heat, bring to a gentle boil, reduce heat to low and simmer for about 30 minutes. Add turkey, celery root, onion, carrots, and cabbage. Using medium-high heat, return to boil; reduce heat to low and simmer for about 1½ hours, adding water if needed. Add salt and peppers; continue to cook 15-20 minutes more or until everything is tender.

Yield: 6 (1¼ cups) servings

1 serving contains:

| Cal | Prot | Fat | Carb | Fiber | Chol | Sodium |
|-----|------|-----|------|-------|------|--------|
| 172kc | 10g | 1g | 28g | 6g | 9mg | 741mg |

S O U P S

# M e a t b a l l   S t e w

*An easy, quick Mexican-type stew*

1 (14 oz.) can stewed tomatoes

2 cups low-fat, low-sodium chicken broth

½ teaspoon chili powder

¼ teaspoon thyme

½ teaspoon Italian seasoning

½ lb. ground turkey breast, no skin added

1 cup frozen or fresh corn

1 (15 oz.) can kidney beans

½ teaspoon Louisiana Hot Sauce (optional)

In a medium soup kettle, combine tomatoes, broth, chili powder, thyme, and Italian seasoning. Cover. Bring to a boil over high heat. Reduce heat to low and simmer about 15 minutes. While tomatoes are cooking, shape ground turkey into 12 meatballs, place on broiler rack and broil until no longer pink inside, turning to brown evenly. Remove to paper towel to drain thoroughly. Adjust heat to medium-high, add corn, beans, and meatballs. Bring to a boil; reduce heat to low and simmer about 15-20 minutes. Add Louisiana Hot Sauce as desired.

Yield: 4 (1¼ cups) servings

1 serving contains:

| Cal | Prot | Fat | Carb | Fiber | Chol | Sodium |
|-----|------|-----|------|-------|------|--------|
| 283kc | 28g | 3g | 40g | 5g | 129mg | 287mg |

SOUPS

# Mushroom Chowder

*Fresh mushrooms lend a subtle flavor to this soup.*

½ cup chopped onion

¼ cup chopped celery

¼ cup green or red pepper

¼ cup water

6 oz. sliced fresh mushrooms

2 cups low-fat, low-sodium chicken broth

1½ cups peeled and diced potatoes

½ teaspoon dried thyme

¼ teaspoon garlic powder

1 cup evaporated skimmed milk

1 cup skim milk

5 tablespoons unbleached or all-purpose flour

¼ teaspoon salt or to taste

¼ teaspoon freshly ground black pepper

In a medium kettle, over medium heat, cook onion, celery, and peppers in ¼ cup water for 3 minutes; add mushrooms, continuing to cook until vegetables are tender. Add broth, potatoes, and thyme; cover, bring to a boil, reduce heat to low and simmer for about 30 minutes or until potatoes are very tender. Adjust heat to medium-low and add evaporated milk to vegetables. In a small jar, combine 1 cup milk and flour, shaking until all the flour is dissolved. Slowly add to the chowder, stirring frequently until it begins to thicken. (Do not let it come to a hard boil.) Add salt and pepper to taste.

Yield: 3 (1½ cups) servings

1 serving contains:

| Cal | Prot | Fat | Carb | Fiber | Chol | Sodium |
|------|------|-----|------|-------|------|--------|
| 250kc | 17g | 2g | 48g | 3g | 5mg | 158mg |

S O U P S

# M i x e d   B e a n   S o u p

*An interesting combination of beans and spices*

1 boneless chicken breast half, skinned

3 cups water

1 (14 oz.) can stewed tomatoes

1 (10 oz.) pkg. frozen baby lima beans

1 bay leaf

2 cloves garlic, minced

½ onion, chopped (approx. ½ cup)

½ teaspoon chili powder

½ teaspoon paprika

dash red pepper

dash Tabasco sauce (optional)

2 cups fresh or frozen green beans

2 cups cooked black beans

In a medium soup kettle, combine chicken and 2 cups water. Cook until tender, about 30-40 minutes. Remove chicken from broth, set aside. Add remaining water, tomatoes, lima beans, bay leaf, garlic, onion, chili powder, paprika, pepper, and Tabasco sauce. Bring to a boil on high heat, reduce heat and simmer about 30 minutes or until lima beans are tender. Meanwhile, cut chicken into bite-sized pieces; add chicken, green beans, and black beans to the kettle. Using medium heat, bring to a boil, reduce heat to simmer, uncover and continue to cook about 20 minutes or until vegetables are tender.

Yield: 2 (1½ cups) servings

1 serving contains:

| Cal | Prot | Fat | Carb | Fiber | Chol | Sodium |
|------|------|-----|------|-------|------|--------|
| 573kc | 48g | 4g | 110g | 22g | 37mg | 634mg |

SOUPS

# Navy Bean Soup

*Add corn bread for a real "down-home" meal.*

*2 cups dried navy beans (1 lb.)*

*½ cup onion, chopped*

*1 cup carrot, cubed*

*1 clove garlic, minced*

*2 bay leaves*

*1½ tablespoons chopped, fresh parsley*

*2 beef bouillon cubes*

*1 teaspoon salt (optional)*

Sort and wash beans, and put in a large kettle. Cover with about 6 cups of water and let stand overnight in a cool place. Next day, rinse beans, return to large kettle, cover with fresh water. Bring to a boil, reduce heat and simmer over low heat for about 1 hour. Add onion, carrot, garlic, bay leaves, parsley, and bouillon. Continue to cook about another hour or until the beans are tender. Add salt if desired.

Yield: 4 (2 cup) servings

1 serving contains:

| Cal | Prot | Fat | Carb | Fiber | Chol | Sodium |
|-----|------|-----|------|-------|------|--------|
| 406kc | 26g | 2g | 75g | 5g | 0mg | 229mg |

*I freeze the remaining beans in small containers and use them later in soups or for refried beans.*

S O U P S

# R a v i o l i   S o u p

*Ravioli adds a totally new dimension to this soup.*

*1 (18 oz.) can low-sodium V-8 juice*

*1 (10½ oz.) can low-fat, low-sodium beef broth*

*3 cups water*

*1 cup sliced carrots*

*1 cup chopped potato*

*¼ cup chopped onion*

*½ cup marinara sauce*

*2 cups low-fat fresh ravioli\**

*1 cup packed, chopped fresh spinach*

*¼ teaspoon Louisiana Hot Sauce (optional)*

*1 teaspoon Worcestershire sauce*

*1 tablespoon fresh parsley, chopped*

*dash freshly ground black pepper*

In a medium soup kettle, combine V-8 juice, broth, water, carrots, potato, and onion. Bring to a boil, reduce heat, cover and simmer about 20-25 minutes or until vegetables are tender. Add marinara sauce, ravioli, spinach, hot sauce, Worcestershire sauce, parsley, and pepper. Bring to a boil, reduce heat, and continue to cook about 15 minutes.

Yield: 5 (2 cup) servings

1 serving contains:

| Cal | Prot | Fat | Carb | Fiber | Chol | Sodium |
|-----|------|-----|------|-------|------|--------|
| 180kc | 9g | 2g | 39g | 1g | 12mg | 296mg |

*\*I use DiGiorno "Light Varieties" Tomato and Cheese Ravioli found in the deli case at the grocery.*

S O U P S

# C r e a m   o f   P o t a t o   S o u p

*Flavorful, creamy, and a good source of calcium*

1 teaspoon olive oil

2 cloves garlic, minced

⅓ cup onion, chopped

⅓ cup celery, chopped

½ cup carrot, chopped fine

3 cups potatoes, peeled and cubed

1 tablespoon unbleached or all-purpose flour

1 tablespoon fat-free powdered milk

2 cups skim milk

¾ teaspoon salt

½ teaspoon freshly ground black pepper

1/16 teaspoon Tabasco sauce (or more according to taste)

Using medium heat, heat oil in a small nonstick skillet; add garlic, cook 2 seconds, then add onion and celery; cook until tender. Transfer to a large saucepan, add carrots, potatoes, and enough water to cover. Adjust heat to medium-high, cover and bring to a boil. Reduce heat to low and simmer until tender, about 40-45 minutes. (At this point you can either place the vegetables in a blender to puree, or for chunky soup, proceed with recipe.) In a jar with a lid, combine flour, powdered milk, and skim milk; shake until flour is dissolved. Reduce heat to low and slowly add milk-flour mixture to the potatoes, stirring constantly until thickened. Add seasonings.

Yield: 6 (1 cup) servings

1 serving contains:

| Cal | Prot | Fat | Carb | Fiber | Chol | Sodium |
|-----|------|-----|------|-------|------|--------|
| 147kc | 5g | 1g | 29g | 2g | 2mg | 354mg |

Serving Suggestions: Garnish with chopped chives. Garnish with whole grain croutons and a dusting of paprika.

Variation: For Potato-Spinach soup, substitute 1 cup fresh or frozen spinach for the carrots, add 1 teaspoon chicken bouillon granules. When ready to serve, dust lightly with ground nutmeg.

# C a j u n   S e a f o o d   G u m b o

*This is wonderful alone or extra special served over rice.*

3 tablespoons unbleached or all-purpose flour

¾ cup water, divided

1 cup chopped onion

½ cup chopped green pepper

½ cup diced celery

½ cup diced carrots

2 cloves garlic, minced

1 (10 oz.) pkg. frozen okra or 1 ½ cups fresh sliced

1 (8 oz.) bottle clam juice

1 (14½ oz.) can stewed tomatoes

1 tablespoon chopped, fresh parsley

1 teaspoon paprika

½ teaspoon dried thyme

½ teaspoon dried oregano

1 bay leaf

⅛ teaspoon white pepper

⅛ teaspoon red pepper

dash freshly ground black pepper

⅓ lb. smoked turkey sausage, sliced

1 (6.5 oz.) can minced clams, drained

½ lb. small fresh shrimp, peeled and deveined

¼ lb. fresh crabmeat, drained

Preheat oven to 350 degrees. Place flour in a shallow baking pan. Bake at 350 degrees for 1 hour or until brown, stirring occasionally. In a large soup kettle, combine ¼ cup water, onion, green pepper, celery, carrots, garlic, and okra. Cook over medium heat until vegetables are barely tender. Stir in browned flour. Add remaining water, all the clam juice and tomatoes. Stir well; add next 8 ingredients. Cover. Using medium heat, bring to a boil, reduce

heat and barely simmer for 1 hour. Add sausage, clams, shrimp, and crabmeat; simmer for 5-10 minutes or until shrimp and crab are cooked.

Yield: 8 (1 cup) servings

1 serving contains:

| Cal | Prot | Fat | Carb | Fiber | Chol | Sodium |
|-----|------|-----|------|-------|------|--------|
| 156kc | 19g | 4g | 12g | 3g | 83mg | 477mg |

## S O U P S

# Split Pea Soup

*A nutritious, colorful soup full of flavor*

*½ lb. green split peas*

*4 cups water*

*½ stalk celery*

*1 small carrot, sliced (about ½ cup)*

*½ small onion, cut into wedges (about ¼ cup)*

*1 clove garlic, minced*

*½ teaspoon dried rosemary*

*1 bay leaf*

*1 beef bouillon cube*

*dash cayenne*

*½ teaspoon salt*

*½ cup skim milk (if needed)*

Sort and wash peas. In a medium pan, combine peas, water, celery, carrot, onion, and garlic. Cover. On high heat bring peas and vegetables to a boil. Reduce heat to medium, cook about 15 minutes. Reduce heat to low, add rosemary, bay leaf, bouillon cube, and cayenne; simmer for about 1 hour or until peas are tender. Add salt. Remove celery and bay leaf, discard. Put 1 cup of the peas in a blender, process until pureed, pour into a bowl. Proceed with the remaining peas until all are processed. Return the pureed peas to the pan, return to heat, add milk until the desired consistency is achieved. Heat, but do not boil.

Yield: 3 (1 cup) servings

1 serving contains:

| Cal | Prot | Fat | Carb | Fiber | Chol | Sodium |
|-----|------|-----|------|-------|------|--------|
| 295kc | 21g | 1g | 53g | 6g | 1mg | 439mg |

Serving Suggestions: Serve ½ cup portions as a first course with dinner. Serve a bowl along with a salad or sandwich for a special lunch.

S O U P S

# C r e a m   o f   T o m a t o   S o u p

*Fresh chopped tomatoes give this a special texture.*

*1 tablespoon low-fat margarine*

*1 tablespoon chopped onion*

*4 cups tomato juice*

*1 teaspoon minced, fresh tarragon*

*1 teaspoon minced, fresh basil*

*4½ tablespoons unbleached or all-purpose flour*

*3 teaspoons sugar*

*¾ teaspoon salt*

*3 cups skim milk*

*1 medium tomato peeled and chopped*

In a medium kettle, melt margarine over medium heat; add onion and cook until soft. Add tomato juice, tarragon, and basil; cook about 10 minutes. In a jar, combine flour, sugar, salt, and 1 cup of milk; shake until thoroughly blended. Reduce heat to low. Spoon about ¼ cup of hot tomato mixture into the milk-flour mixture, then return to saucepan, stirring constantly with a whisk; add remaining milk, continuing to stir constantly. Add chopped tomato and continue to cook until heated through.

Yield: 6 (1 cup) servings

1 serving contains:

| Cal | Prot | Fat | Carb | Fiber | Chol | Sodium |
|-----|------|-----|------|-------|------|--------|
| 112kc | 6g | 1g | 20g | 1g | 3mg | 930mg |

S O U P S

# T o r t i l l a   S o u p

*This is just as good the next day; you will love the leftovers.*

1 tablespoon olive oil

7 corn tortillas, divided

6 cloves garlic, minced

1 cup chopped onion

2 cups tomato sauce

1 tablespoon chopped parsley

½ tablespoon ground cumin

1 teaspoon chili powder (or more to taste)

2 bay leaves

4 tablespoons canned tomato puree

2 quarts low-fat, low-sodium chicken broth

1 teaspoon salt (or to taste)

dash cayenne pepper

1 cooked chicken breast half, cut into small cubes

½ cup shredded fat-free cheddar cheese

Coarsely chop 4 tortillas, heat oil in large sauce-pan over medium heat. Add chopped tortillas and garlic, sauté until tortillas are soft; don't let garlic brown. Add onion, tomato sauce, parsley, cumin, chili powder, bay leaves, to-mato puree, and chicken broth. Bring to a boil, reduce heat to low and simmer, uncovered, for about 30 minutes. Add salt and cayenne pep-per. While soup is cooking: Preheat oven to 450 degrees; cut 3 remaining tortillas into thin strips, place on nonstick baking sheet and bake 5 minutes; turn and continue to bake about 5 minutes more or until brown and crisp.

To Serve: Ladle soup into individual soup bowls, put a few chunks of chicken and about a teaspoon of cheese on top, then garnish with a few crisp tortilla strips.

Yield: 8 (1 cup) servings

1 serving contains:

| Cal | Prot | Fat | Carb | Fiber | Chol | Sodium |
|------|------|-----|------|-------|------|--------|
| 125kc | 9g | 4g | 13g | 2g | 11mg | 737mg |

S O U P S

# T u r k e y   S t e w

*This is a great-tasting low-fat version.*

1 tablespoon unbleached or all-purpose flour

12 oz. turkey breast, cubed in ½" pieces

1 tablespoon olive oil

½ cup celery, sliced

1 small onion, sliced

2 cups tomato quarters or stewed tomatoes

3 cups water

½ cube of Knorr chicken bouillon

1 teaspoon chopped, fresh oregano or ½ teaspoon dried

3 tablespoons fresh parsley or 1½ tablespoons dried

¼ cup wild rice

1 cup lima beans

1 cup carrot chunks

½ teaspoon salt or to taste

⅓ teaspoon freshly ground white pepper

2 teaspoons white Worcestershire sauce

Toss flour with turkey to coat. Heat oil in a non-stick skillet; brown the turkey in the oil, transfer turkey to a medium soup kettle. Add celery, onion, tomato, water, bouillon, oregano, and parsley to the turkey. Using medium-high heat, bring to a boil, reduce heat to low and simmer uncovered for 45 minutes. Add rice, simmer for 15 minutes. Adjust heat to medium, add beans and carrots, cover, bring to a boil. Reduce heat to low, uncover and simmer for 45 minutes to one hour. Add salt and pepper, and Worcestershire sauce.

Yield: 4 (1½ cups) servings

1 serving contains:

| Cal | Prot | Fat | Carb | Fiber | Chol | Sodium |
|------|------|-----|------|-------|------|--------|
| 327kc | 31g | 7g | 368g | 5g | 68mg | 75mg |

Serving Suggestion: Serve with Mary's Oatmeal Molasses Bread.*

*This recipe can be found in the Breads section of this book.*

# I t a l i a n   V e g e t a r i a n   S o u p

*A flavorful combination of herbs, vegetables, and spices*

¼ cup chopped celery

¼ cup chopped onion

1 (8 oz.) can stewed tomatoes

1 (4 oz.) can tomato sauce

1 (14 oz.) can low-fat, low-sodium beef broth

1 (14 oz.) can water

1 tablespoon dried parsley

⅛ teaspoon thyme

1 teaspoon Italian seasoning

½ teaspoon dried basil

1 bay leaf

1 clove garlic, minced

1 cup cooked white beans, navy, cannelloni, or great
northern*

⅓ cup uncooked pasta (bow ties, spirals, etc.)

¼ cup fat-free mozzarella cheese

In a medium soup kettle over medium heat, cook celery and onions in ½ cup water for 4-5 minutes. Using high heat, add tomatoes, tomato sauce, beef broth, water, parsley, thyme, Italian seasoning, basil, bay leaf, and garlic. Bring to a boil, reduce heat to low and simmer for 40-50 minutes or until tomatoes break up easily. Add pasta and beans. Continue to cook on low for 20-25 minutes, or until pasta is tender.

To Serve: Ladle soup into bowl, sprinkle 1 tablespoon cheese on top.

Yield: 6 (1 cup) servings

1 serving contains:

| Cal | Prot | Fat | Carb | Fiber | Chol | Sodium |
|------|------|-----|------|-------|------|--------|
| 152kc | 90g | 2g | 27g | 3g | 9mg | 239mg |

*When I need a small quantity of beans, I use beans I have previously frozen or canned beans. If using canned, make sure you get the beans with no added fat.*

S O U P S

# Vegetable and Bean Soup

*A perfect supper for after the ice-skating party*

1 cup dried beans (½ lb. or 2 cups cooked)*

3 cups water

1 beef bouillon cube

1 carrot, chopped (about ½ cup)

1 potato, diced (about 1 cup)

¼ cup onion, chopped

½ cup cabbage, chopped

1 tablespoon chopped, fresh parsley

¼ cup tomato sauce

dash teaspoon black pepper

dash Tabasco sauce (or to taste)

½ teaspoon salt

Sort and wash beans; put in a medium kettle, cover with about 3 cups water and let stand overnight in a cool place. Next day, rinse beans. Return to kettle, add water, and cook over low heat until almost tender. Add bouillon, carrots, potato, onion, cabbage, parsley, tomato sauce, pepper, and Tabasco sauce. Cook until the vegetables are tender. Add salt.

Yield: 4 (1½ cups) servings

1 serving contains:

| Cal | Prot | Fat | Carb | Fiber | Chol | Sodium |
|------|------|-----|------|-------|------|--------|
| 149kc | 9g | 1g | 28g | 5g | 0mg | 495mg |

*When I need a small quantity of beans, I use beans I have previously frozen or canned beans. If using canned, make sure you get the beans with no added fat.

S O U P S

# White Chili

*A different approach to a favorite recipe*

1 teaspoon olive oil

½ cup chopped onion

1 clove garlic, minced

2 boneless chicken breast halves, skinned, cut into small cubes

3 cups cooked white beans (great northern or navy)

2 cups water

1 (4 oz.) can chopped green chilies (or to taste)

½ cup tomato sauce

1 teaspoon cumin

½ teaspoon Italian seasoning

dash ground cloves

dash cayenne pepper

½ cup shredded fat-free cheddar cheese

In a medium kettle over medium-high heat, add oil and onion, cooking until wilted; add garlic. Toss, then add chicken cubes, cooking quickly until tender and no longer pink. Add beans, water, chilies, tomato sauce, cumin, Italian seasoning, cloves, and pepper, stir. Cover, reduce heat to low and simmer about 1 hour. When ready to serve, sprinkle a little cheese over each individual serving.

Yield: 4 (1½ cups) servings

1 serving contains:

| Cal | Prot | Fat | Carb | Fiber | Chol | Sodium |
|------|------|-----|------|-------|------|--------|
| 320kc | 30g | 4g | 42g | 6g | 51mg | 354mg |

SOUPS

# Zucchini-Buttermilk Soup

*A slightly tart, flavorful soup*

2 chopped green onions

1 cup low-fat, low-sodium chicken broth

2 cups shredded zucchini

1 tablespoon minced, fresh parsley

½ teaspoon dried thyme

1 cup low-fat buttermilk

1 cup skim milk

3 tablespoons unbleached or all-purpose flour

½ teaspoon salt

freshly ground black pepper to taste

2 tablespoons shredded fat-free Swiss cheese

In a medium saucepan over medium-high heat, cook onions in 3 tablespoons chicken broth until tender. Add remaining broth, zucchini, parsley, and thyme; cover, reduce heat to low and simmer 30-40 minutes until zucchini is very tender. Uncover; slowly add buttermilk and ½ cup skim milk to vegetables. In a small jar, combine remaining ½ cup milk and flour; shake until flour is dissolved. Slowly add to soup, stirring frequently until it begins to thicken. (Do not bring to a boil.) Add salt and pepper. Sprinkle 1 teaspoon of cheese over individual servings as served.

Yield: 3 (1½ cups) servings

1 serving contains:

| Cal | Prot | Fat | Carb | Fiber | Chol | Sodium |
|-----|------|-----|------|-------|------|--------|
| 113kc | 10g | 1g | 18g | 1g | 3mg | 472mg |

SOUPS

# Ann's Zucchini - Macaroni Soup

*A colorful, tasty soup great for lunch*

1 teaspoon olive oil

1 clove garlic, minced

2 tablespoons chopped green onion

2½ cups low-fat, low-sodium chicken broth

1 cup zucchini, cut into chunks

1 cup fresh tomato, peeled and chopped

1 cup shell macaroni

¼ teaspoon dried rosemary (or more as desired)

dash freshly ground black pepper

1 tablespoon grated Parmesan cheese, made with skim milk

Heat oil in a medium soup kettle over medium heat; add garlic and onion, cook until tender. Add broth, zucchini, tomato, macaroni, and rosemary; cook until macaroni is tender. Add pepper. Spoon into individual serving bowls; sprinkle cheese over soup.

Yield: 3 (1½ cups) servings

1 serving contains:

| Cal | Prot | Fat | Carb | Fiber | Chol | Sodium |
|-----|------|-----|------|-------|------|--------|
| 123kc | 6g | 3g | 18g | 2g | 1mg | 40mg |

SOUPS

# Cold Cantaloupe Soup

*Refreshing, simple, and delicious*

1 cup coarsely chopped cantaloupe

¾ cup orange juice

1 tablespoon fresh lemon juice

fresh mint leaves

ground ginger (optional)

Place cantaloupe in a food processor; process until pureed; stir in orange and lemon juice. Cover and chill at least 1 hour.

Yield: 4 (½ cup) servings

1 serving contains:

| Cal | Prot | Fat | Carb | Fiber | Chol | Sodium |
|------|------|-----|------|-------|------|--------|
| 50kc | 1g | 0g | 12g | 0g | 0mg | 12mg |

Serving Suggestions: Garnish with mint leaves and sprinkle with ground ginger. Garnish with additional chunks of cantaloupe.

SOUPS

# Carrot Soup

*A colorful way to start your meal*

2 cups carrots, sliced

2 cups low-fat, low-sodium chicken broth

1 ½ teaspoons lemon juice

¼ teaspoon curry

In a medium saucepan, combine carrots and broth. Cover. On high heat bring to a boil; reduce heat to simmer and cook for about 30 minutes or until tender. Working with 1 cup at a time, put carrots and broth through a blender or food processor until smooth. Add lemon juice and curry, blend well. Chill.

Yield: 2 (1 cup) servings

1 serving contains:

| Cal | Prot | Fat | Carb | Fiber | Chol | Sodium |
|-----|------|-----|------|-------|------|--------|
| 49kc | 6g | 1g | 12g | 4g | 0mg | 39mg |

Serving Suggestions: Serve hot with whole grain croutons sprinkled with chopped chives. Serve with carrot curls sprinkled with minced cilantro.

S O U P S

# C u c u m b e r - Y o g u r t  S o u p

*A wonderfully cool, refreshing soup with fresh cucumbers*

1 medium cucumber (approx. 1 cup)

2 tablespoons onion, chopped

1 (8 oz.) fat-free plain yogurt

4 tablespoons fat-free sour cream substitute

¼ teaspoon garlic powder

⅛ teaspoon dried dill weed (or more)

⅛ teaspoon white pepper

Cut about a 1" circle from the cucumber, set aside. Do not peel; cut remaining cucumber into quarters lengthwise. Remove seeds, cut into large chunks. Put in blender container with onion, yogurt, sour cream, garlic powder, dill, and pepper. Whirl in blender until smooth. Chill. Slice the remaining cucumber into very thin slices. Pour soup into individual serving bowls, garnish with cucumber slices and a light dusting of dill.

Yield: 2 (1 cup) servings

1 serving contains:

| Cal | Prot | Fat | Carb | Fiber | Chol | Sodium |
|------|------|-----|------|-------|-------|--------|
| 82kc | 8g | 0g | 12g | 1g | 15mg | 103mg |

Serving Suggestion: Garnish with croutons and sprinkle with nutmeg.

SOUPS

# Gazpacho

*A cold Mexican soup—refreshing, nutritious, and exciting*

*1 (16 oz.) can stewed tomatoes*

*2 oz. green pepper chunks*

*6 green onions, chopped*

*4 oz. cucumber chunks*

*2 small tomatoes, chunks (approx. 1 cup)*

*1 tablespoon vinegar*

*3 tablespoons red wine*

*2 tablespoons canned, diced green chilies*

*¼ teaspoon salt*

*dash black pepper*

Place stewed tomatoes in food processor and process until pureed; place in a large container. Process green pepper and onions until very finely chopped; add to stewed tomato puree. Process cucumbers until finely chopped; add to vegetables in container. Process tomatoes until finely chopped; add to vegetables in container. Stir in vinegar, wine, chilies, salt, and pepper. Cover and refrigerate several hours or overnight to let flavors blend.

Yield:  8 (½ cup) servings

1 serving contains:

| Cal | Prot | Fat | Carb | Fiber | Chol | Sodium |
|------|------|-----|------|-------|------|--------|
| 37kc | 1g | 0g | 7g | 1g | 0mg | 238mg |

Serving Suggestions: Garnish with thinly sliced lime wedge. Garnish with additional cucumber, coarsely chopped.

Variations: For traditional Gazpacho, add 1 tablespoon minced fresh basil.

# BREADS

**B**reads, along with cereals, pasta, and rice, provide complex carbohydrates for our diets and play an important part in providing energy and fiber to our diet. We must keep in mind, however, not to load these foods with butter or fatty sauces.

I personally enjoy making bread from scratch, but for those who don't, the automatic bread makers are a wonderful addition to your kitchen, and most groceries today offer a wide variety of freshly baked breads. Carefully read labels as you purchase bread; try to use breads that are made with whole grains and very low in fat and sugar.

Never try to cut hot bread; let cool completely and then reheat. To heat bread in the microwave, wrap bread in a cloth napkin, heat for twenty to twenty-five seconds on high in the microwave. I am extra cautious to not overheat bread because it will make the bread tough; experiment a little to find the best time on your microwave. To heat in a conventional oven, simply wrap bread in aluminum foil and place in a 400-degree oven and heat for about four to five minutes. Include six to eleven servings of bread, cereal, rice, or pasta daily.

BREADS

# Banana Pancakes

*A delightful, flavorful change*

1 egg white, slightly beaten

1½ cups baking mix*

¾ cup skim milk (or more if needed)

½ cup mashed banana

⅓ teaspoon poppy seeds

vegetable spray

In a medium mixing bowl, using a wire whisk, beat egg white until slightly frothy. Add baking mix and milk; beat. Stir in banana and poppy seeds. Spray a nonstick skillet or griddle with vegetable spray; heat on medium-high heat. When hot, pour about ¼ cup batter into skillet. Cook until tiny bubbles appear all over pancake; turn and continue to cook until lightly browned. Serve immediately.

Yield: 4 servings (2 cakes each)

1 serving contains:

| Cal | Prot | Fat | Carb | Fiber | Chol | Sodium |
|-----|------|-----|------|-------|------|--------|
| 204kc | 7g | 3g | 38g | 0g | 1mg | 535mg |

*I prefer to use a popular low-fat baking mix.*

BREADS

# Banana Bran Muffins

*A moist, flavorful muffin*

vegetable spray

¾ cup unbleached or all-purpose flour

⅛ cup whole wheat flour

½ cup oat bran

¼ cup sugar

1 teaspoon soda

2 egg whites, slightly beaten

¼ cup mashed, very ripe banana

½ cup skim milk

1 tablespoon canola oil or oil of choice

Preheat oven to 400 degrees. Spray muffin tin with vegetable spray. In a medium mixing bowl, combine flour, bran, sugar, and soda. In a small bowl, combine egg whites, banana, milk, and oil; add liquids to the dry ingredients; stir just until well blended. Spoon into muffin cups, filling about ⅔ full or more. Bake in a 400-degree oven for 18 minutes.

Yield: 6 servings

1 serving contains:

| Cal | Prot | Fat | Carb | Fiber | Chol | Sodium |
|-----|------|-----|------|-------|------|--------|
| 159kc | 5g | 3g | 28g | 1g | 0mg | 97mg |

Variation: Add ½ cup chopped apricots. If your diet allows, sprinkle poppy seeds over the tops of muffins.

B R E A D S

# Beer Muffins

*Beer and onion combination gives a pleasing flavor.*

vegetable spray

1½ cups baking mix*

½ teaspoon sugar

1 tablespoon minced onion

6 oz. warm beer

Preheat oven to 425 degrees. Spray a 6-cup muffin tin with vegetable spray. In a medium mixing bowl, combine baking mix, sugar, and onion. Add beer and stir only until mixed. Spoon into prepared pan and bake in a 425-degree oven for 15 minutes.

Yield: 3 servings (2 muffins each)

1 serving contains:

| Cal | Prot | Fat | Carb | Fiber | Chol | Sodium |
|-----|------|-----|------|-------|------|--------|
| 329kc | 4g | 3g | 65g | 1g | 0mg | 615mg |

*I use a popular low-fat baking mix.

B R E A D S

# California Bran Bread

*A sweet, nutritious treat; serve with fruit for breakfast.*

vegetable spray

1 cup low-fat buttermilk

1 cup All-Bran cereal

1 cup all-purpose flour

1 ¼ teaspoons soda

¾ cup packed brown sugar

2 egg whites

¾ cup gold raisins

Preheat oven to 350 degrees. Spray 9x5 loaf pan with vegetable spray. In a small bowl, combine buttermilk and cereal; set aside. In a medium mixing bowl, combine flour, soda, and brown sugar. Add egg whites to cereal; mix; add to dry ingredients, stirring until well blended; add raisins; stir. Spoon into 9x5 loaf pan and bake in 350-degree oven for 60 minutes or until wooden pick comes out clean. Let cool in pan 5 minutes. Turn onto wire rack and cool completely.

Yield: 10 servings (1 slice each)

1 serving contains:

| Cal | Prot | Fat | Carb | Fiber | Chol | Sodium |
|-----|------|-----|------|-------|------|--------|
| 148kc | 4g | 1g | 35g | 3g | 0mg | 195mg |

BREADS

# Herbed Cheer Bread

*Beer gives this a slight tangy flavor.*

vegetable spray

2½ cups self-rising flour

3 tablespoons sugar

2 tablespoons parsley flakes

1½ teaspoons dill weed

1 (12 oz.) can warm beer

Preheat oven to 350 degrees. Spray 9x5 loaf pan with vegetable spray. In a large mixing bowl, combine flour, sugar, parsley, and dill. Add beer and stir only until mixed. Spoon into pan and bake in 350-degree oven for 55-60 minutes or until browned and sounds hollow when you tap it with knuckles. Cool on a wire rack.

Yield: 10 servings (1 slice each)

1 serving contains:

| Cal | Prot | Fat | Carb | Fiber | Chol | Sodium |
|-----|------|-----|------|-------|------|--------|
| 143kc | 3g | 0g | 29g | 0g | 0mg | 339mg |

BREADS

# Corn Cakes Tex-Mex

*Little cakes go great with fish.*

vegetable spray

1 ½ tablespoons all-purpose flour

½ cup cornmeal

½ teaspoon baking powder

¼ teaspoon salt

⅓ cup skim milk

1 egg white, slightly beaten

2 tablespoons picante sauce

¼ cup frozen corn, thawed, drained on paper towel

1 tablespoon diced green or red pepper

Spray a nonstick griddle with vegetable spray; heat over medium-high. In a small mixing bowl, combine flour, cornmeal, baking powder, and salt. In another small bowl, combine milk, egg white, picante sauce, corn, and pepper; add to dry ingredients, mixing just until moistened. Spoon 3 tablespoons batter onto hot griddle. Cook until bubbles appear on top; turn, and cook until brown. Serve immediately.

Yield: 2 servings

1 serving contains:

| Cal | Prot | Fat | Carb | Fiber | Chol | Sodium |
|-----|------|-----|------|-------|------|--------|
| 131kc | 6g | 0g | 24g | 1g | 0mg | 444mg |

# C o r n m e a l   S u g a r - C o a t e d   M u f f i n s

*These are surprisingly different.*

vegetable spray

¼ cup + 1 tablespoon cornmeal, divided

½ cup + 1 tablespoon brown sugar, divided

2 cups unbleached or all-purpose flour

2 teaspoons baking powder

¾ teaspoon salt

1 cup  fat-free vanilla yogurt, artificially
   sweetened

½ cup skim milk

1 teaspoon low-fat margarine, melted

1 teaspoon vanilla flavoring

2 egg whites, slightly beaten

Preheat oven to 400 degrees. Spray 12-cup muffin tin with vegetable spray. In a small bowl, combine 1 tablespoon cornmeal and 1 tablespoon brown sugar; set aside. In a medium mixing bowl, combine ¼ cup cornmeal, ½ cup brown sugar, flour, baking powder, and salt; set aside. In another small bowl, combine yogurt, milk, margarine, vanilla, and egg whites. Pour liquids into dry ingredients, stirring just until moistened. Spoon batter into muffin tins; sprinkle with cornmeal-sugar crumbs. Bake at 400 degrees for 15-18 minutes or until a wooden pick comes out clean.

Yield: 12 muffins

1 serving contains:

| Cal | Prot | Fat | Carb | Fiber | Chol | Sodium |
|------|------|-----|------|-------|------|--------|
| 127kc | 4g | 0g | 26g | 1g | 1mg | 104mg |

*These freeze very well; freeze any extra to use another day for breakfast.*

BREADS

# Corn-Tomato Muffins

*A delightfully different recipe*

vegetable spray

¾ cup cornmeal

½ cup unbleached or all-purpose flour

1 tablespoon sugar

3 teaspoons baking powder

¼ teaspoon salt

⅔ cup skim milk

1 egg white, slightly beaten

½ cup seeded, diced plum tomato

1 tablespoon minced, fresh basil or oregano

Preheat oven to 400 degrees. Spray muffin tin with vegetable spray. In a medium mixing bowl, combine cornmeal, flour, sugar, baking powder, and salt, set aside. In a small bowl, combine milk, egg white, tomato, and herbs. Pour liquids into flour mixture, stirring just until blended. Spoon into muffin cups and bake in 400-degree oven for 20 minutes.

Yield: 6 muffins

1 serving contains:

| Cal | Prot | Fat | Carb | Fiber | Chol | Sodium |
|------|------|-----|------|-------|------|--------|
| 120kc | 4g | 1g | 25g | 1g | 0mg | 327mg |

BREADS

# Grits Casserole

*A low-fat version of a favorite southern recipe*

2½ cups water

⅔ cup regular grits, uncooked

¼ cup chopped onion

1 clove garlic, minced

¼ teaspoon salt

vegetable spray

dash freshly ground black pepper

¼ cup evaporated skim milk

2 egg whites

1 tablespoon chopped red or green pepper

½ cup shredded fat-free cheddar cheese

Bring water to a boil. Gradually stir in grits, onion, garlic, salt; reduce heat and simmer covered about 20 minutes or until thick, stirring occasionally. Preheat oven to 350 degrees. Spray 1-quart baking dish with vegetable spray.

In a small bowl, combine pepper, milk, and egg whites. Stir in about ½ cup cooked grits, then pour into pan with remaining grits. Add pepper and cheese; stir well. Spoon into prepared dish and bake in 350-degree oven for 45 minutes, or until set.

Yield: 4 servings (1 cup each)

1 serving contains:

| Cal | Prot | Fat | Carb | Fiber | Chol | Sodium |
|-----|------|-----|------|-------|------|--------|
| 133kc | 7g | 1g | 50g | 0g | 18mg | 313mg |

Serving Suggestion: Serve this with your favorite omelet, made with egg substitute.

*This is good left over; just reheat in microwave oven.*

BREADS

# Herbs and Corny Corn Bread

*The herbs add a distinctively new taste.*

vegetable spray

⅓ cup unbleached or all-purpose flour

¾ cup yellow cornmeal

½ tablespoon sugar

½ tablespoon baking powder

⅛ teaspoon dried dill weed

⅛ teaspoon lemon pepper

¼ teaspoon salt

1 egg white, slightly beaten

¾ cup skim milk

2 teaspoons chopped chives

⅓ cup fresh or frozen corn kernels

Preheat oven to 400 degrees. Spray a 6" iron skillet or a 1-quart flat baking dish with vegetable spray. In a medium mixing bowl, combine flour, cornmeal, sugar, baking powder, dill, lemon pepper, and salt. In a small bowl, combine egg white and milk; pour into dry ingredients, mixing well. Add chives and corn; mix well. Pour into prepared pan and bake in 400-degree oven for 15-20 minutes or until browned. Invert onto a plate or cake rack; remove pan and turn corn bread upright. Let cool slightly before cutting.

Yield: 4 servings

1 serving contains:

| Cal | Prot | Fat | Carb | Fiber | Chol | Sodium |
|-----|------|-----|------|-------|------|--------|
| 163kc | 6g | 0g | 34g | 0g | 1mg | 314mg |

BREADS

# Miniature Lemon Muffins

*Always a hit, deliciously simple*

vegetable spray

1 ¼ cups unbleached or all-purpose flour

1 ½ teaspoons baking powder

½ cup low-fat margarine

1 cup sugar

2 egg whites, slightly beaten

¼ cup skim milk

4 tablespoons fresh lemon juice, divided

1 teaspoon freshly grated lemon zest

1 teaspoon poppy seeds

¾ cup powdered sugar

Preheat oven to 350 degrees. Spray miniature muffin tins with vegetable spray. In a small bowl, combine flour and baking powder; set aside. In a large bowl, beat margarine and granulated sugar until light and fluffy. Add egg whites, milk, and 3 tablespoons lemon juice; gradually add flour, mixing well. Stir in lemon zest and poppy seeds. Spoon into prepared muffin tins. Bake in 350-degree oven for 15 minutes or until top springs back when touched. Let cool in pan 5 minutes; remove from pan and cool. In a small bowl, combine powdered sugar and remaining 1 tablespoon lemon juice, beating until smooth. Spread glaze over top and let set until glaze hardens.

Yield: 48 miniature muffins

1 serving contains:

| Cal | Prot | Fat | Carb | Fiber | Chol | Sodium |
|------|------|------|------|-------|------|--------|
| 45kc | 1g | 1g | 9g | 0g | 0mg | 37mg |

*The batter will hold for you to use the same muffin tins for two different batches if you only have two 12-cup tins.*

BREADS

# Multigrain Banana-Lemon Bread

*A nutritious, moist, very easy-to-make bread*

vegetable spray

2 tablespoons canola oil or oil of choice

¾ cup molasses

2 egg whites, slightly beaten

3 teaspoons lemon zest

½ cup skim milk

½ cup very ripe, mashed banana

¼ cup oat bran

1½ cups whole wheat flour

1 cup unbleached or all-purpose flour

1½ teaspoons soda

Preheat oven to 350 degrees. Spray a 9x5 loaf pan with vegetable spray. In a medium bowl, combine oil and molasses; add egg whites, lemon zest, milk, and banana; set aside. In a small bowl, combine oat bran, flour, and soda. Gradually add flour mixture to molasses; stir until combined. Pour into prepared pan. Bake in a 350-degree oven for 40 minutes or until a wooden pick comes out clean. Turn out on a rack to cool. Cool completely before cutting.

Yield: 10 servings (1 slice each)

1 serving contains:

| Cal | Prot | Fat | Carb | Fiber | Chol | Sodium |
|-----|------|-----|------|-------|------|--------|
| 227kc | 5g | 3g | 45g | 1g | 0mg | 72mg |

BREADS

# Oatmeal Cakes

*A hearty addition served with scrambled eggs for brunch*

3 tablespoons old-fashioned oats, uncooked

⅓ cup water

¼ cup unbleached or all-purpose flour

1 teaspoon baking powder

dash of salt

1 egg white, slightly beaten

½ cup skim milk

1 teaspoon low-fat margarine, melted

vegetable spray

½ cup sweetened applesauce

Prepare oatmeal and water according to directions; set aside to cool. (This should be thick.) In a small bowl, combine flour, baking powder, and salt; in a medium bowl, combine egg white, milk, margarine, and oatmeal; stir well. Continuing to stir, gradually add flour mixture to liquids, stirring to just moisten the dry ingredients. Spray a nonstick griddle or skillet with vegetable spray and heat on medium-high heat. When hot, reduce heat to medium and spoon 2 tablespoons of batter in skillet. Cook until the top begins to bubble and the edges start to look a little dry. Turn and continue to cook until underside is brown. (These need to be cooked slower and turned gently, more like potato cakes than pancakes.) Place a paper towel on a tray, placing the cooked cakes on paper towel and covering with another paper towel until all the cakes are cooked. To serve, top with a tablespoon of applesauce.

Yield: 3 servings (2 cakes each)

1 serving contains:

| Cal | Prot | Fat | Carb | Fiber | Chol | Sodium |
|-----|------|-----|------|-------|------|--------|
| 100kc | 4g | 1g | 20g | 1g | 1mg | 180mg |

B R E A D S

# O r a n g e   P a n c a k e s

*A refreshing new taste with fresh oranges*

*1 egg white, slightly beaten*

*1½ cups baking mix\**

*¾ cup skim milk (or more if needed)*

*½ cup fresh orange juice*

*2 teaspoons grated orange zest*

*½ teaspoon orange flavoring*

*vegetable spray*

In a medium mixing bowl, using a wire whisk, beat egg white until slightly frothy. Add baking mix, milk, orange juice, zest, and flavoring; stir just until blended. Spray a nonstick skillet or griddle with vegetable spray and heat on medium-high heat. When hot, pour about ¼ cup batter into skillet; cook until tiny bubbles appear all over pancake; turn and continue to cook until lightly browned. Serve immediately.

Yield: 4 servings (2 cakes each)

1 serving contains:

| Cal | Prot | Fat | Carb | Fiber | Chol | Sodium |
|-----|------|-----|------|-------|------|--------|
| 192kc | 6g | 3g | 35g | 0g | 1mg | 535mg |

*\*I prefer to use a popular low-fat baking mix.*

B R E A D S

# P a n c a k e s ' n ' F r u i t

*Use fresh seasonal fruits for the sweet, rich fruit flavors.*

½ cup cooked fruit—thinly sliced peaches, apples,
    pears, or any kind of berries

¼ cup sugar

½ teaspoon cinnamon

batter for 6 (6") pancakes*

Sprinkle 1 tablespoon of sugar over warm fruit. In a small bowl, blend remaining sugar and cinnamon. Prepare pancakes according to directions. Place pancakes on individual serving plate. Spoon warm fruit over them; sprinkle with cinnamon-sugar mixture. Serve immediately.

Yield: 2 (3 cakes each) servings

1 serving contains:

| Cal | Prot | Fat | Carb | Fiber | Chol | Sodium |
|---|---|---|---|---|---|---|
| 323kc | 5g | 4g | 68g | 2g | 0mg | 660mg |

*I use a popular low-fat baking mix.*

B R E A D S

# P u m p k i n - C r a n b e r r y   T e a   B r e a d

*A deliciously moist new version of an old standby.*

vegetable spray

2¼ cups unbleached or all-purpose flour

1½ teaspoons baking soda

2½ teaspoons cinnamon

½ teaspoon cloves

¼ teaspoon nutmeg

⅓ cup canola oil or oil of choice

1½ cups sugar

1 cup pumpkin, cooked and mashed (fresh or canned)

3 egg whites, slightly beaten

1 cup raw cranberries, chopped

Preheat oven to 350 degrees. Spray 9x5 loaf pan with vegetable spray. In a large mixing bowl, combine flour, soda, cinnamon, cloves, and nutmeg. In a small bowl, combine oil, sugar, pumpkin, and egg whites. Pour liquids into flour mixture, stirring just until moistened. Stir in cranberries. Spoon batter into prepared loaf pan and bake in 350-degree oven for 75 minutes or until wooden pick comes out clean. Cool for 5 minutes before removing from pan; invert onto wire rack to cool.

Yield: 12 servings (1 slice each)

1 serving contains:

| Cal | Prot | Fat | Carb | Fiber | Chol | Sodium |
|-----|------|-----|------|-------|------|--------|
| 245kc | 4g | 6g | 46g | 1g | 0mg | 112mg |

BREADS

# Pumpkin Muffins

*A moist, slightly sweet treat; serve with any meal or for snacks.*

1½ cups unbleached or all-purpose flour

¼ cup brown sugar, packed

1 tablespoon baking powder

½ teaspoon cinnamon

¼ teaspoon nutmeg

2 egg whites, slightly beaten

1 cup pumpkin, cooked and mashed (fresh or canned)

2 tablespoons canola oil or oil of choice

2 tablespoons sour skim milk*

vegetable spray

Preheat oven to 400 degrees. Spray 12-cup muffin tin with vegetable spray. In a medium mixing bowl, combine flour, sugar, baking powder, cinnamon, and nutmeg. In a small bowl, combine egg whites, pumpkin, oil, and sour milk, slowly add liquids, stirring just until moistened. Spoon batter into muffin tins. Bake in 400-degree oven for 20 minutes.

Yield: 12 large muffins

1 serving contains:

| Cal | Prot | Fat | Carb | Fiber | Chol | Sodium |
|-----|------|-----|------|-------|------|--------|
| 99kc | 2g | 3g | 17g | 1g | 0mg | 47mg |

Using miniature muffin tin, bake at 400 degrees for 14 minutes or until done.

Yield: 40 miniature muffins

*Add ⅛ teaspoon lemon juice to 2 tablespoons milk; mix; remove ⅛ teaspoon and discard.

B R E A D S

# R a i s i n   F r e n c h   T o a s t

*A delightfully simple, simply delicious treat*

½ cup egg substitute

2 tablespoons skim milk

dash cinnamon

4 slices raisin bread

vegetable spray

1 teaspoon powdered sugar

In a shallow bowl, beat together egg substitute, skim milk, and cinnamon; dip bread slices in mixture, turning to coat both sides; leave in bowl until all the egg mixture is absorbed. Spray a large nonstick skillet or griddle with vegetable spray and heat on medium-low heat. When hot, gently lift bread into skillet. Cook about 4 minutes on each side until brown and no longer soggy. Remove to serving plate and sprinkle with powdered sugar.

Yield: 2 servings

1 serving contains:

| Cal | Prot | Fat | Carb | Fiber | Chol | Sodium |
|-----|------|-----|------|-------|------|--------|
| 171kc | 10g | 1g | 30g | 2g | 2mg | 280mg |

Serving Suggestion: Serve with maple syrup or applesauce.

B R E A D S

# R a s p b e r r y   M u f f i n s

*Serve with fruit for a delightful, delicious breakfast.*

vegetable spray

3 cups unbleached or all-purpose flour

1 tablespoon baking powder

⅛ teaspoon soda

¼ teaspoon nutmeg

6 tablespoons low-fat margarine, soft

1 cup sugar

1 teaspoon vanilla

3 egg whites, slightly beaten

1 cup water

1 cup fresh or frozen raspberries

Preheat oven to 400 degrees. Spray muffin pans with vegetable spray. In a small mixing bowl, combine flour, baking powder, soda, and nutmeg; set aside. In a large mixing bowl, beat margarine and sugar until creamy; add vanilla and egg whites. Gradually add flour mixture and water alternately to margarine mixture, beating just until blended; gently fold in raspberries. Spoon batter into prepared muffin pans. Bake in 400-degree oven for 18-20 minutes or until wooden pick comes out clean.

Yield: 18 muffins

1 serving contains:

| Cal | Prot | Fat | Carb | Fiber | Chol | Sodium |
|-----|------|-----|------|-------|------|--------|
| 141kc | 3g | 2g | 28g | 1g | 0mg | 123mg |

*These make nice miniature muffins. Place in miniature muffin pans and bake for 9-10 minutes.*

BREADS

# Refrigerator Bran Muffins

*Keep this batter in the refrigerator for quick, flavorful muffins.*

1 (14 oz.) box bran flakes

1¼ cups sugar

5 cups unbleached or all-purpose flour

5 teaspoons soda

1 cup egg substitute

¾ cup canola oil or oil of choice

1 quart low-fat buttermilk

1½ cups raisins, dates, or apricots

vegetable spray

Using an extra large mixing bowl, combine bran flakes, sugar, flour, soda. Add egg substitute, oil, and buttermilk; stir well; add raisins, stir well. Store in a covered container in the refrigerator for 4-5 weeks. If the batter becomes stiff, add milk until moist enough to spoon. When ready to use: Preheat oven to 350 degrees; spray muffin tin with vegetable spray; fill muffin tins about ¾ full; bake in 350-degree oven for 16-18 minutes or until wooden pick comes out clean.

Yield: 55 muffins

1 serving contains:

| Cal | Prot | Fat | Carb | Fiber | Chol | Sodium |
|-----|------|-----|------|-------|------|--------|
| 123kc | 3g | 4g | 22g | 3g | 0mg | 69mg |

*These muffins also freeze very well.*

BREADS

# Rice Pancakes

*An interesting change from traditional pancakes*

1 cup unbleached or all-purpose flour

¼ teaspoon salt

2 teaspoons baking powder

1 cup skim milk

2 egg whites, slightly beaten

3 teaspoons canola oil or oil of choice

2 cups cooked white rice

vegetable spray

In a medium bowl, combine flour, salt, and baking powder. In a small bowl, combine milk, egg whites, and oil; stir into dry ingredients, blending well. Add rice. Set aside for 10-15 minutes. Spray a nonstick griddle or skillet with vegetable spray and heat on medium-high heat. When hot, reduce heat to medium, pour batter into griddle or skillet and cook until bubbles appear on top and edges start to look a little dry. Turn and continue to cook until brown on both sides (only turning once). Serve immediately.

You can make little silver-dollar size cakes or larger, depending on how you are serving them.

Yield: 3 servings (4 medium cakes each)

1 serving contains:

| Cal | Prot | Fat | Carb | Fiber | Chol | Sodium |
|-----|------|-----|------|-------|------|--------|
| 350kc | 12g | 5g | 66g | 3g | 2mg | 553mg |

Serving Suggestion: Serve with maple syrup or cooked fruit.

BREADS

# Zucchini-Lemon Bread

*This is one of my favorites, especially good with zucchini fresh from the garden.*

vegetable spray

2 cups unbleached or all-purpose flour

1 cup whole wheat flour

1 teaspoon baking powder

1 teaspoon baking soda

2 teaspoons cinnamon

1 teaspoon ground cloves

1½ cups sugar

¾ cup canola oil or oil of choice

2 teaspoons grated lemon peel

2 egg whites, slightly beaten

¼ cup egg substitute

3 cups grated zucchini

1 cup gold raisins

Preheat oven to 350 degrees. Spray two 9x5 loaf pans with vegetable spray. In a medium bowl, combine flour, baking powder, soda, cinnamon, and cloves; set aside. In a large mixing bowl, using an electric mixer, combine sugar, oil, and lemon peel; add egg whites, egg substitute, and zucchini. Add the dry ingredients in about 3 parts, beating the batter well after each addition. Fold in raisins. Divide the batter evenly between the 2 loaf pans. Bake in a 350-degree oven for 45 minutes or until a wooden pick comes out clean. Invert on a cooling rack. Cool before slicing.

Yield: 24 servings (1 slice each)

1 serving contains:

| Cal | Prot | Fat | Carb | Fiber | Chol | Sodium |
|-----|------|-----|------|-------|------|--------|
| 187kc | 2g | 7g | 30g | 1g | 0mg | 59mg |

*Freezes beautifully for up to 3 months.*

BREADS

# Potato Bread

*Mashed potatoes make this nice and moist.*

vegetable spray

½ teaspoon canola oil or oil of choice

2¼ cups unbleached or all-purpose flour

1 cup whole wheat flour

1 package rapid rise yeast

1 teaspoon salt

1¼ cups warm water (115°-125° F)

¼ cup molasses, room temperature

1 cup smooth, fairly stiff mashed potatoes, room temperature

Lightly oil large bowl; spray 2 small round casseroles or baking dishes with vegetable spray. In another large bowl, combine 2 cups flour, yeast, and salt; add water, molasses, and mashed potatoes; mix well. Place in heavy-duty mixer. Add 1 cup flour, ¼ cup at a time, until it forms a soft dough. Turn out on a lightly floured surface and knead in remaining flour. Place in prepared bowl, turning to grease dough all over; cover and let rise in a warm, draft-free place until doubled in size, about 30 minutes. Punch down, turn out on floured surface and knead about 1-2 minutes. Preheat oven to 375 degrees. Shape dough into 2 small round loaves and place in prepared pans. Cover and let rise in a warm, draft-free place until doubled in size, about 25 minutes. Bake at 375 degrees about 30-35 minutes; the loaves should sound hollow when baked.

Yield: 16 servings (1 slice each)

1 serving contains:

| Cal | Prot | Fat | Carb | Fiber | Chol | Sodium |
|-----|------|-----|------|-------|------|--------|
| 118kc | 3g | 0g | 25g | 1g | 0mg | 153mg |

BREADS

# Crusty French Rolls

*These little rolls freeze beautifully.*

2 teaspoons canola oil or oil of choice

vegetable spray

1 teaspoon cornmeal

1 egg white

1 teaspoon water

3¼ cups unbleached or all-purpose flour

1 pkg. active dry yeast

1 teaspoon salt

1¼ cups warm water (115-125° F)

Put oil in a large, clean bowl. Lightly spray baking sheet with vegetable spray and sprinkle cornmeal over the pan. In a small bowl, lightly beat the egg white and water together; set aside. In a large mixing bowl, combine 2 cups flour, yeast, and salt; add water and mix well. Gradually add ½ cup flour and mix well. Using a dough hook, start to knead, gradually adding remaining flour ½ cup at a time until dough clings to the hook and cleans the sides of the bowl. Continue to knead for about 7-8 minutes, adding flour 1 tablespoon at a time (to keep dough from sticking to the bowl). When dough is smooth, make indentation with fingers in dough; if it springs back, the dough has been kneaded enough. (If you are kneading by hand, turn out onto a lightly floured surface and knead until smooth and satiny, adding last ¼ cup of flour as necessary.) Place dough in greased bowl, turning to grease all

over. Cover with a plain cloth and let rise in a warm, draft-free place until doubled in size. Press your finger lightly into dough. If indentation remains, dough is ready for next step. Punch down and let rise again until doubled in size; this won't take nearly as long. Turn out onto a floured surface and knead lightly. Cut into 14 equal pieces. Form each piece into a round ball. Place on prepared baking sheet and brush each roll with egg white wash. Place in a warm, draft-free place to rise. Preheat oven to 375 degrees and place a pan of hot water on the bottom rack. When rolls have doubled in size, brush again with glaze and bake on the rack above steaming water 15 minutes, brush again and bake about 15 minutes longer or until brown.

Yield: 14 rolls

1 serving contains:

| Cal | Prot | Fat | Carb | Fiber | Chol | Sodium |
|-----|------|-----|------|-------|------|--------|
| 115kc | 4g | 1g | 23g | 1g | 0mg | 173mg |

BREADS

# Italian Bread Sticks

*A nice addition to your favorite pasta dish*

vegetable spray

1 egg white, slightly beaten

1 teaspoon water

1 pkg. active dry yeast

1 tablespoon sugar

1 teaspoon salt

3 cups unbleached or all-purpose flour

¼ cup olive oil

1 ¼ cups warm water (115-125° F)

Spray 2 baking sheets with vegetable spray. In a small bowl, lightly beat the egg white and water together; set aside. In a large mixing bowl, combine yeast, sugar, salt, and 2 cups flour; add oil and water. Using a heavy-duty mixer, beat at medium speed for 2 minutes. Scrape sides, add ½ cup flour and continue to beat for 2 minutes more. Using a dough hook, knead dough, gradually adding enough remaining flour, 1 tablespoon at a time, until dough clings to the hook and cleans the sides of the bowl. Turn out onto lightly floured surface and knead another minute or 2 until dough is smooth and springy. Make indentation with finger in dough; if it springs back, the dough has been kneaded enough. (If you are kneading by hand, turn out onto a lightly floured surface and knead until smooth and satiny, adding last ½ cup flour as needed.) Preheat oven to 350 degrees. Divide dough into 3 equal

pieces. Taking 1 piece at a time, cut into 5 equal pieces; shape each piece into a roll. (You can make them as thick or as thin as you like.) Continue with remaining 2 pieces of dough until all is used. Arrange on prepared baking sheets and cover; let rise in a warm, draft-free place until just puffy, about 20 minutes. Brush each stick with egg white wash. Bake in 350-degree oven for about 15-18 minutes or until brown.

Yield: 15 bread sticks

1 serving contains:

| Cal | Prot | Fat | Carb | Fiber | Chol | Sodium |
|------|------|-----|------|-------|------|--------|
| 97kc | 2g | 3g | 15g | 1g | 0mg | 121mg |

*Freezes beautifully.*

BREADS

# Mary's Oatmeal Molasses Bread

*Wonderfully moist with a tang of molasses*

½ teaspoon canola oil or oil of choice

vegetable spray

1 teaspoon cornmeal

¾ cup old-fashioned oats, uncooked

2 cups skim milk

⅓ cup molasses

1 tablespoon low-fat margarine

1 package active dry yeast

1 teaspoon salt

4 to 4½ cups unbleached or all-purpose flour

Put oil in a large, clean bowl. Spray two 9x5 pans with vegetable spray and sprinkle with cornmeal.

Place oats and milk in a small saucepan over medium heat and bring to a gentle boil; reduce heat to simmer and continue to cook 10 minutes, stirring constantly; remove from heat. Add molasses and shortening. Cool to luke-warm (115-125 degrees). In a large mixing bowl, combine yeast, salt, and 2 cups of flour; add liquids and oats, stirring well. Using a heavy-duty mixer, knead, adding 2 cups flour ½ cup at a time or until dough clings to dough hook and cleans sides of bowl.

Continue to knead for about 8-9 minutes, adding flour 1 tablespoon at a time (to keep dough from sticking to the bowl) or until dough is smooth and springs back when touched. (If you are kneading by hand, turn out onto a lightly floured surface and knead until smooth

and satiny, adding last ¼ cup of flour as necessary.) Turn dough out onto lightly floured surface and knead 1-2 minutes more. Place dough in greased bowl, turning to grease all over. Cover and let rise in a warm, draft-free place until doubled in size. Press your finger lightly into dough; if indentation remains, dough is ready. Turn out again on lightly floured surface and knead a few seconds. Shape into 2 loaves, place in prepared 9x5 pans, cover and let rise again in a warm, draft-free place. Preheat oven to 400 degrees. Sprinkle 1 teaspoon oats over the bread. Bake in 400 degree oven for 5 minutes, reduce heat to 350 degrees and continue to bake 45-50 minutes or until loaves sound hollow when thumped.

Yield: 2 loaves or 20 servings (1 slice each)

1 serving contains:

| Cal | Prot | Fat | Carb | Fiber | Chol | Sodium |
|-----|------|-----|------|-------|------|--------|
| 134kc | 4g | 1g | 27g | 1g | 0mg | 150mg |

*Freezes very well.*

BREADS

# Honey-Wheat Muffins

*A moist, sweet muffin*

vegetable spray

¾ cup shredded wheat cereal

½ cup skim milk

1 egg white, slightly beaten

2 tablespoons honey

1 tablespoon low-fat margarine

2 tablespoons applesauce

⅔ cup unbleached or all-purpose flour

2 teaspoons baking powder

¼ teaspoon cinnamon

⅛ teaspoon nutmeg

½ cup raisins

Preheat oven to 400 degrees. Spray muffin tin with vegetable spray. In a small mixing bowl, combine cereal and milk, let set for about 5 minutes.

Add egg white, honey, margarine, and applesauce to cereal mixture. Combine flour, baking powder, cinnamon, and nutmeg in a medium mixing bowl; add cereal mixture, stirring just until moistened. Add raisins, stir. Spoon into muffin cups, filling about ⅔ full or more. Bake in a 400-degree oven for 15 minutes.

Yield: 6 servings

1 serving contains:

| Cal | Prot | Fat | Carb | Fiber | Chol | Sodium |
|---|---|---|---|---|---|---|
| 154kc | 4g | 1g | 37g | 2g | 0mg | 39mg |

Variation: Substitute ½ cup chopped apricots for raisins. If your diet allows, sprinkle poppy seeds over the tops of muffins.

# SALADS

**S**alads are a wonderful way to ensure the eating of raw vegetables and fruits suggested for every day. They can fit a number of needs in your meals: Serve as a first course in place of an appetizer, with the meal as an accompaniment to the entrée, or serve as the main entrée for lunch or "lite" suppers. You can even use dessert salads such as fruit and yogurt combinations for dessert.

If possible, use only the freshest ingredients available, even though it means shopping every few days. Nothing can compare with the fresh crispness and deep colors of fresh fruits and vegetables.

I simply refrigerate most vegetables until ready to use; however, I do prepare salad greens when I bring them home from the grocery. Rinse the greens in cold water, drain in a colander, then spread out on a towel to dry. Or, you can use a salad spinner. When almost dry, put in a zip-lock plastic bag and refrigerate. Greens will keep several days when prepared like this. I prefer to tear salad greens; cutting with a knife can cause them to discolor, and tearing makes a nicer appearance.

When choosing combinations for your salad, keep in mind the various colors, textures, and flavors.

To prevent darkening of freshly cut fruit, dip in lemon juice or in an ascorbic-acid mixture such as Fruit Fresh.

Choose a variety of fresh fruits, fruit juices, dried, canned, or frozen fruits; just be aware of the syrup in prepackaged fruits. Choose the fruits packed in their own juices or "lite" syrup.

When reaching for a glass of fruit juice, remember the whole fruit has much more fiber than the juice.

When making tossed salad, don't add extra fat with the salad dressing; serve the salad dressings in a small bowl separate from the salad itself, dipping your fork in the dressing before taking salad onto the fork. Keep a variety of nonfat dressing in the refrigerator.

Add citrus juice or citrus zest to green tossed salads or fresh fruit for added flavor.

Include three to five servings of vegetables and two to four servings of fruit daily.

SALADS

# Asparagus-Raspberry Salad

*An exciting, colorful way to begin the meal*

*8 fresh asparagus spears*

*4 large lettuce leafs*

*¼ cup Raspberry Salad Dressing\**

*¼ cup fresh raspberries*

Wash asparagus, break off tough ends, discard. Place asparagus spears in microwave-safe dish, cover and cook on high for 2 minutes. Submerge in ice water then drain. Arrange lettuce on serving plates. Place 4 asparagus spears on each plate. Drizzle with dressing and garnish with fresh raspberries.

Yield: 2 servings

1 serving contains:

| Cal | Prot | Fat | Carb | Fiber | Chol | Sodium |
|------|------|-----|------|-------|------|--------|
| 18kc | 2g | 0g | 4g | 1g | 1mg | 85mg |

*\*This recipe can also be found in this section.*

S A L A D S

# A s p a r a g u s - T u n a   S a l a d

*A special way to serve the old favorite—canned tuna*

1 (6½ oz.) can white tuna, packed in water

3 tablespoons minced celery

¼ cup low-fat French dressing*

1 cup fresh asparagus tips, approx. 4 oz.

lettuce to garnish

Combine tuna, celery, and dressing; chill for 10-15 minutes for flavors to blend. Arrange lettuce on individual serving plates; spoon tuna mixture on lettuce; arrange asparagus tips around tuna.

Yield: 2 servings

1 serving contains:

| Cal | Prot | Fat | Carb | Fiber | Chol | Sodium |
|-----|------|-----|------|-------|------|--------|
| 146kc | 29g | 1g | 7g | 1g | 0mg | 534mg |

*This recipe can also be found in this section.

SALADS

# Asparagus and Tomatoes

*The subtle flavor of balsamic vinegar enhances the salad.*

*8 fresh asparagus spears*

*1 sliced tomato*

*1 tablespoon chopped, fresh basil*

*1 tablespoon balsamic vinegar*

*2 lettuce leaves (optional)*

Wash asparagus, break off tough ends, discard. Place asparagus in a microwave-safe dish, cover and cook on high for 1 minute; submerge in ice water, then drain. If desired, arrange lettuce on serving plate, place asparagus on lettuce, sprinkle with chopped basil, then drizzle vinegar over all.

Yield: 2 servings

1 serving contains:

| Cal | Prot | Fat | Carb | Fiber | Chol | Sodium |
|-----|------|-----|------|-------|------|--------|
| 32kc | 3g | 1g | 6g | 1g | 1mg | 9mg |

S A L A D S

# C a b b a g e   W a l d o r f

*I especially like the sweet, tart flavor.*

¼ cup chopped pineapple tidbits, packed in its own juice

1 cup shredded cabbage

½ cup chopped crisp red apple

¼ cup low-fat salad dressing (mayonnaise type)

½-2 tablespoons reserved pineapple juice

Drain pineapple; reserve juice. In a medium mixing bowl, combine pineapple, cabbage, and apple. In a small bowl, blend mayonnaise and pineapple juice; spoon over cabbage and toss gently to mix.

Yield: 2 (¾ cup) servings

1 serving contains:

| Cal | Prot | Fat | Carb | Fiber | Chol | Sodium |
|------|------|-----|------|-------|------|--------|
| 153kc | 1g | 6g | 24g | 3g | 0mg | 247mg |

SALADS

# Caesar Salad

*Our daughter revised this old fat-laden favorite to a delicious low-fat version.*

½ lb. romaine lettuce

1 clove garlic, minced

½ tablespoon olive oil

½ teaspoon chile rojo olive oil*

½ tablespoon water

½ tablespoon Dijon mustard

½ tablespoon balsamic vinegar

2 teaspoons grated Parmesan cheese, made with skim milk

½ cup croutons

Using a small salad bowl, rub bowl with minced garlic; leave garlic in bowl. Tear romaine into bite-sized pieces and place in salad bowl. In a small bowl, combine oils, water, mustard, and vinegar; using a tiny whisk, whisk to emulsify. When ready to serve, drizzle over romaine; add Parmesan cheese and croutons, and toss gently. Serve immediately.

Yield: 4 (salad course) servings (or 2 servings to be used as main course)

1 serving contains:

| Cal | Prot | Fat | Carb | Fiber | Chol | Sodium |
|-----|------|-----|------|-------|------|--------|
| 50kc | 2g | 3g | 4g | 1g | 1mg | 125mg |

*If you can't find this product, soak ¼ teaspoon crushed red pepper in 2 tablespoons olive oil for several hours, strain and use. Save remainder for later use.*

S A L A D S

# Chinese Salad

*There are many variations for this popular salad, however, none are low-fat. I think you will enjoy this version.*

1 tablespoon rice vinegar

2 tablespoons sugar

½ tablespoon low-sodium soy sauce

½ tablespoon olive oil

1 teaspoon almond slices

1 teaspoon sesame seeds

2 cups coarsely shredded napa cabbage *

3 green onions, sliced

½ package Ramen noodles, crushed (do not use spices)

Combine vinegar, sugar, and soy sauce in a small microwave cup. Heat 30 seconds, stir; heat another 20 seconds, stir, repeating until sugar is dissolved. Set aside to cool; when cool add olive oil. Place almond and sesame seeds in 350-degree oven and bake 15-20 minutes until slightly toasted. Cool. In a small salad bowl, combine cabbage, onions, and Ramen noodles; toss gently. Pour cooled sauce over all and toss gently. Sprinkle almonds and sesame seeds on top. Serve immediately.

Yield: 4 servings

1 serving contains:

| Cal | Prot | Fat | Carb | Fiber | Chol | Sodium |
|-----|------|-----|------|-------|------|--------|
| 109kc | 3g | 3g | 19g | 2g | 13mg | 54mg |

*Save the unused portion of cabbage and use in Judy's Napa Cabbage-Chicken found in the Poultry Section.*

SALADS

# Chicken-Stuffed Tomatoes

*An attractive hearty salad*

½ cup cooked long grain and wild rice combined (cooked without added fat or salt)

⅓ cup chopped water chestnuts

1 cup cooked shredded chicken breast

1½ tablespoons chopped onion

2 teaspoons chopped pimiento

2 teaspoons chopped chives

¼ cup fat-free mayonnaise

1 tablespoon fat-free plain yogurt

1 teaspoon chive vinegar (or white)

⅛ teaspoon salt

dash black pepper

2 medium tomatoes

⅛ lb. spinach leaves

In a medium mixing bowl, combine rice, water chestnuts, chicken, onion, pimiento, and chives; toss gently. In a small bowl, combine mayonnaise, yogurt, vinegar, salt, and pepper; pour over chicken salad, tossing gently. Cover and refrigerate until ready to serve. Cut the top from the tomatoes, scoop out pulp, fill with chicken salad. Serve on a bed of spinach leaves.

Yield: 2 servings

1 serving contains:

| Cal | Prot | Fat | Carb | Fiber | Chol | Sodium |
|-----|------|-----|------|-------|------|--------|
| 177kc | 17g | 8g | 25g | 2g | 40mg | 356mg |

S A L A D S

# Citrus Salad with Orange Vinaigrette

*This is especially good when the citrus is fresh and juicy.*

2 tablespoons fresh orange juice

1 teaspoon basil vinegar (or white)

1 teaspoon olive oil

1 teaspoon water

1 teaspoon fresh orange zest

dash ground ginger

2 cups loosely packed torn leaf lettuce

½ small grapefruit, sectioned

½ small orange, sectioned

In a small bowl, combine juice, vinegar, oil, water, orange zest, and ginger. Cover and let set at least 30 minutes to blend flavors. Arrange lettuce and fruit on individual salad plates. When ready to serve, drizzle vinaigrette over all.

Yield: 2 servings

1 serving contains:

| Cal | Prot | Fat | Carb | Fiber | Chol | Sodium |
|------|------|-----|------|-------|------|--------|
| 66kc | 1g | 3g | 11g | 2g | 0mg | 5mg |

SALADS

# Corn - Pea Salad

*An easy, colorful addition to the meal*

1 cup frozen corn

1 cup frozen peas

½ cup chopped tomato

2 tablespoons sliced green onion

3 tablespoons Herb Vinaigrette*

Place corn and peas in a small microwave-safe bowl, cover, microwave on high 3 minutes. Submerge corn and peas in cold water, then drain. In a small bowl, combine corn, peas, tomato, and onion. Drizzle with Herb Vinaigrette, toss gently.

Yield: 2 servings

1 serving contains:

| Cal | Prot | Fat | Carb | Fiber | Chol | Sodium |
|-----|------|-----|------|-------|------|--------|
| 149kc | 5g | 4g | 24g | 5g | 0mg | 98mg |

*This recipe can be found in this section.*

SALADS

# Couscous with Marinated Vegetables

*Crunchy vegetables and tangy dressing add special interest.*

½ cup couscous

¾ cup boiling water

½ cup sliced carrots

¼ cup fat-free Italian dressing

1 teaspoon Dijon mustard

2 dashes of Louisiana Hot Sauce

½ cup cubed cucumber or green zucchini

1 tablespoon chopped fresh basil

⅓ cup sliced green onion

Prepare couscous according to package directions (without added fat or salt). Spoon into a medium bowl and set aside. Place carrots in a small microwave-safe bowl, cover and cook on high for 2 minutes. Place in ice water to stop cooking, and drain. In a small bowl, combine Italian dressing, mustard, and Louisiana Hot Sauce, and mix well. Add carrots, cucumber, basil, and green onion to couscous; add dressing mixture to couscous and vegetables and toss gently to combine.

Yield: 4 (⅔ cup) servings

1 serving contains:

| Cal | Prot | Fat | Carb | Fiber | Chol | Sodium |
|------|------|-----|------|-------|------|--------|
| 104kc | 3g | 0g | 22g | 1g | 0mg | 206mg |

S A L A D S

# C r a b   S a l a d

*A delightfully refreshing salad for lunch*

3 cups coarsely shredded cabbage

3 tablespoons minced onion

2 tablespoons minced celery

⅓ lb. imitation crabmeat

⅓ cup fat-free mayonnaise

½ tablespoon olive oil

1 tablespoon Dijon mustard

1 tablespoon basil vinegar (or white)

3 drops Louisiana Hot Sauce

⅛ teaspoon salt

⅛ teaspoon garlic powder

½ tablespoon sugar

Place cabbage, onion, and celery in a medium bowl. Chop crabmeat; add to vegetables. Place mayonnaise in a small bowl; using a whisk, slowly pour olive oil in, whisking until it is all incorporated in the mayonnaise. Whisk in mustard, vinegar, and hot sauce, then add salt, garlic powder, and sugar. Drizzle over crab and vegetables, tossing gently.

Yield:   2 (lunch entrée) servings

4 (salad course) servings

1 serving contains:

| Cal | Prot | Fat | Carb | Fiber | Chol | Sodium |
|-----|------|-----|------|-------|------|--------|
| 179kc | 11g | 5g | 26g | 3g | 13mg | 680mg |

Serving Suggestion: Serve with sliced tomato and fat-free, low-sodium crackers or rolls.

SALADS

# Cranberry Salad

*A great alternative to cranberry sauce*

2 (3 oz.) pkg. sugar-free strawberry or raspberry Jell-O

2 cups boiling water

1 (16 oz.) can whole cranberry sauce

1 (8 oz.) can crushed pineapple and juice

1 cup chopped apple

⅓ cup finely chopped celery

Dissolve jello in boiling water. Add cranberry sauce, using a fork to break it up; stir until well blended. Add pineapple and juice. Chill until the consistency of egg whites. Fold in apples and celery. Pour into a 10x10 pan or similar size. Chill until firm.

Yield: 8 servings

1 serving contains:

| Cal | Prot | Fat | Carb | Fiber | Chol | Sodium |
|-----|------|-----|------|-------|------|--------|
| 116kc | 0g | 0g | 30g | 1g | 0mg | 21mg |

*Add ¼ cup chopped nuts if your diet permits.*

SALADS

# Creamy Tomato and Cucumber Salad

*An easy, quick summer salad*

1 medium tomato, cubed

1 small cucumber, cubed

2 tablespoons chopped onion

2 tablespoons fat-free mayonnaise

½ teaspoon balsamic or white wine vinegar

1 teaspoon sugar

2 teaspoons skim milk

dash Louisiana Hot Sauce

8 spinach leaves

Combine tomato, cucumber, and onion in a small bowl. In another small bowl, combine mayonnaise, vinegar, sugar, milk, and hot sauce; blend well and pour over vegetables. Toss gently. Arrange spinach leaves on serving plates; distribute tomato mixture evenly over spinach.

Yield: 2 servings

1 serving contains:

| Cal | Prot | Fat | Carb | Fiber | Chol | Sodium |
|-----|------|-----|------|-------|------|--------|
| 28kc | 2g | 0g | 7g | 1g | 0mg | 127mg |

SALADS

# Crunchy Oriental Turkey Salad

*Celery and water chestnuts make this a nice crunchy salad.*

1 cup cooked turkey breast, chopped

⅓ cup celery, chopped fine

1 tablespoon water chestnuts, chopped

1 tablespoon green onion, sliced

2 tablespoons raisins

½ medium banana, cubed (approx. ⅓ c.)

⅓ cup pineapple tidbits, drained

⅓ cup mandarin oranges, drained

2 tablespoons low-fat salad dressing (mayonnaise type)

1 tablespoon fat-free plain yogurt

1 tablespoon pineapple juice

¼ teaspoon ginger

⅛ teaspoon dry mustard

4 pieces leaf lettuce (garnish)

In a medium mixing bowl, combine turkey, celery, water chestnuts, onion, raisins, banana, pineapple, and oranges; toss gently. In a small bowl, combine salad dressing, yogurt, pineapple juice, ginger, and dry mustard, pour over turkey mixture, and toss gently. To serve, place leaf lettuce on plate and spoon the turkey salad over it.

Yield: 2 servings

1 serving contains:

| Cal | Prot | Fat | Carb | Fiber | Chol | Sodium |
|-----|------|-----|------|-------|------|--------|
| 270kc | 26g | 6g | 31g | 3g | 68mg | 178mg |

SALADS

# C u c u m b e r - P e a   S a l a d

*Use garden-fresh cucumbers for a wonderfully crunchy salad.*

2 medium-small cucumbers

½ cup frozen peas, thawed

1 cup chicken breast, cooked, minced

¼ cup low-fat mayonnaise

¼ teaspoon dried dill weed

dash paprika

4 lettuce leaves

1 large tomato, sliced

Cut cucumbers in half lengthwise, scoop out pulp and chop. (Remove about ¾ cup chopped pulp, use if needed, but probably will be too much to refill the shells.) Set shells aside. Combine pulp, peas, chicken, mayonnaise, dill weed, and paprika. Gently spoon into cucumber shells. Place lettuce on individual serving plate; place 2 cucumber shells on lettuce; arrange tomato slices around.

Yield: 2 servings

1 serving contains:

| Cal | Prot | Fat | Carb | Fiber | Chol | Sodium |
|------|------|-----|------|-------|------|--------|
| 226kc | 17g | 8g | 21g | 2g | 37mg | 333mg |

S A L A D S

# Endive-Raspberry Salad with Raspberry Vinaigrette

*An especially attractive salad*

¼ head endive

6 leaves red-leaf lettuce

4 slices sweet onion

¼ cup Raspberry Vinaigrette *

2 tablespoons fresh raspberries (optional)

Wash and dry lettuce; arrange on serving plates. Evenly divide onion slices over lettuce, drizzle with dressing, and garnish with fresh raspberries.

Yield: 4 servings

1 serving contains:

| Cal | Prot | Fat | Carb | Fiber | Chol | Sodium |
|------|------|-----|------|-------|------|--------|
| 40kc | 0g | 4g | 2g | 1g | 1mg | 5mg |

*This recipe can be found in this section.

S A L A D S

# E n g l i s h   P e a   S a l a d

*A delicious old recipe from my childhood*

1 (17 oz.) can peas, drained*

1 tablespoon chopped pimientos

1 small crisp apple, chopped

2 tablespoons chopped dill pickle

2 tablespoons low-fat mayonnaise

1 teaspoon sugar

freshly ground black pepper

lettuce for garnish

Combine all ingredients except lettuce. Chill for about 20 minutes to blend flavors. Serve on bed of lettuce.

Yield: 2 (1 cup) servings

1 serving contains:

| Cal | Prot | Fat | Carb | Fiber | Chol | Sodium |
|------|------|-----|------|-------|------|--------|
| 230kc | 9g | 4g | 41g | 5g | 0mg | 1083mg |

*To reduce the sodium content, use fresh or frozen peas, cook in the microwave for 2-3 minutes on high.*

SALADS

# Fruit Salad with Lemon-Honey Dressing

*An attractive and tasty summer salad*

2 tablespoons lemon juice

1 teaspoon canola oil or oil of choice

1 teaspoon water

2 tablespoons honey

2 cups leaf lettuce

½ banana, cubed

¼ cup strawberries, quartered

½ peach, sliced

In a small bowl, combine lemon juice, oil, water, and honey; let set 20-30 minutes to blend flavors. In a medium bowl, tear lettuce into bite-sized pieces, add banana, strawberries, and peaches. Toss lightly with dressing (using just enough to moisten); serve immediately.

Yield: 2 servings

1 serving contains:

| Cal | Prot | Fat | Carb | Fiber | Chol | Sodium |
|-----|------|-----|------|-------|------|--------|
| 147kc | 1g | 3g | 33g | 2g | 0mg | 7mg |

SALADS

# Italian Potato Salad

*Red potatoes and Parmesan cheese make a great team.*

4 small red potatoes (approx. ¾ lb.)

2 tablespoons green onion, sliced

½ tablespoon chopped, fresh parsley

1 ½ tablespoons canola oil or oil of choice

1 teaspoon grated Parmesan cheese, made with skim milk

1 teaspoon white Worcestershire sauce

1 ½ teaspoons white vinegar

dash salt

dash freshly ground black pepper

Steam potatoes until just barely tender; set aside to cool slightly. When cool enough to handle, cut into quarters. In a medium bowl, combine potatoes, onion, and parsley. In a small mixing bowl, combine oil, Parmesan cheese, Worcestershire sauce, vinegar, salt, and pepper. Pour dressing over potatoes, cover and let set 10-15 minutes to let the flavor penetrate the potatoes.

Yield: 2 servings

1 serving contains:

| Cal | Prot | Fat | Carb | Fiber | Chol | Sodium |
|------|------|-----|------|-------|------|--------|
| 424kc | 7g | 11g | 77g | 6g | 1mg | 65mg |

SALADS

# Lemony Cucumber and Onions

*A sweet, tart side dish*

½ medium cucumber, sliced (approx. 4 oz.)

2 tablespoons chopped onion

1 tablespoon lemon basil vinegar (or white)

1 package artificial sweetener

dash black pepper

2 very thin slices of lemon (optional)

Arrange the cucumbers and onions in a shallow serving dish. In a small bowl, combine vinegar, sweetener, and pepper; pour over vegetables; cover and refrigerate at least 30 minutes. Garnish with lemon slices.

Yield: 2 servings

1 serving contains:

| Cal | Prot | Fat | Carb | Fiber | Chol | Sodium |
|------|------|-----|------|-------|------|--------|
| 10kc | 1g | 0g | 3g | 3g | 0mg | 2mg |

SALADS

# Mandarin Orange Salad with Raspberry Vinaigrette

*An easy, attractive salad for winter*

5 oz. can mandarin oranges

6 leaves romaine lettuce

3 tablespoons Raspberry Vinaigrette *

1 teaspoon toasted almond slivers

Drain orange slices. Wash and dry lettuce; arrange lettuce on serving plates. Evenly divide orange slices over lettuce, drizzle with dressing, and garnish with almond slivers.

Yield: 2 servings

1 serving contains:

| Cal | Prot | Fat | Carb | Fiber | Chol | Sodium |
|------|------|-----|------|-------|------|--------|
| 82kc | 1g | 6g | 8g | 1g | 2mg | 8mg |

*This recipe can be found in this section.*

SALADS

# Marinated Cucumbers and Tomatoes

*Garden-fresh ingredients are essential for this dish.*

1 large tomato, sliced (approx. 1 cup)

½ medium cucumber, sliced

1 tablespoon chive vinegar (or white vinegar)

1 teaspoon olive oil

1 tablespoon minced, fresh basil

1 teaspoon minced, fresh chives

1 tablespoon chopped onion

1 small clove garlic, minced

dash salt

dash black pepper

2 sprigs fresh basil (optional)

Arrange the tomato and cucumbers in a shallow serving dish. In a small bowl, combine vinegar, oil, basil, chives, onion, garlic, salt, and pepper; pour over vegetables. Garnish with basil.

Yield: 2 servings

1 serving contains:

| Cal | Prot | Fat | Carb | Fiber | Chol | Sodium |
|-----|------|-----|------|-------|------|--------|
| 41kc | 1g | 3g | 5g | 1g | 0mg | 8mg |

SALADS

# Barbara's Pasta-Dijon Salad

*The Dijon mustard adds an interesting tang to an old favorite.*

8 ounces uncooked spiral pasta (3 cups)

½ cup broccoli flowerettes

½ cup diced carrots

1 cup fat-free Italian salad dressing

1½ tablespoons Dijon mustard

⅛ teaspoon freshly ground black pepper

½ cup cubed green or yellow zucchini

½ cup diced green pepper

½ cup diced sweet onion

¼ cup sliced black olives

2 tablespoons chopped pimientos

Cook pasta according to directions (without added fat or salt), using minimum cooking time; drain well. Place broccoli and carrots in microwave-safe bowl, cover and cook on high for 2 minutes. Drain and plunge into ice water to cool; drain again.

In a small bowl, combine salad dressing, mustard, and pepper; set aside. Place pasta in a large mixing bowl, add vegetables, pepper, onion, olives, and pimientos; toss very gently. Pour dressing over all and toss very gently once more. Chill slightly before serving.

Yield: 7 (one-cup) servings

1 serving contains:

| Cal | Prot | Fat | Carb | Fiber | Chol | Sodium |
|------|------|-----|------|-------|------|--------|
| 83kc | 3g | 1g | 16g | 2g | 0mg | 469mg |

Serving suggestions: Add diced, cooked chicken and serve on a bed of lettuce.
Add canned oil-free white tuna served on a bed of lettuce sprinkled with almond slivers.

*I make this large of a quantity because it stays fresh for several days, and I can serve it many different ways.*

SALADS

# Pear-Raspberry Salad

*This is a very flavorful as well as attractive salad.*

1 medium firm pear, cubed

1 small banana, cubed

½ cup red seedless grapes

¼ cup Raspberry Vinaigrette*

spinach leaves

In a small bowl, combine pear, banana, and grapes. Carefully drizzle 2 tablespoons of vinaigrette over fruit. Set aside for about 10 minutes. Arrange spinach leaves on individual salad plates; spoon fruit onto spinach. Serve with remaining vinaigrette to be used as desired.

Yield: 2 servings

1 serving contains:

| Cal | Prot | Fat | Carb | Fiber | Chol | Sodium |
|-----|------|-----|------|-------|------|--------|
| 162kc | 1g | 4g | 34g | 4g | 0mg | 1mg |

Variation: Use cantaloupe, nectarine, and blueberries for a refreshing summer fruit salad.

*This recipe can be found in this section.*

SALADS

# Caroline's Pineapple - Cranberry Mousse

*This is quickly becoming a Shriver family Thanksgiving tradition.*

1 (20 oz.) can crushed pineapple (packed in its own juice)

2 (6 oz.) pkg. of sugar-free raspberry gelatin

1 medium orange, cut into 8 wedges

1 (12 oz.) pkg. of fresh cranberries

1½ cups sugar

2 cups fat-free plain yogurt or fat-free sour cream

lettuce for garnish

Drain pineapple, reserving 1 cup juice. Set pineapple aside. Heat juice to boiling; stir in gelatin, stirring until dissolved. Slice orange, peel included. In food processor, chop orange and cranberries with sugar to make a relish. Add pineapple to relish, then stir into gelatin. Chill until slightly thickened. Fold in yogurt, pour into a 2- quart mold, and chill until firm. When ready to serve, unmold onto lettuce-lined serving plate.

Yield: 10 servings

1 serving contains:

| Cal | Prot | Fat | Carb | Fiber | Chol | Sodium |
|------|------|-----|------|-------|------|--------|
| 198kc | 3g | 0g | 48g | 1g | 1mg | 36mg |

Serving suggestion: Pour into individual molds, serve on individual beds of lettuce.

SALADS

# Salmon-Pasta Salad

*The blending of herbs, salmon, and pasta makes a delightfully refreshing salad.*

¼ cup fat-free mayonnaise

1 tablespoon fat-free plain yogurt

1 teaspoon basil-lemon vinegar (or white)

1 teaspoon dried dill weed

⅛ teaspoon salt

dash black pepper

1¼ cups uncooked spiral macaroni

1 (6½ oz.) can pink salmon, drained

⅓ cup fresh pea pods, sliced

1 tablespoon chopped onion

1 teaspoon chopped red pepper

1 teaspoon sliced black olives

2 slices onion, separated into rings (approx. ¼ c.)

lettuce for garnish

fresh fruit for garnish

In a small mixing bowl, combine mayonnaise, yogurt, vinegar, dill weed, salt, and pepper. Cover and refrigerate for about 1 hour to blend flavors. Cook pasta according to directions (without added fat or salt). Drain. In a large mixing bowl, combine pasta, salmon, pea pods, onion, red pepper, black olives, and onion rings, and toss gently. Spoon sauce over pasta mixture; toss gently. Serve on a bed of lettuce; garnish with fresh fruit.

Yield: 2 servings (to be used as a main course)

1 serving contains:

| Cal | Prot | Fat | Carb | Fiber | Chol | Sodium |
|-----|------|-----|------|-------|------|--------|
| 364kc | 27g | 6g | 50g | 2g | 0mg | 720mg |

Serving Suggestion: Serve with Cornmeal Sugar-Coated Muffins*.

*This recipe can be found in the Bread Section of this book.

S A L A D S

# Smoked Chicken with Cantaloupe

*Cantaloupe, smoked poultry, and honey-and-mustard dressing make a winning combination.*

¼ cantaloupe (about 1 cup), cut into cubes

½ cup fresh or frozen peas, thawed

⅓ lb. cubed smoked chicken or turkey

3 cups leaf lettuce

¼ cup onion rings, sliced thin

⅓ cup Honey Mustard vinaigrette*

Combine cantaloupe, peas, and chicken in a small bowl. Moisten with 2 tablespoons vinaigrette; set aside. Tear lettuce into bite-sized pieces and arrange on individual serving plates. Divide chicken mixture evenly between the 2 salad plates; garnish with onion rings. Serve immediately with remaining dressing.

Yield: 2 servings

1 serving contains:

| Cal | Prot | Fat | Carb | Fiber | Chol | Sodium |
|-----|------|-----|------|-------|------|--------|
| 243kc | 19g | 10g | 20g | 1g | 33mg | 766mg |

*This recipe can also be found in this section.*

SALADS

# Smoked Turkey Rice Salad

*The nutty taste of the rice and the smoky flavor of the turkey make an interesting combination.*

¼ cup wild rice

¼ cup brown rice

1 cup low-fat, low-sodium chicken broth

1 cup cubed smoked turkey

2 tablespoons chopped pimiento

2 tablespoons chopped green onion

1 tablespoon chopped parsley

2 tablespoons balsamic vinegar

½ tablespoon olive oil

¼ teaspoon fresh ginger, minced

1 clove garlic, minced

8 cherry tomatoes

4 leaves lettuce

Preheat oven to 350 degrees. Place rice in an oven-proof pan over medium-high heat, stirring constantly for about 2 minutes. Add broth. Cover and bake in 350-degree oven for 20-25 minutes until rice is tender. Set aside to cool. In a medium bowl, combine rice, turkey, pimiento, onion, and parsley. In a small bowl, combine vinegar, oil, ginger, and garlic, pour over turkey-rice, and toss gently; add tomatoes. Let set 10-15 minutes to let flavors blend. Serve on a bed of lettuce.

Yield: 2 servings

1 serving contains:

| Cal | Prot | Fat | Carb | Fiber | Chol | Sodium |
|-----|------|-----|------|-------|------|--------|
| 185kc | 18g | 6g | 19g | 1g | 34mg | 507mg |

SALADS

# Spaghetti Squash—Sun-Dried Tomatoes

*Tossed gently with Herb Vinaigrette, this makes an exciting side dish.*

1 small spaghetti squash, 3-4 lbs.

8 pieces sun-dried tomatoes

½ cup boiling water

2 sliced green onions

½ zucchini, thinly sliced

1 clove garlic, minced

1 recipe Herb Vinaigrette Dressing*

Wash squash, cut in half lengthwise; scoop out seeds and discard. Place squash halves in microwave-safe dish; add water to cover. Cover, and microwave on high 10-12 minutes or until flesh of squash separates nicely into strands. Drain and cool. While squash is cooking, place tomatoes in boiling water, cover, and let stand 10 minutes. Drain and rinse tomatoes, drain again, set aside. Using a fork, remove the spaghetti-like strands of the squash flesh and place in large mixing bowl. Add tomatoes, onion, and zucchini to squash. Combine minced garlic with dressing, pour over vegetables, toss gently. Serve at room temperature.

Yield: 6 servings

1 serving contains:

| Cal | Prot | Fat | Carb | Fiber | Chol | Sodium |
|------|------|-----|------|-------|------|--------|
| 144kc | 1g | 8g | 27g | 1g | 0mg | 20mg |

*This recipe can be found in this section.

S A L A D S

# Sweet-Tart Marinated Vegetables

*Serve with sandwiches or add to a green salad.*

½ cup broccoli flowerettes

½ cup cauliflower flowerettes

¼ cup sliced carrots

2 tablespoons chopped onion

¼ cup Honey-Mustard Vinaigrette*

In a small bowl, combine broccoli, cauliflower, carrots, and onion. Drizzle vinaigrette over all, toss gently; cover and refrigerate at least one hour or overnight.

Yield: 2 servings

1 serving contains:

| Cal | Prot | Fat | Carb | Fiber | Chol | Sodium |
|-----|------|-----|------|-------|------|--------|
| 48kc | 2g | 2g | 8g | 2g | 0mg | 61mg |

*This recipe can be found in this section.*

S A L A D S

# T a b o u l i   S a l a d

*An exciting, colorful addition to your entrée*

½ cup dry bulgur wheat (tabouli)

¾ cup boiling water

¼ teaspoon salt

¼ cup + 1 tablespoon fresh lemon juice

1 tablespoon olive oil

1 clove garlic, minced

freshly ground black pepper to taste

2 green onions, finely minced

2 tablespoons minced, fresh parsley

1 medium tomato, diced

Combine bulgur and boiling water in a medium mixing bowl; cover and let stand about 30 minutes or until the bulgur is tender. In a small bowl, combine salt, lemon juice, olive oil, garlic, pepper, and bulgur; mix. Cover and refrigerate for about 30 minutes or until cool. Stir in onion, parsley, and tomato; cover and chill until ready to serve.

Yield: 4 (½ cup) servings

1 serving contains:

| Cal | Prot | Fat | Carb | Fiber | Chol | Sodium |
|-----|------|-----|------|-------|------|--------|
| 70kc | 2g | 4g | 9g | 1g | 0mg | 247mg |

SALADS

# Tomato Squash Basil

*This salad is truly a summer delight.*

½ *zucchini squash, sliced about* ¼"

½ *yellow squash, sliced about* ¼"

*1 medium tomato cut into wedges*

*1 tablespoon chopped, fresh basil*

*1 tablespoon basil vinegar (or white)*

*1 teaspoon olive oil*

*1 small clove garlic, minced*

*fresh basil leaves for garnish*

Arrange zucchini and squash in a small bowl, cover and microwave on high for 45 seconds; plunge into ice water; drain well. In a small bowl, combine zucchini, squash, tomato wedges, and basil; set aside. In another small bowl, combine vinegar, oil, and garlic. To serve: Spoon squash and tomatoes into small, clear, glass bowls; pour dressing over all; garnish with fresh basil leaf.

Yield: 2 servings

1 serving contains:

| Cal | Prot | Fat | Carb | Fiber | Chol | Sodium |
|-----|------|-----|------|-------|------|--------|
| 44kc | 1g | 3g | 5g | 2g | 0mg | 7mg |

SALADS

# Tropical Salad

*A creamy, fruity-tasting salad; try a variety of fruits.*

2 tablespoons fat-free plain yogurt

2 tablespoons fat-free cottage cheese

½ medium banana, cubed

1 teaspoon lemon extract

¼ lb. spinach, rinsed and dried

1 cup pineapple chunks

1 papaya, cubed

1 banana, cubed

1 orange, in segments

Combine yogurt, cheese, banana, and lemon extract in a blender bowl; process until smooth. Layer spinach on individual serving plates, arrange fruit on spinach, drizzle dressing over all. Serve immediately

Yield: 4 servings (or 2 servings to be used as the main course)

1 serving contains:

| Cal | Prot | Fat | Carb | Fiber | Chol | Sodium |
|------|------|-----|------|-------|------|--------|
| 125kc | 4g | 1g | 29g | 4g | 1mg | 31mg |

Serving Suggestion: Serve with assorted crackers for a delightful lunch or light supper.

SALADS

# Tuna Macaroni Salad

*The cucumber and dill give it an unusual flavor.*

1 cup elbow macaroni

¼ cup diced cucumber

1 tablespoon herb-flavored vinegar

¼ teaspoon minced dill weed

½ cup low-fat mayonnaise

¼ cup fat-free plain yogurt

½ teaspoon dry mustard

½ teaspoon salt

dash white pepper

¼ cup sliced green onions

1 oz. diced pimiento

3 oz. can white tuna packed in water, drained, flaked

lettuce leaves

Cook macaroni according to directions (without added fat or salt); drain. While macaroni is cooking, combine cucumber, vinegar, and dill weed; set aside. In a small bowl, combine mayonnaise, yogurt, mustard, salt, and pepper; blend. In a large bowl, combine macaroni, cucumbers, mayonnaise mixture, green onions, and pimiento. Cover and chill about 30 minutes. To serve, arrange lettuce leaves on serving plate, spoon macaroni salad on top of lettuce, and top with tuna.

Yield: 4 servings

1 serving contains:

| Cal | Prot | Fat | Carb | Fiber | Chol | Sodium |
|------|------|------|------|-------|-------|--------|
| 174kc | 11g | 10g | 23g | 1g | 12mg | 559mg |

Serving suggestions: Serve as an entrée 1 day, and the next serve the macaroni salad without the tuna, perhaps with grilled chicken. Make tuna salad sandwiches with the remaining tuna.

SALAD DRESSINGS

# Basil Buttermilk Dressing

*A distinct flavor using fresh basil*

*¼ cup low-fat mayonnaise*

*⅓ cup low-fat buttermilk*

*1 tablespoon fresh basil, minced*

*1 teaspoon tarragon vinegar (or white)*

*2 teaspoons minced onion*

*dash freshly ground pepper*

In a small bowl, combine all ingredients. Cover and chill for at least 30 minutes.

Yield: 5 (2 tablespoons each) servings

1 serving contains:

| Cal | Prot | Fat | Carb | Fiber | Chol | Sodium |
|------|------|-----|------|-------|------|--------|
| 40kc | 1g | 3g | 3g | 0g | 0mg | 104mg |

SALAD DRESSINGS

# Creamy Basil Dressing

*The combination of fresh basil and dry mustard is refreshing.*

⅓ cup low-fat mayonnaise

2 tablespoons fat-free plain yogurt

1 teaspoon chopped fresh basil

⅛ teaspoon dry mustard

In a small bowl, combine all ingredients. Cover and chill for at least 30 minutes.

Yield: 6 servings (2 tablespoons each)

1 serving contains:

| Cal | Prot | Fat | Carb | Fiber | Chol | Sodium |
|-----|------|-----|------|-------|------|--------|
| 43kc | 1g | 3g | 4g | 0g | 4mg | 78mg |

Serving Suggestions: Serve over sliced tomatoes and cucumbers or onions. Serve over mixed green salad.

SALAD DRESSINGS

# Berry-Flavored Vinegar

*These combinations result in a more subtle, fruity vinegar.*

2 cups ripe berries*

4 cups white vinegar

Rinse berries and drain very well. Evenly divide berries between 2 pint jars. Heat vinegar not quite to boiling; pour over berries. Cover jars with plastic wrap or any nonmetal covering. Let set about 2 weeks. Strain through cheesecloth until clear. Pour into nice bottles and seal with cork or plastic lid. If fresh berries are not available, use unsweetened frozen berries.

Yield: 4 cups

*Blueberries, blackberries, cranberries, or any firm berry.*

S A L A D   D R E S S I N G S

# S o f t   B e r r y   V i n e g a r

*1½ cups white vinegar*

*1 cup berries\**

Rinse berries and drain very well. Place berries in a clean pint jar. Heat vinegar not quite to boiling, pour vinegar over berries. Cover with plastic wrap or any nonmetal covering. Let stand at room temperature 5-7 days. Proceed with vinegar as directed on page 131.

Yield: 1½ cups

1 serving contains:

| Cal | Prot | Fat | Carb | Fiber | Chol | Sodium |
|-----|------|-----|------|-------|------|--------|
| 41kc | 1g | 0g | 10g | 2g | 0mg | 4mg |

*\*Strawberries, raspberries, chinaberries, or any soft berry.*

SALAD    DRESSINGS

# Buttermilk-Garlic Creamy Dressing

*Very similar to the popular commercial product*

½ cup low-fat mayonnaise*

½ cup low-fat buttermilk

2 teaspoons minced onion

¼ teaspoon garlic powder

1 teaspoon chopped, fresh parsley

In a small bowl, combine all ingredients. Cover and chill for at least 30 minutes.

Yield: 8 (2 tablespoons each) servings

1 serving contains:

| Cal | Prot | Fat | Carb | Fiber | Chol | Sodium |
|------|------|-----|------|-------|------|--------|
| 50kc | 1g | 5g | 2g | 0g | 6mg | 96mg |

*You can use nonfat mayonnaise to further reduce the fat and cholesterol.*

SALAD DRESSINGS

# Creamy French Dressing

*A wonderful fresh taste for your fresh salad greens*

*½ cup fat-free mayonnaise*

*½ cup fat-free plain yogurt*

*¼ cup catsup*

*dash hot sauce*

*dash vinegar*

In a small bowl, combine all ingredients; cover and chill for at least 30 minutes.

Yield: 8 (2 tablespoons) servings

1 serving contains:

| Cal | Prot | Fat | Carb | Fiber | Chol | Sodium |
|-----|------|-----|------|-------|------|--------|
| 20kc | 1g | 0g | 8g | 10g | 0mg | 312mg |

SALAD DRESSINGS

# Gourmet Herb Vinegar

*These vinegars add a special flavor to salads. They are very simple to make or you can purchase them in gourmet shops.*

1 cup clean herbs, oregano, chives, marjoram, etc.

1 quart white wine vinegar

Variations:

## Festive Italian Vinegar

1 cup clean oregano or marjoram

5 large garlic cloves, peeled

1 quart white wine vinegar (or use red wine vinegar for a more hearty flavor)

## Mexican Fiesta Vinegar

½ cup clean oregano

¼ cup clean cilantro

4 large garlic cloves, peeled

3-4 small, hot, red peppers

1 quart white wine vinegar

Place the herbs in a clean, 1-quart jar; pour vinegar over. Cover with plastic wrap or any nonmetal covering. Let stand for 2-3 weeks. You may leave the herbs in or strain through cheesecloth to remove the pieces of herbs, then add fresh herbs to the mixture for a more attractive presentation.

There is no fat, cholesterol, sodium, or protein, and only minimal calories and carbohydrates in vinegar.

SALAD DRESSINGS

# Herb Vinaigrette Dressing

*A wonderfully subtle blend of fresh herb flavors, vinegar, and oil.*

3 tablespoons oregano vinegar (or white)

¼ cup olive oil

2 tablespoons water

1 teaspoon sugar

1 clove garlic, minced

1 tablespoon minced, fresh basil

⅛ teaspoon black pepper

In a small bowl, combine all ingredients; cover and chill for at least 30 minutes.

Yield: 10 (2 tablespoons) servings

1 serving contains:

| Cal | Prot | Fat | Carb | Fiber | Chol | Sodium |
|------|------|-----|------|-------|------|--------|
| 49kc | 0g | 5g | 1g | 0g | 0mg | 0mg |

S A L A D   D R E S S I N G S

# Honey-Mustard Creamy Dressing

*A nice creamy, dressing with a bite*

¼ cup fat-free plain yogurt

2 tablespoons fat-free mayonnaise

2 tablespoons honey

1 tablespoon + 1 teaspoon Dijon mustard

1 teaspoon lemon juice

In a small bowl, combine all ingredients; cover and chill for at least 30 minutes.

Yield: 5 servings (2 tablespoons each)

1 serving contains:

| Cal | Prot | Fat | Carb | Fiber | Chol | Sodium |
|------|------|-----|------|-------|------|--------|
| 37kc | 1g | 0g | 8g | 0g | 1mg | 133mg |

SALAD DRESSINGS

# Honey-Mustard Vinaigrette

*The mild, delicate flavors compliment any salad.*

1 tablespoon canola oil or oil of choice

1 tablespoon water

2 teaspoons Dijon mustard (or any brown, spicy mustard)

2 teaspoons honey

1 teaspoon sherry

1 teaspoon minced, fresh lemon basil*

dash white pepper

In a small bowl, combine all ingredients; cover and chill for at least 30 minutes.

Yield: 4 (1 tablespoon) servings

1 serving contains:

| Cal | Prot | Fat | Carb | Fiber | Chol | Sodium |
|------|------|-----|------|-------|------|--------|
| 45kc | 0g | 4g | 3g | 0g | 0mg | 75mg |

*If fresh lemon basil is not available, use 1 teaspoon basil plus ½ teaspoon lemon zest.

SALAD DRESSINGS

# Raspberry Salad Dressing

*A colorful, exciting new taste*

¼ cup raspberry vinegar

2 tablespoons balsamic vinegar

2½ tablespoons fat-free mayonnaise

2 teaspoons white Worcestershire sauce

1 tablespoon sugar

In a small bowl, combine all ingredients; chill and cover for at least 30 minutes.

Yield: 5 (2 tablespoons) servings

1 serving contains:

| Cal | Prot | Fat | Carb | Fiber | Chol | Sodium |
|-----|------|-----|------|-------|------|--------|
| 9kc | 0g | 0g | 2g | 0g | 1mg | 84mg |

SALAD DRESSINGS

# Raspberry Vinaigrette

*2 tablespoons raspberry vinegar*

*1 tablespoon canola oil or oil of choice*

*1 tablespoon water*

*1 package artificial sweetener*

*dash cinnamon*

In a small bowl, combine all ingredients; chill and cover for at least 30 minutes.

Yield: 2 (2 tablespoons) servings

1 serving contains:

| Cal | Prot | Fat | Carb | Fiber | Chol | Sodium |
|------|------|-----|------|-------|------|--------|
| 60kc | 0g | 7g | 0g | 0g | 0mg | 0mg |

# MEATS

**B**eef, pork, poultry, and fish are good sources of protein, B vitamins, iron, and zinc. Include in your diet sources of protein that contain only moderate amounts of fat. Always use lean cuts of meat: Use white meat of poultry when possible; when using beef, use flank steak, round or sirloin, and extralean ground beef, or for pork use the tenderloin cuts.

You can greatly reduce the fat in your diet by using low-fat cooking tech-niques: Bake rather than fry; use non-stick pans with water or broth instead of fat, or use only a small amount of fat.

Take care in purchasing and handling all meats. Make certain to buy only the finest available. Prepare or freeze within a short time of purchase. When preparing, be careful to wash cutting boards, utensils, and hands carefully after handling meat.

Include two to three servings from this group, which also includes eggs, dry beans, and nuts.

# P O U L T R Y

The special flavor and texture of poultry make it adaptable to a wide and seemingly endless variety of recipes. I have included an extensive collection of poultry recipes because I think the reason people get bored with poultry is due to the fact that they have a very limited number of ways to prepare it. The diversity of ground poultry is just as great as with ground beef, however, it does not have quite the deep flavor as beef and when overcooked tends to be dry.

When purchasing ground poultry, try to buy ground white meat; it is not always available, but some grocers do offer it. Never use ground poultry which includes the skin or added fats. You can grind your own using a small food grinder; just be extra cautious when washing utensils, before and after grinding.

I have found the success to using ground poultry is to add more distinctive flavors to it by using herbs, garlic, onion, etc. Most importantly, *do not overcook*; cook just until juices are no longer pink. When we do burgers on the grill, I use BBQ sauce or some other source of moisture. Once you get the knack of cooking poultry burgers, just add a slice of onion, tomato and lettuce, and serve on a good bun for a delicious burger.

BAKED   POULTRY

# Balsamic-Thyme Chicken

*A very mild, tangy flavor*

vegetable spray

1 teaspoon low-fat margarine

2 boneless chicken breast halves, skinned

¼ cup low-fat, low-sodium chicken broth

⅓ red pepper, cut into wedges (optional)

⅓ green pepper, cut into wedges

⅓ cup onion slices

½ teaspoon fresh thyme

2 tablespoons balsamic vinegar

1 teaspoon sugar

dash freshly ground black pepper

Preheat oven to 350 degrees. Spray shallow 1-quart baking dish with vegetable spray. Heat margarine in a medium nonstick skillet over medium-high heat. Add chicken and cook just until slightly browned; remove chicken to baking dish. Pour broth into skillet, add peppers, onion, and thyme; simmer about 10 minutes. Lift vegetables from skillet with a slotted spoon and arrange on top of chicken. In a small bowl, combine vinegar, sugar, salt, and pepper. Pour into skillet, bring to a boil and simmer about 5 minutes. Pour over chicken. Cover. Bake in 350-degree oven for 20 minutes or until chicken is tender.

Yield: 2 servings

1 serving contains:

| Cal | Prot | Fat | Carb | Fiber | Chol | Sodium |
|------|------|-----|------|-------|------|--------|
| 172kc | 28g | 4g | 5g | 1g | 73mg | 89mg |

BAKED POULTRY

# Chicken with Artichokes

*A simple, thickened sauce, tangy and with a hint of tarragon*

vegetable spray

2 boneless chicken breast halves, skinned

1 cup canned oil-free artichokes, drained and quartered

4 onion slices (approx. 3 oz.)

¼ cup low-fat, low-sodium chicken broth

¼ cup Sauterne wine

¼ teaspoon tarragon

freshly ground black pepper to taste

1 teaspoon cornstarch

2 teaspoons water

Preheat oven to 350 degrees. Spray a 1-quart shallow oven-proof and range-top-proof dish with vegetable spray. Lightly spray a nonstick skillet with a vegetable spray. Place skillet over medium-high heat. When skillet is hot, add chicken, cook until brown on both sides. Remove chicken to baking dish. Arrange artichokes around chicken. In skillet, add onions and broth; cook until onions are wilted. Stir in wine, tarragon, and pepper; pour over chicken and artichokes. Cover and cook in a 350-degree oven for about 40 minutes or until chicken is tender. Lift chicken, artichokes, and onions from juices and place on serving plate. Place the baking dish with juices on medium-low heat. In a small bowl, combine cornstarch and water; slowly stir into the juices, cooking just until thick. Spoon over chicken and vegetables. Serve immediately.

Yield: 2 servings

1 serving contains:

| Cal | Prot | Fat | Carb | Fiber | Chol | Sodium |
|------|------|-----|------|-------|-------|--------|
| 222kc | 33g | 4g | 12g | 2g | 73mg | 124mg |

Serving Suggestion: Serve with Twice-Baked Potatoes*.

*This recipe can be found in the Vegetables section of this book.

BAKED POULTRY

# Chicken Breast in Orange Sauce

*Fresh orange juice and zest give this a yummy flavor.*

2 boneless chicken breast halves, skinned

1 teaspoon orange zest

½ cup fresh orange juice

1 tablespoon white wine

1 tablespoon brown sugar

½ teaspoon prepared mustard

dash ground ginger

1 tablespoon cornstarch

¼ cup water

Preheat oven to 350 degrees. Place chicken in a 1-quart shallow baking dish. In a small bowl, combine zest, juice, wine, brown sugar, mustard, and ginger; pour over chicken. Bake covered in a 350-degree oven for 30 minutes or until tender. Remove chicken to serving dish; keep warm. Pour juices into a small saucepan. In a small bowl, combine cornstarch and water; add to juices. Cook over medium-low heat until it starts to thicken. Spoon sauce over chicken. Serve immediately.

Yield: 2 servings

1 serving contains:

| Cal | Prot | Fat | Carb | Fiber | Chol | Sodium |
|-----|------|-----|------|-------|------|--------|
| 208kc | 27g | 3g | 15g | 0g | 73mg | 83mg |

BAKED POULTRY

# Chicken Zucchini Crisp

*Add a salad for an easy, colorful, one-dish meal.*

*vegetable spray*

*1 cup fresh bread crumbs*

*2 tablespoons unbleached or all-purpose flour*

*1 tablespoon grated Parmesan cheese, made with skim milk*

*½ teaspoon Italian seasoning*

*dash black pepper*

*1 egg white, slightly beaten*

*1 teaspoon water*

*2 boneless chicken breast halves, skinned*

*1 zucchini, cut into wedges (approx. ⅓ lb.)*

*1 tablespoon low-fat margarine, melted*

*dash cayenne pepper*

Preheat oven to 350 degrees. Lightly spray a 10x7 shallow baking dish with vegetable spray. In another shallow dish, combine crumbs, flour, cheese, Italian seasoning, and black pepper; set aside. In another shallow dish, combine egg white and water; dip chicken in egg mixture then into crumbs, coating all sides. Place in baking dish. Repeat the above steps to prepare the zucchini, placing the zucchini around the chicken. Pour margarine over all and sprinkle with cayenne pepper. Bake, uncovered, in a 350-degree oven for 50-60 minutes or until chicken and zucchini are tender.

Yield: 2 servings

1 serving contains:

| Cal | Prot | Fat | Carb | Fiber | Chol | Sodium |
|-----|------|-----|------|-------|------|--------|
| 280kc | 33g | 7g | 19g | 1g | 76mg | 321mg |

BAKED POULTRY

# Cornish Hens Baked in Wine

*An easy, yet elegant entrée*

vegetable spray

2 Cornish hens

1 bay leaf

5 juniper berries

10 peppercorns

freshly ground black pepper

¼ teaspoon salt

1 cup pearl onions

2 tablespoons balsamic vinegar

2 tablespoons water

½ cup white wine

Preheat oven to 350 degrees. Prepare small clay roaster per directions or spray a small roasting pan with vegetable spray. Rinse hens and pat dry. Combine bay leaf, juniper berries, peppercorns, ground pepper, and salt, and rub around the cavities of hens. Stuff onions into the cavities. Combine vinegar, water, and wine. Place hens in roaster and pour liquid over them. Place in 350-degree oven and bake for 50-60 minutes or until tender.

Yield: 2 servings

1 serving contains:

| Cal | Prot | Fat | Carb | Fiber | Chol | Sodium |
|-----|------|-----|------|-------|------|--------|
| 218kc | 21g | 3g | 5g | 1g | 63mg | 400mg |

BAKED POULTRY

# Glazed Turkey Breast

*The glaze helps keep it moist while giving it a subtle fruity flavor.*

*4-5 lb. turkey breast*

*⅛ teaspoon salt*

*¼ cup apricot preserves (all fruit; no sugar added)*

*dash ground ginger*

Preheat oven to 325 degrees. Rinse turkey breast and pat dry. Rub inside with salt. Place turkey breast skin side up on rack in shallow baking dish. Cook in 325-degree oven for about 1½ to 2 hours or until meat thermometer registers 185°F internal temperature. In a small bowl, combine fruit spread and ginger. After about 45 minutes, brush glaze on turkey, and continue to brush on glaze every 30 minutes until done. If turkey is getting too brown, gently tent a piece of foil over entire breast, removing the foil the last 20 minutes. Cool about 30 minutes before slicing.

Yield: 8 servings (enough for leftovers)

1 serving contains:

| Cal | Prot | Fat | Carb | Fiber | Chol | Sodium |
|-----|------|-----|------|-------|------|--------|
| 300kc | 60g | 4g | 1g | 0g | 114mg | 175mg |

B A K E D   P O U L T R Y

# Gourmet Chicken

*A festive entrée, yet so simple to put together*

vegetable spray

2 boneless chicken breast halves, skinned

¼ cup orange juice

1 tablespoon currants

1 tablespoon chutney

⅛ teaspoon cinnamon

dash curry

dash thyme

2 cups cooked long grain brown rice (cooked
  without added fat or salt)

½ cup fresh pineapple chunks

1 banana, cut into chunks

Preheat oven to 350 degrees. Spray a shallow 1-quart baking dish with vegetable spray. Spray a medium nonstick skillet with vegetable spray, and heat over medium-high. Add chicken and sauté quickly until brown on both sides; place in prepared baking dish. In a small bowl, combine orange juice, currants, chutney, cinnamon, curry, and thyme; pour over chicken. Cover and bake in a 350-degree oven for about 30 minutes, or until tender. To serve, arrange chicken around a bed of long grain brown rice and garnish with fruit. Serve extra sauce in a small bowl.

Yield: 2 servings

1 serving contains:

| Cal | Prot | Fat | Carb | Fiber | Chol | Sodium |
|-----|------|-----|------|-------|------|--------|
| 511kc | 32g | 4g | 89g | 1g | 73mg | 69mg |

BAKED POULTRY

# Hungarian Chicken with Dried Tomatoes

*The chicken will melt in your mouth.*

vegetable spray

2 boneless chicken breast halves, skinned

½ cup sliced onion

3 cloves garlic, minced

1½ cups chopped fresh tomatoes

½ cup low-sodium tomato sauce

⅛ teaspoon nutmeg

¼ teaspoon paprika

1 Knorr chicken bouillon cube

⅓ cup chopped dried tomatoes

2 tablespoons sherry

Preheat oven to 325 degrees. Spray a shallow 2-quart baking dish with spray. Spray a medium nonstick skillet with vegetable spray, and heat to medium-high. Add chicken and sauté quickly until brown on both sides; place in prepared baking dish. Add onion to the skillet and sauté about 1 minute; add garlic and continue to cook about 30 seconds. Add tomatoes, tomato sauce, nutmeg, paprika, and bouillon cube. Bring to a boil; pour over chicken. Place in 325-degree oven and bake for 2 hours or until chicken falls apart. While chicken is baking, soak dried tomatoes in sherry; add to chicken the last hour.

Yield: 2 servings

1 serving contains:

| Cal | Prot | Fat | Carb | Fiber | Chol | Sodium |
|------|------|-----|------|-------|-------|--------|
| 233kc | 30g | 4g | 16g | 0g | 73mg | 657mg |

Serving Suggestions: Serve over yolk-free noodles. Serve over gnoche.

BAKED POULTRY

# Joyce's Connecticut Chicken

*This is a favorite of an outstanding cook*

vegetable spray

½ tablespoon low-fat margarine

2 boneless chicken breast halves, skinned

½ cup sliced fresh mushrooms

½ can low-sodium cream of mushroom soup

2 tablespoons fat-free cream cheese

¼ cup white wine

2 teaspoons Good Seasons Italian dressing mix (dry)

2 teaspoons chopped chives

Preheat oven to 350 degrees. Spray a 1-quart baking dish with vegetable spray. Heat margarine in a medium nonstick skillet over medium-high. Add chicken and cook quickly until brown on both sides; remove to baking dish. Add mushrooms and cook for about 1 minute; spoon over chicken. Add soup and cream cheese to skillet; blend. Add wine, Italian dressing, and chives, stirring to blend well. Pour over chicken. Cover and bake in 350-degree oven for 30 minutes or until chicken is tender.

Yield: 2 servings

1 serving contains:

| Cal | Prot | Fat | Carb | Fiber | Chol | Sodium |
|------|------|-----|------|-------|-------|--------|
| 249kc | 32g | 8g | 5g | 1g | 79mg | 308mg |

BAKED POULTRY

# Lemon-Lime Mustard Baked Chicken

*The combination gives this dish a distinct, tangy taste.*

2 tablespoons fresh lemon juice

2 tablespoons fresh lime juice

1 tablespoon brown mustard

2 boneless chicken breast halves, skinned

dash freshly ground white pepper

⅛ teaspoon curry powder

1 teaspoon grated lemon zest

⅓ cup fine dry bread crumbs

vegetable spray

2 teaspoons melted low-fat margarine

In a small bowl, combine lemon juice, lime juice, and mustard; brush over chicken; cover and refrigerate for about 30 minutes. In another small dish, combine pepper, curry, lemon zest, and bread crumbs. Preheat oven to 400 degrees. Spray small baking pan with vegetable spray. Remove chicken from marinade and roll in crumb mixture, coating both sides. Place chicken in baking pan. Pour melted margarine over chicken. Bake in 400-degree oven for 30-45 minutes or until tender, depending on thickness of chicken.

Yield: 2 servings

1 serving contains:

| Cal | Prot | Fat | Carb | Fiber | Chol | Sodium |
|-----|------|-----|------|-------|------|--------|
| 192kc | 28g | 6g | 7g | 0g | 73mg | 247mg |

BAKED POULTRY

# Oven-Fried Chicken

*A great recipe for crisp, moist, oven-fried chicken*

½ cup crushed cornflakes

2 tablespoons oat bran

1 egg white, slightly beaten

¼ cup skim milk

¼ cup unbleached or all-purpose flour

dash salt

dash black pepper

dash cayenne pepper

2 boneless chicken breast halves, skinned

1 teaspoon melted low-fat margarine

Preheat oven to 400 degrees. Lightly spray an 8x8 shallow baking pan with vegetable spray. Combine cornflake crumbs and oat bran in a shallow dish; set aside. In a small mixing bowl, combine egg white and milk; while stirring with a whisk, gradually add flour, salt, and both peppers, mixing until batter is smooth. Dip chicken in batter then into cereal mixture; place in baking pan. Pour melted margarine over chicken. Bake in 400-degree oven, uncovered, about 30 minutes or until tender.

Yield: 2 servings

1 serving contains:

| Cal | Prot | Fat | Carb | Fiber | Chol | Sodium |
|-----|------|-----|------|-------|------|--------|
| 268kc | 33g | 5g | 19g | 2g | 74mg | 210mg |

BAKED POULTRY

# Chicken with Lemon Artichokes

*Artichokes in a creamy, lemon-flavored sauce*

*vegetable spray*

*2 boneless chicken breast halves, skinned*

*2½ tablespoons unbleached or all-purpose flour, divided*

*2 teaspoons canola oil or oil of choice, divided*

*½ small onion, chopped*

*1 cup canned oil-free artichokes, drained*

*¼ cup white wine*

*1 cup low-fat, low-sodium chicken broth*

*2 teaspoons lemon zest*

*½ cup evaporated skimmed milk*

*½ teaspoon salt*

*⅛ teaspoon freshly ground black pepper*

Preheat oven to 350 degrees. Spray shallow baking dish with vegetable spray. Dredge chicken in 2 tablespoons flour; set aside. Heat 1 teaspoon oil in a medium nonstick skillet over medium heat; add onion; cook until glazed and tender crisp. Transfer to baking dish. Heat remaining oil in skillet over medium-high heat; when hot, add chicken and cook until brown. Transfer to prepared baking dish with onions; add artichokes. Combine wine, broth, and zest in skillet, and cook until heated through; pour over chicken. Cover and bake in 350-degree oven for about 40-45 minutes or until tender. While the chicken is baking, combine milk and flour in a small jar, and shake until well blended. (Make sure mixture is room temperature.) When chicken is tender, transfer about ¼ cup of liquid from baking dish to a small bowl; add to sauce mixture about 1 tablespoon at a time, stirring constantly. Add salt and pepper.

Return all liquids to the chicken, stir, cover and return to oven for 5 minutes. Stir again and bake about 5 minutes more. Sauce should be slightly thickened. Stir before serving.*

Yield: 2 servings

1 serving contains:

| Cal | Prot | Fat | Carb | Fiber | Chol | Sodium |
|-----|------|-----|------|-------|------|--------|
| 348kc | 36g | 8g | 27g | 2g | 76mg | 782mg |

Serving suggestions: Serve over hot yolk-free noodles. Serve over cooked brown rice.

*If sauce starts to curdle, stir briskly with a whisk, and it will smooth out.*

BAKED POULTRY

# Rosemary Lemon Chicken

*Fresh rosemary gives this a marvelous, sultry flavor.*

vegetable spray

2 boneless chicken breast halves, skinned

1 clove garlic, minced

¼ cup white wine

2 small sprigs fresh rosemary

2 very thin slices fresh lemon

Preheat oven to 350 degrees. Spray shallow baking dish with vegetable spray. Spray a non-stick medium skillet with vegetable spray, and heat to medium-high. Add chicken and sauté quickly until brown on both sides; remove to baking dish. Add garlic, cooking about 30 seconds. Remove to baking dish. Pour wine in skillet, swish around, then pour over chicken. Place rosemary over chicken, then lay lemon slices over rosemary. Cover and bake in 350-degree oven for 45 minutes or until tender.

Yield: 2 servings

1 serving contains:

| Cal | Prot | Fat | Carb | Fiber | Chol | Sodium |
|-----|------|-----|------|-------|------|--------|
| 161kc | 27g | 3g | 0g | 0g | 63mg | 81mg |

B A K E D   P O U L T R Y

# S p a n i s h   R i c e

*A delicious variation of a special treat, but low in fat*

vegetable spray

½ lb. ground turkey or chicken (without skin)

¼ cup chopped onion

¼ cup chopped red or green pepper

1 cup stewed tomatoes

1 (8 oz.) can low-sodium tomato sauce

¾ cup water

¼ teaspoon chili powder

⅛ teaspoon black pepper

¼ teaspoon salt

¼ teaspoon garlic powder

½ teaspoon ground cumin

1 teaspoon Worcestershire sauce

1 tablespoon oregano vinegar* (or white)

⅓ cup uncooked brown rice

Preheat oven to 350 degrees. Spray a 2-quart baking dish with spray. Spray a small nonstick skillet with vegetable spray. Using medium heat, cook the ground turkey a few minutes, add onion and pepper and continue to cook until turkey is no longer pink. Add the remaining ingredients; mix well. Spoon into baking dish; cover and bake for 70 minutes.

Yield: 2 servings

1 serving contains:

| Cal | Prot | Fat | Carb | Fiber | Chol | Sodium |
|-----|------|-----|------|-------|------|--------|
| 295kc | 31g | 3g | 41g | 4g | 29mg | 703mg |

* Recipe for this can be found in the Salads section of this book.

Different flavored vinegars may be used; either herb flavored, berry flavored, or plain white.

BAKED POULTRY

# Lou's Spicy Baked Chicken

*Arrange on a platter around a bed of pasta or rice.*

1 teaspoon canola oil or oil of choice

¼ cup onion, chopped

1 clove garlic, minced

2 boneless chicken breast halves, skinned

2 tablespoons flour

1 (4 oz.) can tomato sauce

1 tablespoon brown sugar

½ tablespoon vinegar

dash black pepper

Preheat oven to 350 degrees. Heat oil in a medium nonstick skillet over medium heat. Add onion and garlic; cook until tender. Dredge chicken in flour and cook in skillet until browned on both sides. Place chicken and vegetables in a shallow, 1-quart baking dish. In a small mixing bowl, combine tomato sauce, sugar, vinegar, and pepper; pour over chicken. Bake for 1 hour, covered, at 350 degrees.

Yield: 2 servings

1 serving contains:

| Cal | Prot | Fat | Carb | Fiber | Chol | Sodium |
|---|---|---|---|---|---|---|
| 232kc | 29g | 6g | 16g | 1g | 73mg | 409mg |

P O U L T R Y

# Tur** ...Tomato-Wine Sauce

*easy and quick dish*

veget

*1 large*

*1 (11 oz.) can tom...*

*1 tablespoon chopped, fresh basil*

*⅓ cup white wine*

Preheat oven to 350 degrees. Spray a shallow, 2-quart baking dish with spray. Spray a medium nonstick skillet with vegetable spray, and heat to medium-high. Add cutlets, season with pepper and salt, and sauté quickly until brown and tender. (*Do not overcook.*) Remove to prepared baking dish. Spray the skillet again, add onion, and sauté about 1 minute; add garlic, and sauté about 30 seconds. Add tomatoes, basil, and wine to skillet; bring to a boil, reduce heat and simmer for 10 minutes. Pour sauce over turkey, cover and bake in a 350-degree oven for about 30 minutes or until turkey is tender.

Yield: 2 servings

1 serving contains:

| Cal | Prot | Fat | Carb | Fiber | Chol | Sodium |
|-----|------|-----|------|-------|------|--------|
| 231kc | 36g | 4g | 10g | 0g | 28mg | 393mg |

G R I L L E D   P O U L T R Y

# Angie's Lemon Basil Chicken

*The combination results in a new, exciting taste*

2 boneless chicken breast halves, skinned

1 tablespoon olive oil

2 tablespoons lemon juice

1 tablespoon white wine vinegar

1 teaspoon grated lemon zest

1 clove garlic, minced

2 tablespoons chopped fresh basil or 2 teaspoons
    dried

dash black pepper

sprig of fresh basil (optional)

Place chicken in a Ziploc plastic bag. In a small bowl, combine oil, juice, vinegar, lemon zest, garlic, chopped basil, and pepper. Pour over chicken, seal bag and refrigerate for 30 minutes or longer. When ready to cook, preheat grill. Remove chicken from marinade; save marinade. Place chicken on hot grill; cook 15-20 minutes or until tender, basting frequently with remaining marinade. Garnish with fresh basil leaves.

Yield: 2 servings

1 serving contains:

| Cal | Prot | Fat | Carb | Fiber | Chol | Sodium |
|------|------|-----|------|-------|------|--------|
| 210kc | 27g | 10g | 1g | 0g | 73mg | 64mg |

*Since you don't use all the marinade, the nutritional values will not be as high.*

GRILLED POULTRY

# Chicken Dinner in a Pocket

*An ideal meal to prepare ahead*

*aluminum foil*

*2 boneless chicken breast halves, skinned*

*1 medium potato, sliced (approx. 6 oz.)*

*4 slices onion (approx. 2 oz.)*

*2 small carrots, sliced (approx. 8 oz.)*

*⅛ teaspoon dried dill weed*

*⅛ teaspoon salt*

*dash black pepper*

*dash Louisiana Hot Sauce*

Using 2 layers, make 2 stacks of aluminum foil large enough to wrap ingredients and fold over. Place 1 breast on each stack of foil; divide potato, onion, carrots, dill, salt, pepper, and hot sauce evenly between the 2 stacks. Bring sides of 1 sheet of foil up around chicken and vegetables folding over to seal. Then bring second sheet of foil up in opposite direction, folding over to seal. Repeat for second dinner. When ready to cook, preheat grill*. Reduce flame to medium-high; place on hot grill about 6 inches from coals, grill for about 25 minutes, turn and continue to cook about 20 minutes or until chicken and vegetables are tender.

Yield: 2 servings

1 serving contains:

| Cal | Prot | Fat | Carb | Fiber | Chol | Sodium |
|-----|------|-----|------|-------|------|--------|
| 238kc | 29g | 3g | 22g | 4g | 73mg | 239mg |

*Can be baked in 400-degree oven for 45-50 minutes.

GRILLED POULTRY

# Cornish Hens/Herbs Grilled

*Nice fresh herbs make a distinct difference.*

2 Cornish hens, split in half

2 teaspoons fresh rosemary, stripped from stem

2 teaspoons fresh thyme, stripped from stem

2 teaspoons chopped, fresh parsley

½ teaspoon ground cumin

2 cloves garlic, minced

2 teaspoons olive oil

Rinse the hens and pat dry. In a small bowl, combine rosemary, thyme, parsley, cumin, garlic, and oil. Rub the herb mixture over hens, inside and out. Place in flat dish, cover and refrigerate for 1 hour or more. When ready to cook, preheat grill. Place hens on hot grill, skin side down. Cook for about 15 minutes. When skin is brown, turn and continue to cook 25-30 minutes or until hens are tender.

Yield: 2 servings

1 serving contains:

| Cal | Prot | Fat | Carb | Fiber | Chol | Sodium |
|------|------|-----|------|-------|-------|--------|
| 173kc | 20g | 7g | 0g | 0g | 63mg | 164mg |

GRILLED POULTRY

# Harold's Italian Grilled Chicken

*A family favorite for more than thirty years*

*2 boneless chicken breast halves, skinned*

*¼ cup white wine*

*¼ cup fat-free Italian salad dressing*

*¼ cup lemon juice*

*½ teaspoon low-sodium soy sauce*

*dash black pepper*

Place chicken in a Ziploc plastic bag. In a small bowl, combine wine, salad dressing, lemon juice, soy sauce, and pepper; pour over chicken. Close bag and marinate in refrigerator for 2-3 hours (overnight is even better). When ready to cook, preheat grill. Remove chicken from marinade; reserve marinade. Place chicken on a hot grill, cooking 15-20 minutes or until tender, basting often with remaining marinade.

Yield: 2 servings

1 serving contains:

| Cal | Prot | Fat | Carb | Fiber | Chol | Sodium |
|------|------|-----|------|-------|------|--------|
| 178kc | 27g | 3g | 5g | 0g | 73mg | 386mg |

GRILLED POULTRY

# Spicy Chicken Kabobs

*A nice piquant flavor*

*2 boneless chicken breast halves, skinned, cut into
  1" cubes*

*2 tablespoons chopped onion*

*1 teaspoon marjoram*

*dash crushed red pepper*

*1 tablespoon Worcestershire sauce*

*1 tablespoon white wine*

*1 tablespoon rice vinegar*

*1 tablespoon brown sugar*

*½ onion cut into quarters*

*½ bell pepper cut into quarters*

Place chicken in a Ziploc plastic bag. In a small bowl, combine onion, marjoram, red pepper, Worcestershire sauce, wine, vinegar, and brown sugar; blend well and pour over chicken. Seal bag and refrigerate at least 30 minutes or for several hours. When ready to cook, preheat grill. Remove chicken from marinade with a slotted spoon, draining slightly; reserve marinade. Thread chicken pieces onto metal skewers, alternating with onion and bell pepper. Place skewers on hot grill; cook about 15-20 minutes, basting with remaining marinade and turning occasionally until chicken is tender.

Yield: 2 servings

1 serving contains:

| Cal | Prot | Fat | Carb | Fiber | Chol | Sodium |
|------|------|-----|------|-------|-------|--------|
| 178kc | 27g | 3g | 8g | 1g | 73mg | 140mg |

GRILLED POULTRY

# Grilled Lime Chicken Breast

*A delightfully tart flavor*

*2 boneless chicken breast halves, skinned*

*2 tablespoons fresh lime juice*

*½ tablespoon canola oil or oil of choice*

*1 large garlic clove, minced*

*dash red pepper*

Place chicken in a Ziploc plastic bag. In a small bowl, combine lime juice, oil, garlic, and pepper. Pour marinade over chicken, seal bag and refrigerate for 6-8 hours. When ready to cook, preheat grill. Remove chicken from marinade; save marinade. Place chicken on hot grill, cooking 15-20 minutes or until tender, basting frequently with remaining marinade.

Yield: 2 servings

1 serving contains:

| Cal | Prot | Fat | Carb | Fiber | Chol | Sodium |
|-----|------|-----|------|-------|------|--------|
| 176kc | 27g | 7g | 1g | 0g | 73mg | 64mg |

ITALIAN POULTRY

# Chicken Sun-Dried Tomato Stir-Fry

*Sun-dried tomatoes add an unusual flavor to this quick entrée.*

6 sun-dried tomatoes

½ cup boiling water

2 boneless chicken breast halves, skinned

1 teaspoon olive oil

½ cup sweet onion, cut into rings

2 cloves garlic, minced

½ cup broccoli flowerettes

1 cup low-fat, low-sodium chicken broth

¼ cup white wine

¼ lb. bow-tie pasta

1 tablespoon chopped, fresh basil

Place tomatoes in boiling water, cover, and set aside. Cut chicken into thin strips, set aside. Heat oil in a nonstick wok over medium-high heat (or a medium nonstick skillet). Add chicken; stir-fry until chicken is almost done. Add onion, garlic, and broccoli; continue to cook until chicken becomes white and tender. Drain and thoroughly rinse tomatoes. Add tomatoes, broth, and wine to chicken and vegetables; reduce heat to simmer. Cover and continue to cook about 10 minutes. Cook pasta according to directions without added salt or fat. Add basil and pasta, toss, and serve immediately.

Yield: 2 servings

1 serving contains:

| Cal | Prot | Fat | Carb | Fiber | Chol | Sodium |
|------|------|-----|------|-------|------|--------|
| 549kc | 37g | 7g | 54g | 2g | 73g | 212mg |

Serving suggestions: Serve with any type of pasta. Serve with cooked white rice.

I T A L I A N     P O U L T R Y

# Creamy Chicken and Fettuccine

*So creamy you won't believe it's low-fat*

2 boneless chicken breast halves, skinned

vegetable spray

1 teaspoon olive oil

3 tablespoons chopped onion

1 clove garlic, minced

1 cup evaporated skimmed milk

1 tablespoon unbleached or all-purpose flour

1 tablespoon white wine

2 tablespoons shredded fat-free Swiss cheese

2 cups hot cooked fettuccine (cooked without added salt or fat)

2 teaspoons grated Parmesan cheese, made with skim milk

Place chicken between 2 pieces of plastic wrap, and pound until about ¼" thick. Spray a non-stick skillet with vegetable spray, add oil, then heat to medium-high. Add onion and garlic; sauté quickly, add chicken, and continue to cook about 4-5 minutes or until chicken is tender.

Remove chicken and onions; set aside and keep warm. In a small jar, combine milk and flour; shake until flour is dissolved. Slowly pour into skillet, stirring constantly and scraping sides of skillet; continue to cook until it begins to thicken. Add wine and Swiss cheese, stirring constantly until bubbly and cheese melts. To serve: place fettuccine on plate, place chicken alongside, and pour about 1 teaspoon sauce over each piece of chicken. Pour remaining sauce over pasta. Sprinkle with Parmesan cheese.

Yield: 2 servings

1 serving contains:

| Cal | Prot | Fat | Carb | Fiber | Chol | Sodium |
|------|------|-----|------|-------|-------|--------|
| 493kc | 47g | 7g | 57g | 3g | 124mg | 367mg |

Serving Suggestion: Serve with Asparagus Raspberry Salad and hot bread.

ITALIAN POULTRY

# Chicken Fricassee

*Tender baked chicken, smothered in onion*

vegetable spray

⅛ teaspoon pepper

⅛ teaspoon thyme

1 clove garlic, minced

2 boneless chicken breast halves, skinned

½ teaspoon olive oil

¼ cup unbleached or all-purpose flour

½ medium onion, sliced thin (approx. 3 oz.)

1 cup low-fat, low-sodium chicken broth

1 bay leaf

Preheat oven to 350 degrees. Spray a 2-quart baking dish with vegetable spray. In a small bowl, blend together pepper, thyme, and garlic; rub over chicken. Place chicken in small shallow bowl, cover and refrigerate. Let stand at least 30 minutes. In a small, nonstick skillet, heat oil on medium-high. Roll chicken in flour, place in skillet with oil, cook until lightly browned on both sides. While chicken is browning, separate the onion into rings, put half the rings in prepared baking dish, lay the chicken on them, then put the remaining rings on top. Pour broth into skillet; bring to a boil, scraping the sides; pour over chicken and onions; add bay leaf. Bake, covered, in a 350-degree oven for one hour. Remove bay leaf before serving.

Yield: 2 servings

1 serving contains:

| Cal | Prot | Fat | Carb | Fiber | Chol | Sodium |
|-----|------|-----|------|-------|------|--------|
| 229kc | 29g | 4g | 14g | 1g | 73mg | 67mg |

ITALIAN POULTRY

# Busy Day Goulash

*A very simple, fast, and pleasing entrée*

½ lb. ground turkey, no skin

¼ cup chopped onion

¼ cup chopped green pepper

1 cup frozen mixed vegetables

3 ounces yolk-free noodles

1 ½ cups fat-free, low-sodium marinara sauce*

dash salt

dash black pepper

2 cups water

In a medium saucepan, using medium heat, cook turkey until it begins to lose its pink color. Add onion and green pepper when turkey is about half done; continue to cook until no longer pink. Add mixed vegetables, noodles, marinara sauce, water, salt, and pepper. Reduce heat to low and continue to cook about 20-25 minutes or until vegetables and noodles are tender, adding more water if needed.

Yield: 2 servings

1 serving contains:

| Cal | Prot | Fat | Carb | Fiber | Chol | Sodium |
|-----|------|-----|------|-------|------|--------|
| 483kc | 45g | 7g | 65g | 5g | 47mg | 277mg |

*I use my homemade marinara; if using commercial sauce, be aware of added fat and sodium.*

ITALIAN POULTRY

# Grecian Chicken

*A few olives gives this a unique flavor.*

1 teaspoon olive oil

2 boneless chicken breast halves, skinned, cut into 1 " cubes

½ onion, cut into wedges

4 medium-size mushrooms, sliced

1 clove garlic, minced

½ cup low-fat, low-sodium chicken broth

¼ teaspoon thyme

1 bay leaf

¼ cup red wine

1 large tomato, skinned and cut into wedges

6 small green olives

freshly ground black pepper

Heat oil in a nonstick medium skillet; add chicken, sauté quickly until almost done; add onion, mushrooms, and garlic; sauté 2-3 minutes more. Add broth, thyme, bay leaf, and wine. Cover and simmer on low for about 15 minutes. Add tomato and olives; continue to cook about 5 minutes more.

Yield: 2 servings

1 serving contains:

| Cal | Prot | Fat | Carb | Fiber | Chol | Sodium |
|-----|------|-----|------|-------|------|--------|
| 216kc | 28g | 7g | 8g | 1g | 73mg | 254mg |

Serving Suggestion: Serve with rice.

ITALIAN  POULTRY

# Italian Parmesan Baked Chicken

*The marinade makes this dish so special.*

¼ cup fat-free Italian salad dressing

2 boneless chicken breast halves, skinned

1 egg white, slightly beaten

1 teaspoon water

2 tablespoons grated Parmesan cheese, made with
   skim milk

¼ cup fine, dry bread crumbs

1 teaspoon minced, dried parsley

dash black pepper

¼ teaspoon paprika

⅛ teaspoon garlic powder

Pour salad dressing into a Ziploc plastic bag; add chicken. Seal and refrigerate for 3-4 hours, turning occasionally. Drain chicken, reserving the marinade. Preheat oven to 375 degrees. Spray a shallow baking dish with vegetable spray. In a small bowl, combine egg white and water. In small shallow dish, combine Parmesan cheese, bread crumbs, parsley, pepper, paprika, and garlic powder. Dip chicken in the egg mixture, then in crumbs until coated. Arrange chicken in prepared baking dish and pour remaining marinade over all. Bake in 375-degree oven for 40-45 minutes or until tender.

Yield: 2 servings

1 serving contains:

| Cal | Prot | Fat | Carb | Fiber | Chol | Sodium |
| --- | --- | --- | --- | --- | --- | --- |
| 205kc | 32g | 5g | 3g | 0g | 77mg | 283mg |

ITALIAN POULTRY

# Mediterranean Chicken with Pasta

*Stir-fry chicken and pasta combined in a flavorful dish*

*2 teaspoons olive oil, divided*

*2 tablespoons lemon juice*

*1 small clove garlic, minced*

*¼ teaspoon lemon zest*

*¼ teaspoon oregano*

*2 boneless chicken breast halves, skinned, cut in 1" cubes*

*⅓ cup sliced carrots*

*½ cup broccoli flowerettes*

*½ cup sliced zucchini*

*1 tablespoon black olive slices*

*1 cup low-sodium, low-fat chicken broth*

*1 tablespoon cornstarch*

*½ teaspoon salt*

*¼ lb. linguine or spaghetti*

*2 tablespoons water*

In a small saucepan, combine 1 teaspoon oil, lemon juice, garlic, lemon zest, and oregano. Heat over medium-high heat until bubbly; cool. Place chicken and marinade in a Ziploc plastic bag; seal and refrigerate for at least 30 minutes or longer. In a small bowl, combine chicken broth, cornstarch, and salt, then set aside. Cook pasta according to directions, without added salt or fat. While pasta is cooking, spray a medium nonstick skillet with vegetable spray, add remaining oil, heat to medium-high. Add chicken and marinade, stirring quickly; cook until chicken is no longer pink and is tender. Remove chicken to bowl, set aside, and keep warm. Spray skillet lightly again; add carrots, broccoli, and zucchini, stir-fry about 1 minute, add 2 tablespoons water, cover and steam for about 3 minutes. Return chicken to vegetables, add olives; slowly stir in cornstarch

mixture. Stir constantly, cooking over medium-low heat until it begins to thicken. Arrange pasta in serving bowl, spoon chicken and vegetables over the pasta.

Yield: 2 servings

1 serving contains:

| Cal | Prot | Fat | Carb | Fiber | Chol | Sodium |
|------|------|-----|------|-------|------|--------|
| 321kc | 33g | 9g | 27g | 2g | 73mg | 703mg |

MEXICAN POULTRY

# Acapulco Chicken

*The salsa gives this dish a little zing.*

*vegetable spray*

*2 boneless chicken breast halves, skinned*

*3 tablespoons shredded fat-free cheddar cheese*

*½ teaspoon chopped, dried cilantro or parsley*

*2 teaspoons chopped black olives*

*⅓ cup mild salsa*

Preheat oven to 350 degrees. Spray a 1-quart, shallow baking dish with vegetable spray. Place a piece of chicken between two pieces of plastic wrap and pound until about ¼" thick. On the wide end of the chicken, place 1 tablespoon cheese, ¼ teaspoon cilantro and 1 teaspoon olives. Roll (jelly-roll fashion), starting with wide end; secure with a wooden pick. Spray a small, nonstick skillet with vegetable spray. Heat to medium-high, add chicken and cook, turning gently until browned on both sides.

Remove chicken to a 1-quart, shallow baking dish. Pour the salsa over all, cover and bake at 350 degrees for 30 minutes, basting twice. Sprinkle remaining 1 tablespoon cheese over chicken and bake uncovered for about 5 minutes more or until cheese is melted.

Yield: 2 servings

1 serving contains:

| Cal | Prot | Fat | Carb | Fiber | Chol | Sodium |
|-----|------|-----|------|-------|------|--------|
| 165kc | 30g | 3g | 2g | 1g | 84mg | 200mg |

Serving Suggestion: Serve with Lima Bean-Tomato Treat* and chopped lettuce and tomato. *This recipe found in the Vegetables section.*

MEXICAN POULTRY

# Chicken Chalupas

*A delightfully easy and tasty lunch*

1 boneless chicken breast half, prepared according to
   Harold's Italian Grilled Chicken*

4 corn tortillas

½ cup mashed pinto beans (prepared with no
   added fat)**

2 cups shredded iceberg lettuce

1 chopped tomato

¼ cup shredded reduced-fat cheddar cheese

¼ cup salsa***

Dice chicken. Quickly heat tortillas one at a time in a nonstick skillet or in a toaster oven on "toast." Place two tortillas on each serving plate; spoon 2 tablespoons beans over tortilla. Top with lettuce, tomato, cheese, salsa, and chicken.

Yield: 2 servings

1 serving contains:

| Cal | Prot | Fat | Carb | Fiber | Chol | Sodium |
|-----|------|-----|------|-------|------|--------|
| 268kc | 18g | 5g | 40g | 4g | 26mg | 254mg |

*This recipe can be found in this section.
**If you don't have cooked pinto beans available you can use canned vegetarian-style refried beans.
***This recipe can be found in the Sauces section of this book.

MEXICAN POULTRY

# Cumin Chicken Bake

*For outstanding flavor, marinate for two hours before cooking.*

*2 boneless chicken breast halves, skinned*

*½ cup chunky mild salsa*

*½ teaspoon cumin*

*½ cup fat-free Italian salad dressing*

*vegetable spray*

*1 teaspoon canola oil or oil of choice*

*½ cup onion slices*

*1 clove garlic, minced*

*1 small sliced tomato*

Place chicken in a medium shallow dish. In a small bowl, combine salsa, cumin, and salad dressing; pour over chicken. Cover and marinate in refrigerator at least 2 hours. Preheat oven to 350 degrees. Spray a small, shallow baking dish with vegetable spray. Heat oil in a medium nonstick skillet over medium-high heat. Sauté onions and garlic in oil until limp. Lift chicken from marinade, add to skillet, cook with onions until brown on both sides. Place chicken and onions in a small, shallow baking dish; top with tomato slices, pour remaining marinade over all. Bake uncovered about 30 minutes or until tender.

Yield: 2 servings

1 serving contains:

| Cal | Prot | Fat | Carb | Fiber | Chol | Sodium |
|-----|------|-----|------|-------|------|--------|
| 228kc | 28g | 6g | 9g | 2g | 73mg | 196mg |

# Tex-Mex Sausage-Chili-Cheese Casserole

*A delicious combination for brunch, lunch, or dinner*

vegetable spray

⅓ lb. turkey Italian sausage

¼ cup chopped onion

1 clove garlic, minced

1 (7 oz.) can mild green chilies, chopped

6 corn tortillas, torn into quarters

1 cup shredded fat-free sharp cheddar cheese

½ cup skim milk

1 cup egg substitute

⅛ teaspoon chili powder

¼ teaspoon cumin

dash freshly ground black pepper

1 large tomato, sliced

paprika

2 tablespoons salsa

Several hours or the night before serving, spray a 2-quart baking dish and a nonstick skillet with vegetable spray. Squeeze sausage from tubing into skillet, cook until slightly pink; add onion and garlic, continuing to cook until sausage is no longer pink. Spoon some of the chilies into the bottom of prepared baking dish, top with a layer of tortillas, part of the sausage, and cheese. Repeat until remaining chilies, tortillas, sausage, and cheese are used. In a small bowl, combine milk, egg substitute, chili powder, cumin, and pepper; beat with a wire whisk until well blended; pour over casserole. Arrange tomato over top; sprinkle with paprika. Cover and refrigerate several hours, overnight, or until ready to cook.

To Cook: Preheat oven to 350 degrees. Remove cover, place in 350-degree oven for about 45 minutes or until a knife inserted in center comes out clean. Serve with salsa.

Yield: 4 servings

1 serving contains:

| Cal | Prot | Fat | Carb | Fiber | Chol | Sodium |
|-----|------|-----|------|-------|------|--------|
| 255kc | 26g | 6g | 26g | 3g | 23mg | 1,040mg |

MEXICAN POULTRY

# Chicken Tortilla Casserole

*Can be made a day ahead and refrigerated until time to bake.*

2 boneless chicken breast halves, skinned

1 small carrot, cut in chunks (approx. ½ cup)

1 stalk celery, cut in chunks (approx. ½ cup)

¼ cup onion, cut in chunks

1 clove garlic, minced

1 bay leaf

¼ teaspoon salt

2 teaspoons low-fat margarine

3 large, sliced mushrooms (approx. ½ cup)

⅓ cup unbleached or all-purpose flour

¾ cup low-fat, low-sodium chicken broth

1¼ cups evaporated skimmed milk

¼ teaspoon chili powder

½ teaspoon paprika

½ teaspoon cumin

½ Knorr chicken bouillon cube

4 oz. can chopped green chilies

vegetable spray

6 corn tortillas, torn into quarters

½ cup shredded fat-free cheddar cheese

In a medium saucepan, combine the first 7 ingredients; add water to cover; bring to a gentle boil; reduce heat to low and simmer about 45 minutes or until chicken is tender. Remove chicken from broth; set chicken aside to cool. When cool, tear into bite-size pieces. Strain broth, set aside. Heat margarine in a medium saucepan; add mushrooms and sauté quickly. While mushrooms are cooking, place flour, broth, and milk in a jar; shake to dissolve. Pour flour mixture over mushrooms, stirring constantly until it starts to thicken.

Add chili powder, paprika, cumin, bouillon, and green chilies, reduce heat and let simmer 3-4 minutes. Preheat oven to 325 degrees. Lightly spray a 2-quart baking dish with vegetable spray. Spoon a small amount of sauce in the bottom of prepared dish. Put a layer of torn tortilla pieces, a layer of chicken, and more sauce. Keep layering until all ingredients are used, ending with sauce. Sprinkle with cheese. Cover and bake for 45 minutes in a 325-degree oven or until heated through and cheese is melted.

Yield: 2 servings

1 serving contains:

| Cal | Prot | Fat | Carb | Fiber | Chol | Sodium |
|------|------|-----|------|-------|-------|--------|
| 647kc | 45g | 10g | 81g | 5g | 110mg | 1590mg |

Variation: If you are really in a hurry, you can substitute ½ can low-fat, low-sodium cream of chicken soup plus ½ can of skim milk for the sauce and omit flour, broth, ¾ cup milk, and bouillon cube.

MEXICAN POULTRY

# Turkey - Corn Burritos

*Add chopped lettuce and tomato for a complete meal.*

½ lb. turkey (no skin added)

2 tablespoons chopped onion

¾ cup salsa

¾ cup creamed corn

1 tablespoon chopped green chilies

¼ cup shredded fat-free Monterey jack cheese

¼ cup shredded fat-free cheddar cheese

6 flour tortillas (7-8")

vegetable spray

Preheat oven to 350 degrees; spray 10x10 baking dish with vegetable spray. In a medium nonstick skillet, brown turkey and onion. Add ½ salsa, cook about 12 minutes, uncovered, or until most of the liquid is absorbed. Add corn, chilies, and ⅓ of both cheeses; blend well. Spoon ¼ cup of the meat mixture down the center of a tortilla, fold both sides over, place seam side down in a 10x10 baking dish, continue until all ingredients are used. Pour remaining salsa over all, sprinkle with remaining cheese. Bake in a 350-degree oven for 15 minutes or until cheese melts.

To microwave:
Place meat and onion in a microwave-safe dish, cover and cook on high for 2 minutes, stirring to break up meat after 1 minute. Add ½ of salsa and cook on 50 percent power for about 2-3 minutes, stirring after every 1 minute.

Proceed as before. Assemble burritos as directed above. Cover with wax paper and cook in microwave oven on ¾ power for 1 minute or just until cheese melts.

Yield: 2 servings

1 serving contains:

| Cal | Prot | Fat | Carb | Fiber | Chol | Sodium |
|---|---|---|---|---|---|---|
| 420kc | 23g | 10g | 45g | 2g | 30mg | 710mg |

Variation: This is also good to make in a casserole form. Put a little meat mixture in the bottom of a 1-quart casserole, then a tortilla; continue to layer until all ingredients are used. Sprinkle remaining cheese over all.

MEXICAN POULTRY

# Mexican Turkey in a Pot

*Prepare this in a Crock-Pot or a very low oven.*

*1½ lb. boneless turkey breast, skinned*

*1 (8 oz.) can tomato sauce*

*1 (4 oz.) can chopped green chilies*

*⅓ cup chopped onion*

*2 tablespoons Worcestershire sauce*

*1 tablespoon chili powder*

*¼ teaspoon garlic powder*

*8 flour tortillas (7-8")*

*½ cup shredded fat-free cheddar or Monterey jack cheese*

*1 cup shredded lettuce*

*½ cup diced tomatoes*

*½ cup salsa*

Place turkey in Crock-Pot. In a small bowl, combine tomato sauce, chilies, onion, Worcestershire sauce, chili powder, and garlic powder; add to turkey. Cover and cook on low 10-12 hours or on high 5-6 hours. Stir well. Turkey should pull apart into shreds. To serve: Spoon onto tortilla and roll up, garnish with cheese, lettuce, tomato, and salsa.

To prepare in oven: Place turkey, tomato sauce, chilies, onion, Worcestershire sauce, chili powder, and garlic powder in 2-quart baking dish. Place in 300-degree oven and bake for 3 hours or until very tender.

Yield: 8 (1 tortilla each) servings *

1 serving contains:

| Cal | Prot | Fat | Carb | Fiber | Chol | Sodium |
|------|------|-----|------|-------|-------|--------|
| 236kc | 26g | 4g | 28g | 2g | 17mg | 309mg |

*Wonderful to have a couple of days later; just heat in the microwave.*

# Asparagus / Cheese - Stuffed Chicken Breast

*These are so delicious and simple.*

6 fresh asparagus spears (approx. ⅓ lb.)

2 boneless chicken breast halves, skinned

½ ounce, grated low-fat mozzarella cheese,
   (approx. 2 tablespoons)

1 teaspoon olive oil

dash salt

3 tablespoons white wine

¼ teaspoon dried tarragon

¼ teaspoon lemon pepper

Trim asparagus, place in microwave-safe bowl, cover and cook on high for 2 minutes. Drain and immerse in ice water, drain again, set aside. Place chicken between 2 pieces of plastic wrap and pound until ¼" thick. Place 3 asparagus spears and ½ of cheese on one end of chicken. Roll up; secure with wooden pick. Repeat with remaining chicken. Sprinkle with salt. Heat oil in a small nonstick skillet over medium heat. Add chicken and cook until brown. Add wine, tarragon, and lemon pepper. Reduce heat, cover and simmer 15-20 minutes or until tender.

Yield: 2 servings

1 serving contains:

| Cal | Prot | Fat | Carb | Fiber | Chol | Sodium |
|---|---|---|---|---|---|---|
| 205kc | 30g | 7g | 2g | 0g | 77mg | 99mg |

VARIOUS POULTRY

# Asparagus Chicken Stir-Fry

*Fresh asparagus makes this a springtime favorite.*

*1 boneless chicken breast half, skinned*

*½ lb. fresh asparagus*

*½ cup low-fat, low-sodium chicken broth*

*1 tablespoon cornstarch*

*1 tablespoon sherry*

*1 tablespoon low-sodium soy sauce*

*1 tablespoon olive oil, divided*

*2 cloves garlic, minced*

*¼ teaspoon fresh ginger, minced*

*1 carrot (½ cup), sliced thinly*

*½ cup sweet onion, cut into rings*

*½ tablespoon fresh chives, chopped*

*2 fresh mushrooms, quartered (1 oz.)*

Cut chicken into thin strips; set aside. Snap off tough ends of asparagus; cut diagonally into 1" pieces; set aside. In a small bowl, combine chicken broth, cornstarch, sherry, and soy sauce; stir until well blended; set aside. Heat ½ table-spoon of the oil in a nonstick wok over medium-high heat (or a medium nonstick skillet). Add chicken; stir-fry until chicken becomes white and tender. Add garlic and ginger. Remove chicken, garlic, and ginger to a bowl, cover and set aside. Heat the remaining oil in wok; when hot, add carrot. Stir-fry about 1 minute. Add onions and asparagus; stir-fry about 1 minute. Add mushrooms; stir-fry another minute. Add chicken; stir, add broth mixture. Bring to a boil, stirring constantly. Cook 1 minute or until thick-ened. Serve immediately.

Yield: 2 servings

1 serving contains:

| Cal | Prot | Fat | Carb | Fiber | Chol | Sodium |
|-----|------|-----|------|-------|------|--------|
| 221kc | 20g | 9g | 17g | 3g | 37mg | 293mg |

Serving Suggestions: Serve with cooked white rice. Serve with Golden Risotto.

VARIOUS POULTRY

# Baked Potatoes with Chunky Chicken Topping

*This entrée is so quick and easy, yet satisfying.*

2 medium baking potatoes

1 tablespoon chopped onion

1 tablespoon chopped celery

½ tablespoon water

½ can low-fat, low-sodium cream of chicken soup

2 tablespoons skim milk

1 tablespoon white wine

dash dried thyme

1 chicken breast half, skinned, cooked, and chopped

½ teaspoon dried parsley

dash lemon zest

dash freshly ground black pepper

Scrub potatoes, pierce skin several times with a fork; place in microwave, cook on high for approximately 7 minutes, or until tender; set aside. In a small microwave-safe dish, combine onion, celery, and water; cover and microwave on high about 2 minutes. Add soup, milk, wine, and thyme; cover and microwave on high about 90 seconds. Add chicken, parsley, and lemon zest; continue to microwave about 30 seconds. Place baked potatoes on individual plates, cut lengthwise, squeeze to open slightly. Spoon soup-chicken mixture over potato, add freshly ground pepper. Serve immediately.

Yield: 2 servings

1 serving contains:

| Cal | Prot | Fat | Carb | Fiber | Chol | Sodium |
|-----|------|-----|------|-------|------|--------|
| 367kc | 18g | 4g | 61g | 1g | 44mg | 469mg |

Serving Suggestion: Serve with a green salad and French bread.

VARIOUS POULTRY

# Blueberry Chicken

*A colorful, festive presentation*

1 teaspoon olive oil

2 boneless chicken breast halves, skinned

3 tablespoons chopped onion

2 tablespoons blueberry vinegar* (or white)

¼ cup low-fat, low-sodium chicken broth

1 tablespoon chopped fresh tomato

¼ cup fresh blueberries, for garnish (optional)

Heat oil in a medium nonstick skillet over medium-high heat. Add chicken and sauté quickly until brown on both sides. Remove chicken; set aside. Reduce heat to medium. Add onion; cook until tender. Add vinegar; cook until sauce is reduced by ½. Reduce heat to low. Stir in chicken broth and tomato; simmer for about 1 minute. Return chicken to pan, cover and simmer 35-45 minutes or until tender. Garnish with fresh blueberries.

Yield: 2 servings

1 serving contains:

| Cal | Prot | Fat | Carb | Fiber | Chol | Sodium |
|------|------|-----|------|-------|------|--------|
| 181kc | 27g | 5g | 5g | 1g | 73mg | 67mg |

This can be prepared to the point where you return the chicken to pan, then place in 350-degree oven and bake for 40-45 minutes.

Different flavored vinegars may be used: raspberry, cherry, cranberry, strawberry, etc., using the appropriate fresh fruit.

*The recipe for this can be found in the Salads section of this book.

VARIOUS POULTRY

# Broccoli and Chicken Stir-Fry

*A great, easy meal for a busy day*

2 tablespoons low-sodium soy sauce

1 tablespoon lemon juice

2 boneless chicken breast halves, skinned, cut into 1" cubes

2 teaspoons olive oil

½ cup onion, sliced

2 cups fresh broccoli flowerettes

4 oz. water chestnuts, sliced and drained

1 tablespoon pimiento, chopped

1 tablespoon cornstarch

¼ cup water + 1 tablespoon, divided

In a small bowl, combine soy sauce and lemon juice. Add chicken and refrigerate 1 hour or until ready to cook. Using medium-high heat, heat oil in a wok or a nonstick skillet. Lift chicken from marinade using a slotted spoon to drain; add to wok and sauté on medium-high, stirring quickly until just tender. Remove chicken to a bowl, cover and set aside. Add onion and broccoli to wok, toss quickly for about 1 minute. Add 1 tablespoon water, reduce heat to medium, cover and steam for about 3 minutes. Add chestnuts, pimientos, and chicken; stir. In a small bowl, combine cornstarch, ¼ cup water, and the remaining marinade; blend well. Pour over chicken and vegetables, stirring gently until sauce thickens. Serve immediately.

Yield: 2 (1½ cups) servings

1 serving contains:

| Cal | Prot | Fat | Carb | Fiber | Chol | Sodium |
|------|------|-----|------|-------|-------|--------|
| 278kc | 31g | 8g | 21g | 2g | 73mg | 569mg |

Serving Suggestion: Serve with cooked brown rice.

VARIOUS POULTRY

# Creamy Chicken and Dumplings

*Basil enhances the flavor; carrots add texture and color.*

2 boneless chicken breast halves, skinned

3 cups low-fat, low-sodium chicken broth

½ cup onion, cut into wedges

½ large carrot (approx. ½ cup), cut in chunks

1 stalk celery (approx. ⅓ cup), cut in chunks

½ teaspoon dried thyme

½ Knorr chicken bouillon cube

1 cup frozen peas

1⅔ cups reduced-fat baking mix*

¼ cup shredded carrots

1 teaspoon dried basil, crushed

⅔ cup skim milk

freshly ground black pepper

Place chicken in a medium-sized kettle; add broth, onion, carrot chunks, celery, thyme, and bouillon cube. On high heat, bring to a boil; reduce heat to simmer and cook for about 2 hours, until chicken is very tender. Remove chicken and cut into bite-sized pieces; set aside. Remove vegetables; discard. Add peas and chicken to broth in kettle. In a medium mixing bowl, combine baking mix, shredded carrots, and basil; add milk and stir just until mixed. While you are doing this, return heat to high, bring broth to a gentle boil. Drop dumplings into the broth by the teaspoon. Reduce heat to simmer; cook uncovered for 10 minutes, cover and continue to cook 10 minutes more. Add pepper, then serve.

Yield: 3 (1½ cups) servings

1 serving contains:

| Cal | Prot | Fat | Carb | Fiber | Chol | Sodium |
|------|------|-----|------|-------|------|--------|
| 245kc | 46g | 6g | 46g | 1g | 50mg | 770mg |

*I buy a popular reduced-fat baking mix.

VARIOUS POULTRY

# Creamy Chicken and Noodles

*So creamy, you won't believe it's healthy.*

*vegetable spray*

*½ lb. boneless chicken breast, skinned, cut into chunks*

*2 tablespoons onion, chopped*

*1 clove garlic, minced*

*1 cup evaporated skimmed milk*

*1 tablespoon white wine*

*2 tablespoons shredded fat-free Swiss cheese*

*2 cups cooked "no yolk" noodles (cooked without added fat or salt)*

*1 tablespoon grated Parmesan cheese, made with skim milk*

*freshly ground black pepper*

Spray a medium nonstick skillet with vegetable spray; heat to medium. Add chicken and onion; cook until chicken loses its pink color. Add garlic; continue to cook until chicken is tender. Remove to a serving dish; keep warm. Using the same skillet, heat milk, wine, and Swiss cheese until bubbly,* reduce heat and continue to simmer for about 8-10 minutes or until slightly thickened. Put chicken in sauce. Put noodles in serving dish, spoon chicken and sauce over noodles, and sprinkle with Parmesan cheese and pepper.

Yield: 2 servings

1 serving contains:

| Cal | Prot | Fat | Carb | Fiber | Chol | Sodium |
|------|------|-----|------|-------|------|--------|
| 409kc | 33g | 5g | 53g | 0g | 50mg | 248mg |

*If sauce starts to curdle, stir briskly with whisk and it will smooth out.*

VARIOUS POULTRY

# Chicken Burgers

*These are an exceptionally good replacement for hamburgers.*

*½ lb. freshly ground chicken breast (no skin)*

*1 tablespoon egg substitute*

*1 tablespoon bread crumbs*

*2 tablespoons finely chopped onion*

*½ teaspoon dried parsley*

*⅛ teaspoon garlic powder*

*⅛ teaspoon Italian seasoning*

*dash season salt*

*½ teaspoon Worcestershire sauce*

*1 teaspoon unbleached or all-purpose flour*

*vegetable spray*

*½ teaspoon olive oil*

*2 sandwich buns*

*2 slices tomato (optional)*

*2 slices onion (optional)*

In a medium mixing bowl, combine chicken, egg substitute, bread crumbs, onion, parsley, garlic powder, Italian seasoning, salt, and Worcestershire sauce; set aside. Sprinkle ½ the flour over a small piece of wax paper, shape into 2 patties and place on wax paper, then sprinkle remainder of flour over top side of patties. Spray a nonstick skillet with vegetable spray, then add oil; place over medium-low heat. When hot, add patties; cook about 5 minutes until the patties are brown, turn, cover and cook another 5 minutes or until done. Remove lid and continue to cook another 1-2 minutes. Serve on bun with tomato and onion.

To Grill:

Spray grill rack with vegetable spray; preheat grill. Shape into 2 patties and place on hot rack, and cook about 10-15 minutes or until juices are no longer pink. *Watch closely, because over-cooking makes them dry.*

Yield: 2 servings

1 serving contains:

| Cal | Prot | Fat | Carb | Fiber | Chol | Sodium |
|------|------|-----|------|-------|-------|--------|
| 298kc | 33g | 6g | 26g | 2g | 75mg | 353mg |

VARIOUS POULTRY

# Chicken Dijon

*Tender chicken in a good flavorful sauce*

2 boneless chicken breast halves, skinned

vegetable spray

1 teaspoon olive oil

2 tablespoons chopped onion

¼ cup white wine

1 tablespoon Dijon mustard (or other spicy brown mustard)

⅛ teaspoon fresh, minced rosemary or a pinch of dried rosemary

⅛ teaspoon fresh, minced thyme or a pinch of dried thyme

⅛ teaspoon fresh, minced tarragon or a pinch of dried tarragon

¾ cup evaporated skimmed milk

dash freshly ground black pepper

Place chicken breast between 2 pieces of plastic wrap and pound to flatten. Spray a medium nonstick skillet with vegetable spray, add oil and heat on medium-high. Carefully place chicken in hot oil and cook until brown on one side; turn. Add onion to chicken and continue to cook until tender and brown on other side. Remove to serving dish and keep warm. Reduce heat to low. In a small bowl, combine wine and mustard, stirring to blend well; pour in skillet. Add rosemary, thyme, tarragon, and pepper, and simmer until reduced by ½. Pour most of the wine mixture into a small bowl. Gradually add milk to this mixture, stirring briskly to prevent curdling,* then return to skillet and simmer about 4-5 minutes just until heated. Do not bring to a boil. Strain, pour over chicken breast and serve immediately.

Yield: 2 servings

1 serving contains:

| Cal | Prot | Fat | Carb | Fiber | Chol | Sodium |
|-----|------|-----|------|-------|------|--------|
| 267kc | 34g | 6g | 13g | 0g | 77mg | 398mg |

*If sauce curdles, just continue to stir briskly with whisk and it will smooth out.*

VARIOUS POULTRY

# Audrey's Green Beans and Red Potatoes

*This is a real down-home meal without the "fatback."*

1 lb. fresh green beans

⅛ lb. smoked turkey

½ lb. new red potatoes

¾ teaspoon salt or to taste

Wash, drain, and break beans into 1-2" lengths; place in medium saucepan. Cut turkey into ½" cubes; add to beans. Add enough water to cover. Using medium-high heat, bring beans to a boil. Reduce heat to low. Continue to cook on low for about 1 hour. Scrub potatoes and quarter. Using a slotted spoon, gently lift beans, placing potatoes under beans. Continue to cook until potatoes and beans are tender. Add water as needed to keep from cooking dry.

Yield: 6 cups

1 serving contains:

| Cal | Prot | Fat | Carb | Fiber | Chol | Sodium |
|------|------|-----|------|-------|------|--------|
| 69kc | 5g | 0g | 13g | 2g | 8mg | 298mg |

Serving Suggestion: Serve with coleslaw and corn bread for the perfect "down-home" meal.

VARIOUS POULTRY

# Hawaiian Chicken

*So quick and simple, yet so tasty*

2 boneless chicken breast halves, skinned, cut into
   1" cubes

vegetable spray

¼ cup fresh orange juice

2 tablespoons BBQ sauce

1 cup pineapple chunks with juice (packed in its
   own juice)

2 cups hot cooked rice (cooked without added fat or
   salt)

1 teaspoon almond slices

Spray a nonstick medium skillet with vegetable spray; heat on medium-high. Add chicken; sauté quickly until brown and tender. In a small bowl, combine orange juice, BBQ sauce, pineapple and juice; add to chicken, heat thoroughly, but do not boil. When hot, serve over rice; sprinkle almonds on top.

Yield: 2 servings

1 serving contains:

| Cal | Prot | Fat | Carb | Fiber | Chol | Sodium |
|-----|------|-----|------|-------|------|--------|
| 490kc | 33g | 6g | 76g | 4g | 73mg | 203mg |

VARIOUS POULTRY

# Judy's Napa-Cabbage Chicken

*Napa cabbage and bok choy give this a hearty flavor.*

¼ cup low-sodium soy sauce

2 cloves garlic, minced

1½ tablespoons olive oil, divided

2 boneless chicken breast halves, skinned, cut into cubes

1 cup low-sodium, low-fat chicken broth

1½ tablespoons cornstarch

2 cups napa cabbage, slightly chopped*

1 cup bok choy, sliced (using only a little of the green)

4 green onions, sliced

½ cup water chestnuts, sliced

¼ cup red pepper, sliced

In a plastic bag with zip-lock closing, combine soy sauce, garlic, and ½ tablespoon oil; add chicken, close bag and refrigerate for about 2 hours. In a small bowl, combine cornstarch and broth; set aside. Using medium-high heat, heat ½ tablespoon oil in wok or large nonstick skillet. Lift chicken from marinade with a slotted spoon to drain, add to wok, and stir-fry quickly until chicken becomes white and is tender. Remove from wok, cover and set aside. Add remaining ½ tablespoon oil to wok. Add napa cabbage, bok choy, and green onions; stirring quickly, cook for 2 minutes. Add water chestnuts and red pepper; cook 1 or 2 minutes more. Return chicken to wok. Add broth and cornstarch to the remaining marinade; pour over chicken and vegetables; cook until thick and bubbly. Serve immediately.

Yield: 2 servings

1 serving contains:

| Cal | Prot | Fat | Carb | Fiber | Chol | Sodium |
|-----|------|-----|------|-------|------|--------|
| 326kc | 3g | 14g | 19g | 3g | 73mg | 1073mg |

Serving suggestion: Serve with cooked rice

*Use the remaining cabbage in Chinese Salad found in the Salads section.*

VARIOUS POULTRY

# Lemony Chicken Stir-Fry

*Lemon and spinach give this a unique flavor.*

2 boneless chicken breast halves, skinned, cut into
    ½" strips

1 tablespoon low-sodium soy sauce

2 tablespoons white wine vinegar

1 tablespoon cornstarch

2 teaspoons lemon pepper

1 tablespoon olive oil, divided

⅓ cup onion slices

1 clove garlic, minced

⅓ small lemon, cut into almost paper-thin slivers

½ cup low-sodium, low-fat chicken broth

1½ cups fresh spinach leaves, washed and drained

Place chicken in a plastic bag with zip-lock clos-ing. In a small bowl, combine soy sauce, vinegar, cornstarch, and lemon pepper; pour over chicken, seal bag, and mix thoroughly. Allow to marinate in refrigerator for about 2 hours. Add ½ tablespoon oil to a medium nonstick skillet or wok; heat to medium-high. Add chicken; sauté quickly until tender; remove to serving dish, cover and set aside. Add remaining ½ tablespoon oil. When hot, add onion, cooking until tender. Add garlic, stirring constantly for about 30 seconds. Add lemon slivers; cook another 30 seconds. Add chicken broth; blend. Stir in spinach and cook until just wilted. Add chicken and sauce.

Yield: 2 servings

1 serving contains:

| Cal | Prot | Fat | Carb | Fiber | Chol | Sodium |
|---|---|---|---|---|---|---|
| 245kc | 29g | 10g | 8g | 2g | 73mg | 340mg |

Serving Suggestions: Serve over hot angel hair pasta. Serve with cooked brown rice.

VARIOUS POULTRY

# Salem's Sunshine Chicken

*An easy, quick, and delicious entrée*

3 tablespoons unbleached or all-purpose flour

dash cinnamon

dash cloves

2 boneless chicken breast halves, skinned

vegetable spray

1 teaspoon olive oil

1 clove garlic, minced

⅓ cup frozen orange juice concentrate

⅓ cup water + ¼ cup water, divided

1 tablespoon chopped onion

⅛ teaspoon salt

Combine flour, cinnamon, and cloves in a plastic bag; add chicken and shake. Reserve remaining flour and spices. Spray a nonstick skillet with vegetable spray; add oil; heat over medium-high heat. Add chicken; sauté quickly until brown; add garlic the last few seconds. While the chicken is cooking, combine orange juice, ⅓ cup water and onion. Pour over chicken, cover and reduce heat to simmer, cooking 15-20 minutes or until tender. Remove chicken to serving dish. Combine ¼ cup water, remaining flour, and salt in a small bowl. Stir into liquid in skillet. Cook over medium heat until thick and bubbly*, spoon over chicken and serve.

Yield: 2 servings

1 serving contains:

| Cal | Prot | Fat | Carb | Fiber | Chol | Sodium |
|------|------|-----|------|-------|------|--------|
| 223kc | 28g | 6g | 13g | 1g | 73mg | 202mg |

Serving Suggestions: Serve with cooked rice. Serve with couscous made with chicken broth.

*If sauce curdles, just continue to stir briskly and it will smooth out.

VARIOUS POULTRY

# Sauerkraut and Sausage Casserole

*A favorite combination enhanced with apple and brown sugar*

*vegetable spray*

*½ cup chopped onion*

*⅓ lb. turkey Italian sausage*

*1 tart apple, peeled and cut into sections*

*1 (17 oz.) can sauerkraut, rinsed and drained\**

*½ cup water*

*¼ cup brown sugar*

Preheat oven to 350 degrees. Spray a 2-quart casserole and a large nonstick skillet with vegetable spray. Remove sausage from casing. Using medium-high heat, cook onion and sausage until sausage is no longer pink. Add apple, sauerkraut, water, and brown sugar; stir and spoon into prepared casserole. Cover and bake in a 350-degree oven for one hour.

Yield: 2 servings

1 serving contains:

| Cal | Prot | Fat | Carb | Fiber | Chol | Sodium |
|-----|------|-----|------|-------|------|--------|
| 296kc | 15g | 9g | 35g | 2g | 45mg | 2,133mg |

*\*Rinsing and draining the sauerkraut will reduce the sodium substantially.*

VARIOUS    POULTRY

# Sausage - Basil   and   Wine

*A favorite combination to serve with pasta*

⅓ lb. turkey Italian sausage

2 cloves garlic, minced

½ cup sliced green onion

1 cup red or green pepper, sliced

½ cup red wine

1 cup chopped fresh tomatoes

1 tablespoon balsamic vinegar

⅓ cup chopped fresh basil

4 oz. spaghetti or fettuccine

Spray a large nonstick skillet with vegetable spray. Remove sausage from casing. Using medium-high heat, cook sausage until just slightly pink; add garlic and cook until sausage is no longer pink. Add onion and peppers, continuing to cook until vegetables are tender-crisp. Add wine and simmer about 5 minutes; add tomatoes, vinegar, and basil, and cook about 5 minutes more. While this is simmering, cook spaghetti according to package directions, without added salt or fat; drain well. Place spaghetti in serving bowl, spoon sausage mixture over spaghetti. Serve immediately.

Yield: 2 servings

1 serving contains:

| Cal | Prot | Fat | Carb | Fiber | Chol | Sodium |
|------|------|------|------|-------|------|--------|
| 434kc | 23g | 11g | 57g | 7g | 45mg | 569mg |

# Turkey Cutlets in Mushroom Sauce

*This entrée is so quick and easy, yet interesting.*

vegetable spray

4 fresh turkey slices (approx. ½ lb.)

2 teaspoons low-fat margarine

2 green onions, cut into 1" pieces (approx. ½ cup)

4 fresh, sliced mushrooms (approx. ¾ cup)

½ cup red or green pepper strips

1 tablespoon unbleached or all-purpose flour

¾ cup evaporated skimmed milk

1 teaspoon low-sodium soy sauce

dash lemon zest

dash white pepper

¼ teaspoon salt

Spray a medium nonstick skillet with vegetable spray; heat to medium-high. Add turkey; sauté quickly until just tender. Remove to serving dish, cover and set aside in warm place. Melt marga-rine in skillet. Add onions, mushrooms, and pep-per. Sauté quickly until tender; spoon over tur-key. In a jar with a lid, combine flour and milk; shake until completely dissolved. Slowly add to skillet, and cook 3-4 minutes, stirring constantly. Add soy sauce; continue to stir until sauce thick-ens. Season with lemon zest, pepper, and salt. Pour over turkey and vegetables and serve.

Yield: 2 servings

1 serving contains:

| Cal | Prot | Fat | Carb | Fiber | Chol | Sodium |
|-----|------|-----|------|-------|------|--------|
| 243kc | 36g | 4g | 16g | 1g | 43mg | 570mg |

Serving Suggestions: Serve with White-Wild Rice Pilaf*. Serve with hot linguine.

*This will keep well for a short time if covered with foil and placed in a warm oven.*

*\*This recipe can be found in the Vegetables section.*

VARIOUS POULTRY

# Lemon/Basil-Stuffed Turkey Tenderloins

*Basil and lemon add a refreshing flavor to the turkey.*

*vegetable spray*

*1 turkey tenderloin (approx. ½ lb.)*

*3 teaspoons low-fat margarine*

*½ teaspoon grated lemon zest*

*1 ½ tablespoons fresh basil or 1 teaspoon dried, divided*

*½ cup low-sodium, low-fat chicken broth*

*½ tablespoon lemon juice*

*1 teaspoon unbleached or all-purpose flour*

*3 tablespoons water*

*fresh basil sprigs for garnish (optional)*

Preheat oven to 350 degrees. Spray a 1-quart shallow baking dish with vegetable spray. Using kitchen shears, slit tenderloins down the side to make a pocket; set aside. In a small bowl, combine 2 teaspoons margarine, lemon zest, and 1 tablespoon basil. Stuff tenderloins with margarine mixture; secure with wooden pick. Spray a medium nonstick skillet with vegetable spray; heat on medium-high. Add tenderloins and sauté quickly until browned on both sides. Remove tenderloins to prepared baking dish; set aside. Combine broth, lemon juice, and remaining ½ tablespoon basil in skillet, heat, then pour over tenderloins. Cover and bake in a 350-degree oven, 35-40 minutes or until tender. Remove to serving dish. Pour juices into a small saucepan. In a small bowl, combine flour and water. Add to juices. Bring to a boil over medium heat; cook until it starts to thicken. Add remaining teaspoon margarine,

stirring constantly until melted. Pour over tenderloins. Garnish with basil and serve.

Yield: 2 servings

1 serving contains:

| Cal | Prot | Fat | Carb | Fiber | Chol | Sodium |
|-----|------|-----|------|-------|------|--------|
| 195kc | 33g | 6g | 2g | 0g | 91mg | 114mg |

VARIOUS POULTRY

# Turkey-Ham and Cheese Omelet

*You will be pleased with this variation of an old favorite.*

½ cup egg substitute plus 4 egg whites or enough
    to equal 1 cup

vegetable spray

2 teaspoons olive oil

2 tablespoons chopped onion

1 tablespoon chopped green or red pepper

2 oz. cubed turkey-ham

¼ cup shredded fat-free sharp cheddar cheese

freshly ground black pepper to taste

In a small mixing bowl, combine egg substitute and egg whites; beat slightly with a fork. Spray a 10" nonstick skillet with vegetable spray; heat over medium-high; add 1 teaspoon olive oil. When hot, add onion and green pepper; cook about 3-4 minutes or until tender. Add remaining oil, then turkey-ham; stir until hot. Reduce heat to low; pour egg mixture over ham, tilting the skillet to spread. As it cooks, gently lift the edge with a spatula and tilt the skillet to permit the uncooked eggs to run to the bottom of the pan. When done, sprinkle cheese over egg, sprinkle with pepper, fold in half, and slide onto the serving plate.

Yield: 2 servings

1 serving contains:

| Cal | Prot | Fat | Carb | Fiber | Chol | Sodium |
|-----|------|-----|------|-------|------|--------|
| 149kc | 18g | 6g | 5g | 0g | 19mg | 643mg |

Serving Suggestion: Serve with mixed green salad and hot rolls.

# S E A F O O D

Seafood is an excellent source of protein, B vitamins, and many minerals. It is also low in fat, cholesterol, and calories. While crab, lobster, shrimp, and other shellfish are higher in cholesterol, they are generally lower in fat, and can still be enjoyed in moderation.

Seafood is one of the easiest and quickest to prepare of all entrées, especially broiled fish, which can cook in just a few minutes. The variety of fresh seafood available at today's grocers is quite extensive. Note: Some stores sell a larger volume of fish, and therefore should have the freshest choices.

I am very selective where I buy my fish. If there is a strong, fishy odor to my choice of seafood, I will change my selection. fish should be bright, clear in color; not shriveled, dark, or cloudy looking. Be careful not to overcook seafood, or it will become tough and dry.

Use sauces sparingly; they will detract from the delicate flavor of seafood.

I plan seafood for dinner at least two days a week, also using tuna or imitation crab frequently for lunch.

For a special dinner, try Scallops 'n' Asparagus with Linguine or Pasta Seafood Italiano. A really easy dish is the Barbecued Catfish or Scotty's Lemon Filets. Our favorite recipe for a quick, simple dinner is Brenda's Grilled Fish.

SEAFOOD

# Baked Fried Fish

*A crispy, low-fat alternative to fried fish*

vegetable spray

⅓ cup coarse, fresh bread crumbs

½ tablespoon grated Parmesan cheese, made with
skim milk

⅛ teaspoon dried dill weed

⅛ teaspoon lemon pepper

3 tablespoons egg whites or egg substitute

½ lb. mild white fish (orange roughy, sole,
flounder, cod, etc.)

2 teaspoons low-fat margarine, melted

2 thin slices fresh lemon (optional)

2 small sprigs fresh parsley (optional)

Preheat oven to 400 degrees. Lightly spray a small, shallow baking pan with vegetable spray. In a small, shallow dish, combine bread crumbs, cheese, dill, and lemon pepper. Put egg in another shallow dish; beat lightly. Dip fish in egg, then in crumbs, repeat until all crumbs are used. Place fish in the prepared baking pan; pour margarine over fish. Bake in a 400-degree oven for about 15 minutes or until fish flakes when tested with a fork. Garnish with fresh lemon wedges and parsley.

Yield: 2 servings

1 serving contains:

| Cal | Prot | Fat | Carb | Fiber | Chol | Sodium |
|-----|------|-----|------|-------|------|--------|
| 145kc | 23g | 3g | 4g | 0g | 51mg | 199mg |

S E A F O O D

# B a r b e c u e d    C a t f i s h

*This is so quick and simple you will use it often.*

*vegetable spray*

*2 tablespoons BBQ sauce*

*¼ teaspoon grated lemon zest*

*½ teaspoon lemon juice*

*dash ground cayenne pepper*

*½ lb. catfish*

Preheat oven to 400 degrees. Spray shallow baking pan with vegetable spray. In a small bowl, combine BBQ sauce, lemon zest, juice, and pepper. Place fish in prepared baking pan; spoon sauce over fish. Bake at 400 degrees for about 20 minutes or until fish flakes when tested with a fork.

Yield: 2 servings

1 serving contains:

| Cal | Prot | Fat | Carb | Fiber | Chol | Sodium |
|-----|------|-----|------|-------|------|--------|
| 143kc | 21g | 5g | 2g | 0g | 66mg | 198mg |

SEAFOOD

# Brenda's Grilled Fish

*This mild, yet flavorful recipe is our favorite for grilled fish.*

vegetable spray

½ lb. mild white fish (orange roughy, scrod, cod, etc.)

1 tablespoon white wine

1 tablespoon white Worcestershire sauce

1 tablespoon lemon juice

1 teaspoon low-fat margarine, melted

Spray wire fish basket* with vegetable spray. In a small bowl, combine wine, Worcestershire sauce, lemon juice, and margarine. Place fish on hot grill, basting frequently with marinade. Cook about 5 minutes on high heat or until fish flakes when tested with a fork.

Yield: 2 servings

1 serving contains:

| Cal | Prot | Fat | Carb | Fiber | Chol | Sodium |
|-----|------|-----|------|-------|------|--------|
| 75kc | 20g | 2g | 2g | 0g | 62mg | 159mg |

*Aluminum foil method: If you don't have a fish basket, lay a piece of aluminum foil over grill rack. Using a fork, pierce the foil several times. Place fish directly on foil and proceed as above.*

Serving Suggestion: Serve with baked sweet potato and Garlicky Green Beans.**

**This recipe can be found in the Vegetables section of this book.*

SEAFOOD

# Crab Au Gratin

*The white sauce makes this extra special.*

vegetable spray

½ cup + 2 tablespoons skim milk

½ tablespoon unbleached or all-purpose flour

1 teaspoon low-fat margarine, melted

2 teaspoons chopped fresh chives

1 tablespoon finely chopped green pepper

¼ teaspoon dry mustard

1 teaspoon white Worcestershire sauce

1 tablespoon lemon juice

1½ tablespoons fat-free mayonnaise

1 tablespoon diced pimiento

⅓ lb. imitation crab

¼ cup fresh bread crumbs

dash white pepper

Preheat oven to 350 degrees. Spray a shallow, 1-quart baking dish with vegetable spray. In a small microwave-safe bowl, combine milk, flour, margarine, chives, and green pepper. Cover and microwave on high 2½ to 3 minutes or until thickened, stirring every 25 seconds to prevent boiling over. Stir in mustard, Worcestershire sauce, lemon juice, mayonnaise, and pimiento. Gently fold in crab. Spoon into baking dish and top with bread crumbs and pepper. Bake in a 350-degree oven uncovered for 20 minutes or until heated through.

Stove-top directions: Place green pepper in a small saucepan with 1 tablespoon water. Cook until tender. Add chives. In a small jar with lid, combine milk and flour. Slowly add to green pepper, stirring constantly until thickened. Proceed as above.

Yield: 2 servings

1 serving contains:

| Cal | Prot | Fat | Carb | Fiber | Chol | Sodium |
|-----|------|-----|------|-------|------|--------|
| 168kc | 17g | 3g | 25g | 0g | 21mg | 837mg |

S E A F O O D

# C r a b - S t u f f e d   F l o u n d e r

*This is not only good, but a very attractive dish.*

vegetable spray

½ lb. flounder filet

¼ cup imitation crab, flaked

2 tablespoons chopped fresh chives

½ tablespoon fat-free mayonnaise

1 teaspoon Dijon mustard

½ teaspoon lemon juice

1 teaspoon melted low-fat margarine

1 tablespoon white wine

¼ cup sliced mushrooms (1 large)

dash paprika

Preheat oven to 400 degrees. Lightly spray a shallow baking dish with vegetable spray. Rinse fish and pat dry; set aside. In a small bowl, combine crab, chives, mayonnaise, mustard, and lemon juice. Lay fish out on dry paper towel. Evenly spread crab mixture over the fish, roll up jelly-roll fashion, and secure with wooden picks. Place in prepared baking dish and bake 10 minutes at 400 degrees. While fish is cooking, combine margarine and wine in a small bowl. Remove dish from oven. Sprinkle mushrooms over top of fish, pour margarine mixture over mushrooms, and lightly dust with paprika. Return to oven and continue to cook 10 minutes or more, just until fish flakes when tested with a fork.

Yield: 2 servings

1 serving contains:

| Cal | Prot | Fat | Carb | Fiber | Chol | Sodium |
|-----|------|-----|------|-------|------|--------|
| 120kc | 19g | 2g | 4g | 0g | 78mg | 393mg |

S E A F O O D

# C r i s p y   B a k e d   F i s h

*Cornflake crumbs make this nice and crispy without the fat.*

vegetable spray

½ lb. mild white fish filets (orange roughy, sole, cod, etc.)

¼ cup egg substitute or 1 egg white

½ cup cornflake crumbs

¾ teaspoon Old Bay Seasoning

2 teaspoons low-fat margarine, melted

Preheat oven to 425 degrees. Spray a small, shallow baking pan with vegetable spray. Rinse fish and pat dry; set aside. In a small bowl, beat egg substitute with a fork until frothy. Place cornflake crumbs and seasoning in a small, shallow dish. Dip fish in egg, then in crumbs; place in prepared baking pan. Pour margarine over fish. Bake in a 425-degree oven for about 15 minutes or until fish flakes when tested with a fork.

Yield: 2 servings

1 serving contains:

| Cal | Prot | Fat | Carb | Fiber | Chol | Sodium |
|-----|------|-----|------|-------|------|--------|
| 147kc | 24g | 3g | 5g | 0g | 48mg | 223mg |

Serving Suggestion: Serve with baked potato and Marinated Tomatoes and Cucumbers.*

Variation: Substitute 1 tablespoon oat bran for 1 tablespoon cereal.

*This recipe can be found in the Salads section of this book.*

SEAFOOD

# Filet Dijon

*Dijon mustard adds a subtle tang to this fish.*

vegetable spray

½ lb. mild white fish filet (cod, orange roughy, etc.)

1 tablespoon fat-free mayonnaise

1 teaspoon Dijon mustard

¼ cup cornflake crumbs

dash dried dill weed

dash garlic powder

Preheat oven to 400 degrees. Spray a shallow baking dish with vegetable spray. Rinse fish and pat dry, set aside. In a small bowl, combine mayonnaise and mustard; set aside. Place crumbs in a small plate; set aside. Spread mustard mixture over 1 side of fish, sprinkle with crumb mixture, lay fish in baking pan, crumb side down; repeat with remaining side of fish.

Sprinkle dill weed and garlic powder over fish. Bake in 400-degree oven about 15 minutes or until fish flakes when tested with a fork.

To microwave: Prepare fish as above. Put in microwave-safe glass baking dish with thickest part of fish toward outside of plate; cover with waxed paper. Microwave about 2½-3 minutes on high or until fish flakes nicely.

Yield: 2 servings

1 serving contains:

| Cal | Prot | Fat | Carb | Fiber | Chol | Sodium |
|-----|------|-----|------|-------|------|--------|
| 107kc | 20g | 1g | 3g | 0g | 62mg | 171mg |

SEAFOOD

# Grilled Fish with Vegetable Kabobs

*Fresh vegetables and fish make a delicious, low-fat meal.*

*2 small new potatoes (½ lb.)*

*8 cherry tomatoes (½ lb.)*

*1 yellow or green squash (4 oz.), cut into 4 thick slices*

*1 sweet onion (4 oz.) cut into 4 wedges*

*½ lb. marlin or any mild fish, about ½" thick*

*¼ cup Herb Vinaigrette Dressing\**

*6 fresh basil leaves (optional)*

Preheat grill; spray fish basket** with vegetable spray. Rinse fish and pat dry. Put in basket; set aside. Precook potatoes for 2 minutes on high in microwave oven. Cut potatoes in half. Using half the ingredients, prepare kabobs as follows: Thread ½ potato on skewer, follow with remaining ingredients, tucking a fresh basil leaf in between occasionally, ending with the other potato half. Prepare second skewer in the same order. Place kabobs on hot grill about 4" from heat. Place fish on grill; baste with vinaigrette. Cook on high, turning kabobs occasionally. Continue to cook about 5-8 minutes or until fish flakes with a fork, basting frequently. To serve, slide the vegetables from skewers onto the serving plates along with the fish. Garnish with fresh basil leaf.

Yield: 2 servings

1 serving contains:

| Cal | Prot | Fat | Carb | Fiber | Chol | Sodium |
|------|------|-----|------|-------|------|--------|
| 254kc | 24g | 6g | 31g | 3g | 48mg | 75mg |

*\*This recipe can be found in the Salads section of this book.*

*\*\*Aluminum foil method: If you don't have a fish basket, lay a piece of aluminum foil over grill rack. Using a fork, pierce the foil several times.*

S E A F O O D

# White Fish Baked in Orange Sauce

*Orange sauce adds an interesting change for baked fish.*

vegetable spray

½ lb. mild white fish filets (cod, orange roughy,
   flounder)

¼ cup orange juice

½ cup cornflake crumbs

⅓ teaspoon lemon pepper

2 teaspoons low-fat margarine

1 tablespoon white wine

1 teaspoon cornstarch

1 teaspoon fresh orange rind, finely grated

1 teaspoon honey

2 thin orange slices

Preheat oven to 400 degrees. Spray a shallow baking dish with vegetable spray. Rinse fish and pat dry. Dip in orange juice; set juice aside to use in the sauce. Roll fish in cornflake crumbs. Sprinkle with lemon pepper, then drizzle margarine over fish. Bake at 400 degrees about 15 minutes or until fish flakes when tested with a fork. In a small saucepan, combine remaining orange juice, wine, cornstarch, orange rind, and honey. Cook over medium heat until it starts to thicken, about 1 minute. Pour over fish and serve immediately.

Microwave Directions:
Prepare fish as above. Place in a microwave-safe baking dish with thickest part of fish towards the outside of plate. Sprinkle fish with lemon pepper, then drizzle margarine over fish. Cover with wax paper; vent. Microwave on high for 3 minutes or until fish flakes easily.

Rotate every minute while cooking. In a 2-cup glass bowl, combine remaining orange juice, wine, cornstarch, orange rind, and honey. Microwave on high for about 2-3 minutes or until thickened, stirring frequently. Pour over fish, garnish with orange slices and serve immediately.

Yield: 2 servings

1 serving contains:

| Cal | Prot | Fat | Carb | Fiber | Chol | Sodium |
|-----|------|-----|------|-------|------|--------|
| 142kc | 16g | 2g | 12g | 0g | 77mg | 174mg |

S E A F O O D

# Green-Topped Flounder

*Parsley and green onion make this a colorful entrée.*

*vegetable spray*

*½ lb. flounder filet (or any mild white fish)*

*1 teaspoon lemon juice, divided*

*1 tablespoon grated Parmesan cheese, made with
  skim milk*

*2 teaspoons low-fat margarine*

*2 teaspoons minced, fresh parsley*

*1 tablespoon chopped green onion, tops and all*

*dash of Louisiana Hot Sauce*

Preheat oven to 400 degrees. Lightly spray shallow baking dish with vegetable spray. Rinse fish and pat dry. Place in prepared baking dish and brush with ½ teaspoon lemon juice. In a small bowl, combine cheese, remaining lemon juice, margarine, parsley, onion, and hot sauce; spread evenly over fish. Bake uncovered in 400-degree oven for about 15 minutes or until fish flakes easily when tested with a fork.

Yield: 2 servings

1 serving contains:

| Cal | Prot | Fat | Carb | Fiber | Chol | Sodium |
|-----|------|-----|------|-------|------|--------|
| 98kc | 16g | 3g | 0g | 0g | 79mg | 149mg |

SEAFOOD

# Grilled Salmon Filet

*The tart taste of lemon with the delicate flavor of salmon makes for a delightful combination.*

vegetable spray

1 salmon filet, approx. ½ lb.

½ teaspoon olive oil

1 tablespoon fresh lemon juice

grated zest from 1 lemon

⅛ teaspoon dried dill weed

2 tablespoons white wine

very thin lemon slices (optional)

Spray fish basket or grill rack with vegetable spray. Rinse fish and pat dry; place in shallow dish. In a small mixing bowl, combine oil, lemon juice, zest, dill, and wine; pour over fish, cover and refrigerate for 30 minutes or more. Preheat grill: * Place salmon in fish basket or on grill rack and cook for 4-5 minutes, basting occasionally with the sauce. Turn and baste; continue to cook about 4 more minutes until fish flakes when tested with fork. Garnish with lemon slices and serve immediately.

Yield: 2 servings

1 serving contains:

| Cal | Prot | Fat | Carb | Fiber | Chol | Sodium |
|------|------|-----|------|-------|-------|--------|
| 150kc | 23g | 6g | 1g | 0g | 58mg | 76mg |

*This may also be prepared under the broiler.

Serving Suggestion: Serve with Dirty Rice and Baked Tomatoes Dijon.**

**These recipes can be found in the Vegetables section of this book.

S E A F O O D

# H a l i b u t   I t a l i a n   S t y l e

*This is very flavorful; serve with pasta or rice.*

1 teaspoon olive oil

2 cloves garlic, minced

½ cup stewed tomatoes

½ tablespoon fresh, chopped parsley

½ tablespoon fresh, chopped basil or 1 tsp. dried

½ cup mushrooms, quartered

½ tablespoon lemon juice

½ tablespoon capers, rinsed

¼ teaspoon freshly ground black pepper

vegetable spray

½ lb. halibut or mild fish

Heat oil in a small saucepan over medium heat; add garlic; sauté quickly. Add tomatoes, parsley and basil, reduce heat to low and simmer for about 10 minutes. Add mushrooms, lemon juice, capers, and pepper; cook about 5 minutes. Preheat oven to 400 degrees. Spray a shallow baking dish with vegetable spray. Rinse fish and pat dry. Place in prepared baking dish; pour sauce over fish. Bake in 400-degree oven for about 15 minutes or until fish flakes when tested with a fork.

Yield: 2 servings

1 serving contains:

| Cal | Prot | Fat | Carb | Fiber | Chol | Sodium |
|-----|------|-----|------|-------|------|--------|
| 167kc | 20g | 5g | 5g | 1g | 44mg | 392mg |

S E A F O O D

# T r i p l e   L e m o n   F i l e t s

*Lemon juice, lemon peel, and pepper enhance the taste of this fish.*

½ lb. mild white fish filets (orange roughy, cod,
sole, etc.)

2 teaspoons low-fat margarine, melted

1 teaspoon lemon juice

⅛ teaspoon Italian seasoning

⅛ teaspoon lemon zest

dash lemon pepper

dash garlic powder

2 tablespoons fresh, coarse bread crumbs

½ tablespoon fresh, chopped parsley

Preheat oven to 425 degrees. Spray baking dish with vegetable spray. Rinse fish and pat dry. Place filets in prepared baking dish. In a small bowl, combine melted margarine and lemon juice; pour over fish. Sprinkle with Italian seasoning, lemon zest, pepper, and garlic powder. In a small bowl, toss bread crumbs with parsley; sprinkle over fish. Place in 425-degree oven and bake 12-15 minutes or until fish flakes when tested with a fork.

Yield: 2 servings

1 serving contains:

| Cal | Prot | Fat | Carb | Fiber | Chol | Sodium |
|-----|------|-----|------|-------|------|--------|
| 74kc | 20g | 3g | 2g | 0g | 68mg | 122mg |

Serving Suggestion: Serve with Hash Brown Casserole* and a salad.

Variation: Substitute 1 tablespoon oat bran for 1 tablespoon bread crumbs.

*This recipe can be found in the Vegetables section of this book.

SEAFOOD

# White Fish with Lemon Stuffing

*This makes a most flavorful entrée.*

*vegetable spray*

*½ lb. mild white fish filets (orange roughy, sole, flounder, etc.)*

*¼ cup low-fat, low-sodium chicken broth*

*½ tablespoon finely chopped onion*

*½ tablespoon finely chopped celery*

*½ cup fine dry bread crumbs*

*⅛ teaspoon lemon pepper*

*1 teaspoon chopped chives*

*1 teaspoon fresh lemon juice*

*1 teaspoon low-fat margarine, melted*

*dash paprika*

*2 lemon wedges*

Preheat oven to 400 degrees. Spray small, shallow baking dish with vegetable spray. If only 1 piece of fish, cut in half. Wash fish and pat dry; set aside. In a medium nonstick skillet, heat 1 tablespoon chicken broth; sauté onion and celery. Add bread crumbs, lemon pepper, chives, remainder of broth, and lemon juice; mix together. Place 1 filet in prepared baking pan. Spread the bread stuffing evenly over 1 filet, top with remaining filet. Pour margarine over all; sprinkle with paprika. Bake in a 400-degree oven for about 20 minutes or until fish flakes when tested with a fork.

Yield: 2 servings

1 serving contains:

| Cal | Prot | Fat | Carb | Fiber | Chol | Sodium |
|-----|------|-----|------|-------|------|--------|
| 74kc | 20g | 2g | 6g | 0g | 63mg | 143mg |

Serving Suggestion: Garnish with lemon wedges.

Variation: Substitute 1 tablespoon oat bran for 1 tablespoon bread crumbs.

SEAFOOD

# Marlin in Wine Sauce

*A nice, meaty fish in mild cream sauce*

vegetable spray

½ lb. marlin filet

2 teaspoons cornstarch

3 tablespoons evaporated skimmed milk

3 tablespoons white wine

2 teaspoons low-fat margarine, melted

Preheat oven to 400 degrees. Spray a small, shallow baking dish with vegetable spray. Rinse fish and pat dry. Place in prepared baking dish. Cover with aluminum foil and bake at 400 degrees for about 15 minutes or until fish flakes easily. While fish is cooking, combine cornstarch, milk, wine, and margarine in a small, microwave-safe bowl. Microwave for one minute or until thickened on 80 percent power, stirring every 25 seconds. To serve: Place marlin on dinner plate, spoon sauce over fish and serve immediately.

Yield: 2 servings

1 serving contains:

| Cal | Prot | Fat | Carb | Fiber | Chol | Sodium |
|------|------|-----|------|-------|------|--------|
| 163kc | 22g | 3g | 5g | 0g | 95mg | 156mg |

S E A F O O D

# Mardi Gras Filet

*A spicy, crispy new idea for fish*

vegetable spray

½ lb. mild white fish filet (cod, flounder, orange roughy, etc.)

1 tablespoon fat-free mayonnaise

1 tablespoon fat-free plain yogurt

⅛ teaspoon ground cumin

⅛ teaspoon cayenne pepper

⅛ teaspoon onion powder

⅛ teaspoon garlic powder

¼ cup crushed, crisp cereal (Rice Krispies, etc.)

1 tablespoon wheat germ

2 rings of red or green pepper (garnish)

Preheat oven to 425 degrees. Spray a shallow baking dish with vegetable spray. Rinse fish and pat dry; set aside. In a small bowl, combine salad dressing, yogurt, cumin, cayenne pepper, onion powder, and garlic powder. Combine crushed cereal and wheat germ on a small plate. Using the back of a teaspoon, spread the salad dressing mixture on both sides of fish; gently coat fish with the crumbs. Place fish in prepared baking dish. Bake in 425-degree oven for about 20 minutes or until fish flakes when tested with a fork. Garnish with pepper rings.

Microwave Directions:

Prepare fish as before. Place in a microwave-safe dish with thickest part of the fish toward the outside of dish. Cover with wax paper; vent. Cook on high for 3 minutes or until flaky.

Yield: 2 servings

1 serving contains:

| Cal | Prot | Fat | Carb | Fiber | Chol | Sodium |
|------|------|-----|------|-------|------|--------|
| 132kc | 22g | 2g | 5g | 0g | 93mg | 129mg |

Variation: This is also good using cracker crumbs instead of cereal.

SEAFOOD

# Oriental Scallops

*Prepare all the vegetables ahead for a quick, easy meal.*

½ cup low-fat, low-sodium chicken broth

1 tablespoon cornstarch

2 teaspoons olive oil, divided

⅛ teaspoon fresh ginger, minced

1 clove garlic, minced

¼ cup red pepper slices

2 chopped green onions

1 cup broccoli flowerettes

¼ lb. snow pea pods

1 small yellow squash, sliced (about 1 cup)

1 tablespoon low-sodium soy sauce

½ lb. bay scallops

½ teaspoon freshly grated orange zest

Have all vegetables prepared and ready to add to the wok; set aside. Combine broth and cornstarch; set aside. In a wok or a nonstick skillet, using medium-high heat, heat 1 teaspoon oil. Add ginger and garlic. Cook about 30 seconds, stirring quickly. Add red pepper, onion, and broccoli. Cook, stirring constantly for about 2 minutes. Add peas and squash. Cook, stirring constantly for about 2 minutes. Remove vegetables from wok; set aside (keep warm). Add 1 teaspoon oil, soy sauce, scallops, and orange zest. Stirring quickly, cook just until scallops are opaque and tender. Return vegetables to the wok with scallops. Add the combined broth and cornstarch. Cook until the broth bubbles and thickens. Serve immediately.

Yield: 2 servings (4 cups)

1 serving contains:

| Cal | Prot | Fat | Carb | Fiber | Chol | Sodium |
|------|------|-----|------|-------|------|--------|
| 148kc | 28g | 6g | 31g | 8g | 37mg | 442mg |

Serving Suggestion: Serve with rice.

SEAFOOD

# Pasta Seafood Italiano

*The mild, light flavors and textures blend nicely for a delicious entrée.*

2 cups stewed tomatoes*

2 cloves garlic, minced

½ cup chopped, fresh basil or 2 tablespoons dry

⅛ teaspoon freshly ground black pepper

4 oz. angel hair pasta

vegetable spray

1 teaspoon olive oil

2 cloves garlic

2 tablespoons sliced green onions

½ lb. bay scallops (or sea scallops quartered)

1 tablespoon grated Parmesan cheese, made with skim milk

In a small saucepan, combine tomatoes, garlic, and basil. Bring to a gentle boil, reduce heat to low and simmer, uncovered, for 1 hour. Add pepper. (Sauce can be prepared ahead of time and reheated if desired.) Cook pasta according to package directions, using no added fat or salt; drain. When pasta is almost done, spray a small, nonstick skillet with vegetable spray; heat over medium heat; add oil. When hot, add garlic, then green onions, stirring quickly; do not let garlic brown. Add scallops, stirring frequently. Cook for 3-4 minutes or just until scallops are opaque and tender. Arrange pasta on serving plate or individual plates, spoon tomato/basil sauce in the center, then top with scallops. Sprinkle with Parmesan cheese. Serve immediately.

Yield: 2 servings

1 serving contains:

| Cal | Prot | Fat | Carb | Fiber | Chol | Sodium |
|-----|------|-----|------|-------|------|--------|
| 409kc | 30g | 5g | 58g | 1g | 39mg | 882mg |

*If you are on a sodium-restricted diet, substitute 2½ cups fresh tomato.*

SEAFOOD

# Scallop and Chicken Kabobs

*The orange ginger sauce makes this extra special.*

*1 boneless chicken breast half, skinned*

*10 ocean scallops (approx. ½ lb.)*

*1 tablespoon canola oil or oil of choice*

*½ tablespoon white Worcestershire sauce*

*1 small clove garlic, minced*

*¼ teaspoon ground ginger*

*¼ cup orange juice*

*2 wedges fresh pineapple, cut 1" thick*

*½ red pepper, cut into squares*

*1 small zucchini, cut into ½" slices*

Cut chicken into 1" cubes and put into a small bowl. Rinse and drain scallops, and put into a separate small bowl. In another small bowl, combine oil, Worcestershire, garlic, ginger, and orange juice. Pour ⅛ cup over chicken and ⅛ cup over scallops. Refrigerate for about 1 hour.

Preheat grill. Drain chicken and fish, reserving marinade. Thread chicken, fish, fruit, and vegetables onto 2 long kabobs, alternating ingredients. Place on hot grill; cook, turning occasionally and basting with the reserved marinade. Cook for 10-15 minutes or until the meat is tender and vegetables are tender-crisp.

Yield: 2 servings

1 serving contains:

| Cal | Prot | Fat | Carb | Fiber | Chol | Sodium |
|-----|------|-----|------|-------|------|--------|
| 267kc | 33g | 9g | 11g | 1g | 74mg | 253mg |

Serving Suggestion: Slide meat and vegetables off skewer onto a serving plate and add Cheer Bread* for a complete meal.

*This recipe may be found in the Breads section of this book.*

S E A F O O D

# San Carlos Seafood

*The unique blend of flavors reminds me of a unique vacation.*

*1 clove garlic, minced*

*2 tablespoons chopped green onions*

*1 tablespoon chopped green chilies*

*½ lb. mild white fish filet, about ½" thick
(marlin, swordfish, mahi-mahi, etc.)*

*1 tablespoon fresh lime or lemon juice*

*2 tablespoons salsa*

*1 teaspoon fresh parsley (or cilantro), minced*

*4 slices fresh tomato*

*2 tablespoons fine, dry bread crumbs*

*2 teaspoons grated Parmesan cheese, made with
skim milk*

In a small bowl, combine garlic, green onions, and green chilies; cover and microwave on high for 45 seconds; let cool. Rinse fish and pat dry. Spray a small baking dish with vegetable spray; arrange fish in dish. To the garlic mixture, add lime juice, salsa, and parsley; spoon over fish. Cover with foil and refrigerate for about 30 minutes. Preheat oven to 400 degrees. Bake fish, covered, for about 15 minutes or until almost done. Set oven to broil, arrange tomato slices on top of fish, sprinkle with bread crumb and cheese mixture, return to oven and broil until crumbs are brown and fish flakes easily.

Yield: 2 servings

1 serving contains:

| Cal | Prot | Fat | Carb | Fiber | Chol | Sodium |
|-----|------|-----|------|-------|------|--------|
| 74kc | 20g | 2g | 5g | 1g | 62mg | 81mg |

Serving Suggestion: Serve with Golden Risotto and Spiced Carrots*.

*These recipes can be found in the Vegetables section of this book.

SEAFOOD

# Scallops and Asparagus with Linguine

*A delightfully light entrée*

⅓ lb. fresh asparagus

½ lb. bay scallops

¼ lb. linguine

2 teaspoons lemon zest

2 teaspoons freshly squeezed lemon juice

2 tablespoons olive oil

1 teaspoon dried dill weed

1 tablespoon grated Parmesan cheese, made with skim milk

1 teaspoon low-fat margarine

2 cloves garlic, minced

½ cup clam juice

2 lemon wedges

sprig of fresh dill (optional)

Rinse asparagus. Break off tough ends. Place tops in a microwave-safe dish. Cover; cook on high for 2 minutes. Immediately submerge in cold water; drain. Cut into 2" sections; set aside. Rinse scallops; drain; set aside. Prepare linguine according to directions (without added salt or fat); drain. Return to pan. Add lemon zest, lemon juice, oil, dill, and ½ tablespoon cheese. Toss. Place lid on ajar to keep warm. In a medium nonstick skillet, heat margarine. Add scallops and garlic; sauté until brown and tender. Add asparagus and clam juice. Cook about 2 minutes. Arrange pasta on a serving plate, top with scallops then sprinkle with remaining cheese. Garnish with lemon wedges and fresh dill.

Yield: 2 servings

1 serving contains:

| Cal | Prot | Fat | Carb | Fiber | Chol | Sodium |
|-----|------|-----|------|-------|------|--------|
| 472kc | 30g | 16g | 20g | 0g | 39mg | 387mg |

S E A F O O D

# B r o i l e d   S c a l l o p s   i n   W i n e

*So simple, quick, and delicious*

½ lb. bay scallops

1 clove garlic, minced

2 tablespoons sliced green onion

1 teaspoon low-fat margarine

2 tablespoons white wine

⅓ cup fresh fine bread crumbs

Rinse scallops, drain and set aside. Place garlic, onions, and margarine in a small microwave-safe bowl; cover and microwave on high for 1½ minutes. Add wine. Place scallops in a shallow, glass, 9" round baking dish; pour wine mixture over scallops. (This can be prepared up to this point and refrigerated.) When ready to cook, preheat broiler. When hot, broil scallops for about 4-5 minutes, stirring occasionally to keep moist. When scallops are tender and look opaque sprinkle bread crumbs over all; return to broiler for about 1 minute or less, just until crumbs are browned.

Yield: 2 servings

1 serving contains:

| Cal | Prot | Fat | Carb | Fiber | Chol | Sodium |
|-----|------|-----|------|-------|------|--------|
| 140kc | 20g | 2g | 7g | 0g | 38mg | 227mg |

SEAFOOD

# Scotty's Lemon Filets

*So simple, so good*

½ lb. mild white fish filet (orange roughy, sole,
   cod, etc.)

¼ cup fresh lemon juice

vegetable spray

1 tablespoon grated Parmesan cheese, made with
   skim milk

2 thin lemon slices (optional)

Rinse fish and pat dry. Place fish in a shallow glass pan; pour lemon juice over fish. Cover and refrigerate 45-60 minutes. When ready to cook: Preheat oven to broil; spray small baking pan with vegetable spray. Drain fish and place in prepared pan. Sprinkle with cheese. Broil 4-5 minutes or until fish flakes easily. Garnish with fresh lemon slices.

Yield: 2 servings

1 serving contains:

| Cal | Prot | Fat | Carb | Fiber | Chol | Sodium |
|-----|------|-----|------|-------|------|--------|
| 75kc | 20g | 2g | 3g | 0g | 64mg | 109mg |

Serving Suggestion: Serve with California Carrots* and baked potato.

*This recipe can be found in the Vegetables section of this book.

SEAFOOD

# Shrimp Stir-Fry

*Colorful and easy, yet special enough for guests*

½ lb. fresh, medium shrimp

1 tablespoon cornstarch

½ tablespoon brown sugar

1 tablespoon low-sodium soy sauce

1 cup low-fat, low-sodium chicken broth

1 tablespoon olive oil, divided

1 cup sliced yellow squash

1 cup sliced zucchini

¼ cup chopped red bell pepper (or 2 tablespoons
   pimiento added last thing)

½ cup sliced mushrooms

1 tablespoon water

1 clove garlic, minced

½ teaspoon gingerroot, minced

Rinse, peel, and devein shrimp; set aside. In a small bowl, combine cornstarch, sugar, soy sauce, and broth; blend well; set aside. Heat 1 teaspoon oil in a medium nonstick skillet on medium-high. Add squash, zucchini, red pepper, and mushrooms; stir-fry for about 2 minutes. Add 1 tablespoon water; cover and steam for about 2 minutes. Remove from skillet, cover and set aside. Add the remaining 2 teaspoons oil to skillet, heat to medium-high. Add garlic and gingerroot; stir-fry about 30 seconds. Add shrimp and stir-fry quickly, about 3 minutes or until done. Add vegetables; stir. Add cornstarch mixture, stirring constantly. Cook over medium heat for about 1-2 minutes or until thickened. (If using pimiento, add at this point.)

Serve immediately.

Yield: 2 (1½ cups) servings

1 serving contains:

| Cal | Prot | Fat | Carb | Fiber | Chol | Sodium |
|-----|------|-----|------|-------|------|--------|
| 240kc | 27g | 9g | 13g | 2g | 221mg | 502mg |

Serving Suggestions: Serve over cooked rice. Serve over Golden Risotto*.

*This recipe can be found in the Vegetables section of this book.

SEAFOOD

# Spicy Baked Fish

*A simple, yet tasty way to prepare fish*

vegetable spray

½ lb. mild white fish filet (orange roughy, cod, sole, etc.)

1 teaspoon melted low-fat margarine

1 teaspoon Good Seasons Italian dressing mix, dry

½ tablespoon finely chopped chives

2 green onions, sliced (optional)

Preheat oven to 400 degrees. Lightly spray a small baking pan with vegetable spray. Rinse fish and pat dry; place in baking pan. Pour margarine over fish, sprinkle with dressing mix and chives. Bake in 400-degree oven about 15 minutes or until fish flakes when tested with a fork. Garnish with green onions.

Yield: 2 servings

1 serving contains:

| Cal | Prot | Fat | Carb | Fiber | Chol | Sodium |
|-----|------|-----|------|-------|------|--------|
| 101kc | 20g | 2g | 0g | 0g | 63mg | 85mg |

Serving Suggestion: Serve with Rice with Fresh Herbs and Carrot Zucchini Sauté*.

*These recipes can be found in the Vegetables section of this book.

SEAFOOD

# Fresh Vegetable and Crab Quiche

*Fresh vegetables and crab make a complete meal.*

*vegetable spray*

*1 cup yellow squash cut in half, then quartered (approx. 4 oz.)*

*½ cup broccoli flowerettes*

*¼ cup chopped onion*

*1 cup imitation crab, cut into chunks (approx. 4 oz.)*

*½ cup shredded fat-free Swiss cheese (approx. 2 oz.)*

*2 egg whites*

*1 cup egg substitute*

*½ cup evaporated skimmed milk*

*2 teaspoons Dijon mustard*

*2 teaspoons chopped, fresh basil*

Preheat oven to 400 degrees. Spray 8" pie pan with vegetable spray. Arrange vegetables, crab, and cheese in prepared pan. In a small mixing bowl, combine egg whites, egg substitute, milk, mustard, and basil. Pour over vegetables. Bake in a 400-degree oven for 10 minutes; reduce heat to 350 degrees and continue baking for 25-30 minutes longer or until the filling is set.

Yield: 4 servings

1 serving contains:

| Cal | Prot | Fat | Carb | Fiber | Chol | Sodium |
|-----|------|-----|------|-------|------|--------|
| 104kc | 15g | 1g | 11g | 1g | 7mg | 444mg |

S E A F O O D

# Shrimp and Vegetable Kabobs

*Excellent sweet, tart flavor compliments both shrimp and veggies*

1(8 oz.) can pineapple chunks

½ cup fat-free Italian dressing

1½ tablespoons brown sugar

1 teaspoon Dijon mustard

8-10 large shrimp

½ red pepper, cut into wedges

½ green pepper, cut into wedges

1 medium zucchini, cut into 1" slices

1 sweet onion, quartered

Drain pineapple, set aside. In a small bowl, combine pineapple juice, Italian dressing, brown sugar, and mustard; set aside. Shell and devein shrimp, rinse; using paper towel, pat dry. Place shrimp in a small Ziploc plastic bag, pour marinade over shrimp, seal and refrigerate for at least 4 hours.

When ready to cook:
Heat grill. Remove shrimp, divide marinade into two equal portions, set 1 portion aside. Place the remaining marinade in a microwave-safe bowl, cover and microwave on high 45 seconds, stir. Continue to cook on low power (stirring frequently) for about two minutes or until it thickens slightly; set aside to be served with the kabobs. Thread shrimp, pineapple, peppers, zucchini, and onion alternately on skewers, place on hot grill, and cook about 12-15 minutes, brushing frequently with uncooked marinade. Do not overcook! Serve over a bed of rice with the thickened marinade.

Yield: 2 servings

1 serving contains:

| Cal | Prot | Fat | Carb | Fiber | Chol | Sodium |
|------|------|-----|------|-------|------|--------|
| 214kc | 9g | 1g | 40g | 7g | 54mg | 663mg |

# RED MEAT

Select your choices of red meat very carefully. While they are good sources of protein, B vitamins, iron, and zinc, they can also be very high in saturated fat. Choose only lean cuts of meat with as little marbling as possible. When selecting beef, choose extralean ground sirloin, flank, sirloin, or tenderloin. When selecting pork, choose tenderloin pieces. Let red meat be a special treat you only have occasionally.

RED MEAT

# Spicy Beef Stew

*This is a great meal for a busy day.*

vegetable spray

1 lb. lean sirloin or flank steak, all visible fat trimmed

2 tablespoons unbleached or all-purpose flour

¼ teaspoon freshly ground black pepper

½ teaspoon salt

1 teaspoon olive oil

1 clove garlic, minced

½ cup cubed onion

½ cup sliced celery

4 small carrots cut into chunks (approx. ½ lb.)

1 (14 oz.) can stewed tomatoes

4 small potatoes scrubbed and cut into quarters
 (approx. ¾ lb.)

Preheat oven to 350 degrees. Spray 2-quart baking dish with vegetable spray. Cut steak into bite-sized pieces; set aside. In a shallow dish, combine flour, salt, and pepper; dredge meat in flour until well coated. Heat oil in a non-stick skillet over medium-high heat. Add garlic, stirring quickly for about 30 seconds, then add meat; sauté until meat is browned. Transfer to prepared baking dish. Add onion, celery, carrots, and tomatoes; cover and cook in 350-degree oven for 45 minutes. Add potatoes and cook another 45 minutes, or until all vegetables are tender. Serve hot.

Yield: 6 (1½ cups) servings

1 serving contains:

| Cal | Prot | Fat | Carb | Fiber | Chol | Sodium |
|-----|------|-----|------|-------|------|--------|
| 229kc | 26g | 8g | 26g | 2g | 67mg | 430mg |

HEALTHY
COOKING
FOR TWO

R E D    M E A T

# B a r b ' s    B e e f    S t r o g a n o f f

*Sauce has a subtle flavor and a wonderful, creamy consistency.*

*½ lb. top round steak (or other low-fat steak)*

*vegetable spray*

*1 teaspoon low-fat margarine*

*1 tablespoon minced onion*

*½ cup sliced, fresh mushrooms*

*dash salt*

*dash freshly ground black pepper*

*dash nutmeg*

*2 tablespoons white wine*

*½ cup fat-free sour cream substitute*

*2 cups cooked "yolk-free" noodles (cooked without
   added fat or salt)*

Pound steak until about ¼" thick. Cut steak into ½" slices across the grain, then cut lengthwise into 1" pieces. Spray a medium nonstick skillet with vegetable spray; heat on medium-high; add margarine. When melted, add onion; sauté about 1 minute. Add steak. Sauté quickly for 4-5 minutes or until browned and tender. Remove from skillet, set aside and keep warm. Add mushrooms to skillet, stirring frequently; when mushrooms are brown, return steak to skillet, add salt, pepper, nutmeg, and wine; bring to a gentle boil. Remove from heat and add sour cream substitute, blending in well. Serve immediately over noodles.

Yield: 2 servings

1 serving contains:

| Cal | Prot | Fat | Carb | Fiber | Chol | Sodium |
|-----|------|-----|------|-------|------|--------|
| 489kc | 37g | 18g | 41g | 4g | 80mg | 129mg |

Serving Suggestion: Serve over cooked rice instead of noodles.

RED MEAT

# Veal Cutlets

*A little change in ingredients and you have greatly lowered the fat content of this favorite.*

butter-flavored vegetable spray

2 teaspoons low-fat margarine

½ lb. thin veal cutlets

1 tablespoon unbleached or all-purpose flour

dash salt

¼ cup low-fat, low-sodium chicken broth

2 tablespoons Marsala wine

dash freshly ground black pepper

Spray a medium nonstick skillet with vegetable spray. Heat on medium-high, when hot add margarine. While skillet is heating, dredge cutlets in flour, and sprinkle with salt and pepper; place in hot skillet, sauté quickly for about 3-4 minutes. Turn and continue to cook about 2-3 minutes until meat is tender and browned. Remove cutlets from skillet; keep warm. Add broth and wine to skillet; reduce heat to simmer. Stir around edges of skillet to loosen all particles. Simmer for about 4-5 minutes. Add pepper and pour over the cutlets and serve.

Yield: 2 servings

1 serving contains:

| Cal | Prot | Fat | Carb | Fiber | Chol | Sodium |
|-----|------|-----|------|-------|------|--------|
| 266kc | 24g | 13g | 3g | 0g | 43mg | 80mg |

RED MEAT

# Chinese Pepper Steak

*A very easy, yet special dinner when served over rice*

½ lb. sirloin steak, all visible fat trimmed

2 tablespoons low-sodium soy sauce

½ cup low-fat, low-sodium beef broth

¼ teaspoon minced gingerroot

2 cloves garlic, minced

dash cayenne pepper

vegetable spray

1 teaspoon olive oil

1 green pepper, cut into thin strips (approx. 4 oz.)

½ cup sliced onion

1 tomato, cut into wedges (approx. 4 oz.)

¼ cup cold water

1 ½ tablespoons cornstarch

⅛ teaspoon freshly ground black pepper

⅛ teaspoon salt

Cut meat into ½" strips. In a medium bowl, combine soy sauce, broth, ginger, garlic, and pepper; add beef. Cover and refrigerate for 1 hour or longer. Drain meat, reserving marinade. Spray wok or nonstick skillet with vegetable spray. Add oil and heat on medium-high. When hot, add meat; cook quickly, stirring constantly until meat begins to lose the pink color; add ¼ cup marinade. Reduce heat to simmer, cover and simmer until meat is tender. Add green pepper and onion; cook 5 minutes; add tomatoes. In a small bowl, combine ¼ cup cold water and cornstarch, mixing well; add remaining marinade, pepper, and salt. Gradually stir into meat mixture, stirring constantly until thick.

Yield: 2 servings

1 serving contains:

| Cal | Prot | Fat | Carb | Fiber | Chol | Sodium |
|-----|------|-----|------|-------|------|--------|
| 308kc | 38g | 13g | 10g | 2g | 107mg | 713mg |

RED MEAT

# Sweet 'n' Sour Pork

*Very easy, yet good enough for guests*

⅓ lb. pork loin chops, all visible fat removed

1 (8 oz.) can pineapple chunks, packed in its own juice

2 tablespoons brown sugar

1 tablespoon cornstarch

2 tablespoons vinegar

1 tablespoon low-sodium soy sauce

¼ cup low-fat, low-sodium chicken broth

1 teaspoon olive oil

½ cup green pepper, cut into thin strips

½ cup onion, cut into thin rings

2-3 cups cooked brown rice, cooked without added fat or salt

Cut pork into ½" strips. Drain pineapple; set aside; reserve juice. In a medium mixing bowl, combine brown sugar and cornstarch; add pineapple juice, vinegar, soy sauce, and broth; stir and set aside. Heat oil in medium nonstick skillet on medium-high; add pork stirring quickly until tender and browned. Drain the meat on a paper towel; keep warm. Wipe the skillet with another paper towel to remove any remaining oil. Add the juice mixture to skillet; cook over medium heat until it starts to thicken. Add the meat; simmer for about 5 minutes. Add green pepper and onion, continue to simmer for 5 minutes. Add pineapple; cover and simmer for about 10 minutes more. Serve immediately over rice.

Yield: 2 servings

1 serving contains:

| Cal | Prot | Fat | Carb | Fiber | Chol | Sodium |
|------|------|-----|------|-------|------|--------|
| 621kc | 27g | 14g | 91g | 5g | 97mg | 336mg |

RED MEAT

# Pork Chops with Apples

*The apples add moisture and a nice change of taste.*

vegetable spray

2 pork loin chops (approx. ½ lb.), all visible fat removed

freshly ground black pepper

1 cup apple slices

1 tablespoon brown sugar

⅓ cup apple juice

¼ cup water

Preheat oven to 350 degrees. Spray a shallow baking dish with vegetable spray. Spray a medium nonstick skillet with vegetable spray; heat on medium-high. When hot, add chops; cook quickly to sear. When brown, place chops in prepared baking dish, sprinkle with pepper, gently place apple slices on top of chops, then sprinkle sugar over apples. Pour apple juice and water in the bottom of dish. Cover and bake in 350-degree oven for 40-45 minutes or until very tender.

Yield: 2 servings

1 serving contains:

| Cal | Prot | Fat | Carb | Fiber | Chol | Sodium |
|-----|------|-----|------|-------|------|--------|
| 315kc | 26g | 14g | 20g | 2g | 98mg | 103mg |

R E D   M E A T

# T o m ' s   F r i e d   R i c e

*Here is a low-fat version of an old favorite.*

vegetable spray

⅓ lb. leanest ground round beef

1 teaspoon olive oil

1 clove garlic, minced

½ cup green or red pepper, sliced

1 small onion, sliced (approx. ⅓ lb.)

2 cups cooked white rice (cooked without added fat or salt)

½ cup egg substitute

¼ teaspoon salt

dash freshly ground black pepper

1 tablespoon low-sodium soy sauce

Spray a nonstick skillet with vegetable spray; heat skillet on medium-high heat. When hot, add ground beef; cook, stirring to crumble chunks until no longer pink; place in a bowl and keep warm. Add oil to skillet and return to medium-high. When hot, add garlic, pepper, and onion; cook until just tender-crisp. Return meat to skillet with vegetables, add rice, gently combine. Continuing on medium-high heat, add egg substitute to skillet and stir constantly until it barely cooks; add salt and pepper. Serve with soy sauce.

Yield: 2 (2 cups) servings

1 serving contains:

| Cal | Prot | Fat | Carb | Fiber | Chol | Sodium |
|-----|------|-----|------|-------|------|--------|
| 315kc | 36g | 8g | 29g | 1g | 72mg | 676mg |

RED MEAT

# Venison Sauerbraten

*The marinade gives meat a rich, spicy flavor.*

2 lb. venison roast, all fat removed

½ teaspoon salt

1 medium onion, sliced (approx. ½ lb.)

1½ cups cider vinegar

1½ cups water

¼ cup brown sugar

2 bay leaves

2 cloves garlic, minced

1 teaspoon whole peppercorns

vegetable spray

1 teaspoon canola oil or oil of choice

1 tablespoon unbleached or all-purpose flour

2 teaspoons sugar

4 small gingersnaps, crushed

⅛ teaspoon freshly ground black pepper

¼ cup red wine

Rub roast with salt. Place in glass bowl just large enough to hold the roast. In a small bowl, combine onion, vinegar, water, brown sugar, bay leaves, garlic, and peppercorns; pour over roast. (If this does not cover the meat, add more water until it does.) Marinate in refrigerator for 48 hours, turning each day.

When ready to cook:
Preheat oven to 350-degrees. Spray small baking dish with vegetable spray. Drain roast, reserving marinade. Heat oil in nonstick skillet on medium-high. When hot, add roast. Brown on all sides. Place in baking dish. Stir flour into drippings in skillet, adding marinade as necessary to make a paste. Stirring constantly, add sugar, cookie crumbs, and pepper, then slowly add reserved marinade. Cook until smooth, stirring constantly. Pour over roast, cover and bake at 350-degrees for 1 hour, basting

occasionally. Reduce heat to 300 degrees and continue to cook for 1 hour; add wine and continue to cook about 15-20 minutes or until very tender. Let cool slightly. Remove roast; slice against the grain. Place in serving bowl. Pour gravy over meat and serve.

Yield: 6 servings

1 serving contains:

| Cal | Prot | Fat | Carb | Fiber | Chol | Sodium |
|------|------|-----|------|-------|-------|--------|
| 264kc | 32g | 2g | 20g | 0g | 94mg | 272mg |

RED MEAT

# Healthier Beef Bourguignonne

*I like this best when sliced cold and served on sandwiches.*

*vegetable spray*

*3 lb. very lean rump roast*

*2 carrots*

*½ onion stuck with 4 whole cloves*

*2 cloves garlic, minced*

*½ cup red wine*

*½ cup water*

*1 bay leaf*

*½ teaspoon dried thyme*

*¼ teaspoon salt*

*2 tablespoons chopped, fresh parsley*

Preheat oven to 350 degrees. Spray nonstick skillet with vegetable spray. Heat skillet on medium-high. When hot, add roast; sear until slightly brown. Put meat into small, deep, baking dish.* Add carrots, onion, garlic, wine, water, bay leaf, thyme, salt, and parsley. Cover, place in 350-degree oven and bake 1 hour, basting frequently; reduce heat to 300 degrees and continue to cook about another hour or until very tender. Remove from pan; let stand 10 minutes before slicing. Discard vegetables.

Yield: 8 servings

1 serving contains:

| Cal | Prot | Fat | Carb | Fiber | Chol | Sodium |
|-----|------|-----|------|-------|------|--------|
| 268kc | 36g | 11g | 2g | 0g | 102mg | 110mg |

This is also very good served cold with horseradish-mayonnaise sauce.

*\*The pan should be small enough for the liquids to come up around the meat.*

# MEATLESS

**M**eatless entrées can be made up of a variety of combinations: cheese and vegetables; cheese, egg white or egg substitutes, and vegetables; egg substitute, cheese, and grains; or cheese and pasta. The combination is endless. However, one thing to remember is to be aware of complete or incomplete proteins.

A rule of thumb for combining different proteins to provide a complete protein is to use twice the amount of grain as legumes. Health experts today tell us we can achieve the same results by getting a balance of protein over the entire course of the day. Most Americans eat more protein than they need anyhow.

Plan your meatless entrée for lunch or dinner, then choose other food to provide the complete protein. Meatless entrées can help you to meet the recommended servings in the milk, yogurt, and cheese group; the meat, egg, dry bean group; the vegetable group; and the bread, cereal, rice, and pasta group.

One of my husband's favorite meals is "yolk-free" spaghetti with marinara sauce, served with grated part-skim Parmesan cheese, a salad, and Italian bread. I always keep a supply of marinara sauce on hand for that day when I need a quick and easy dinner.

MEATLESS

# Baked Eggplant

*A one-dish entrée that reminds me of summer gardens.*

vegetable spray

*1 lb. eggplant, peeled and cubed*

*½ cup fresh, coarse bread crumbs*

*½ cup evaporated skimmed milk*

*¼ cup finely chopped onion*

*¼ cup finely chopped green pepper*

*1 tablespoon chopped red pepper\**

*¼ cup egg substitute*

*⅛ teaspoon salt*

*freshly ground black pepper*

*¼ teaspoon dried sage or to taste*

*½ cup shredded fat-free sharp cheddar cheese*

Preheat oven to 350 degrees. Spray a 1-quart baking dish with vegetable spray. Put eggplant in microwave-safe dish, add 1 tablespoon water and a dash of salt; cover and cook for 6 minutes, stirring every 2 minutes. Drain. Spoon into prepared baking dish; set aside. In a small bowl, combine bread crumbs, milk, onion, green and red pepper, egg substitute, salt, black pepper, and sage. Pour over eggplant. Bake in 350-degree oven for 40 minutes. Top with cheese, return to oven and continue to cook until cheese melts.

Yield: 2 servings

1 serving contains:

| Cal | Prot | Fat | Carb | Fiber | Chol | Sodium |
|-----|------|-----|------|-------|------|--------|
| 273kc | 15g | 1g | 34g | 3g | 6mg | 614mg |

Serving Suggestion: Serve with fresh fruit salad and Spiced Carrots.\*\*

\*You can substitute 1 teaspoon pimiento.

\*\*This recipe can be found in the Vegetables section of this book.

M E A T L E S S

# A u d r e y ' s   V e g e t a b l e   L a s a g n a

*Colorful, delicious, and wonderful to have extra in the freezer*

vegetable spray

12 lasagna noodles

1 tablespoon olive oil

3 cloves garlic, minced

1 medium yellow squash, sliced (approx. 6 oz.)

1 medium zucchini, sliced (approx. 6 oz.)

1 small red or green pepper, sliced (approx. 4 oz.)

1 head broccoli (approx. 1 lb.), cut into flowerettes

4 teaspoons fresh thyme

1 teaspoon salt

4 egg whites

15 oz. fat-free ricotta

15 oz. fat-free cottage cheese

2 cups shredded part-skim mozzarella cheese

½ cup chopped, fresh basil leaves

dash red pepper sauce

Preheat oven to 425 degrees. Spray four 2-quart freezer-safe baking dishes with vegetable spray or one 9x13 pan. Cook noodles according to directions without added fat or salt. Heat oil in large nonstick skillet. Add garlic, squash, zucchini, peppers, broccoli, and thyme. Cover and cook about 10 minutes or until tender-crisp. Pour off liquid and sprinkle with salt. Set aside. In a large bowl, beat egg whites until frothy; add ricotta cheese, cottage cheese, 1 cup mozzarella cheese, basil, and red pepper sauce; stir. Distributing among the 4 dishes, place a layer of noodles in bottom of baking dish, spread cheese mixture, another layer of noodles, then vegetable mixture. Sprinkle top with mozzarella. Tightly cover the dishes to be frozen with foil.

To bake immediately: Cover, place in 425-degree oven for 1 hour or until bubbly and heated through. Cool 10 minutes before serving.

To bake the frozen lasagna: Let set at room temperature about 1 hour, place in preheated oven and cook at least 1½ hours, possibly longer, depending on thickness.

Yield: 12 servings

1 serving contains:

| Cal | Prot | Fat | Carb | Fiber | Chol | Sodium |
|------|------|-----|------|-------|-------|--------|
| 161kc | 19g | 8g | 10g | 1g | 63mg | 263mg |

Serving Suggestion: Serve with Caesar salad and Italian Bread Sticks.*

*These recipes can be found in other chapters of this book.

MEATLESS

# Fresh Vegetables and Linguine

*Fresh vegetables and wine highlight this quick entrée.*

¼ lb. linguine

1 teaspoon olive oil

¼ cup chopped onion

1 clove garlic, minced

1 sliced zucchini (approx. ¼ lb.)

¼ cup sliced mushrooms

1 peeled tomato, cut into 8 sections*

½ cup low-fat, low-sodium chicken broth

2 tablespoons white wine

¼ teaspoon dried Italian seasoning

⅛ teaspoon salt

freshly ground black pepper

1 tablespoon grated Parmesan cheese, made with skim milk

Cook linguine according to package directions, without added salt or fat. While linguine is cooking, add oil to a medium nonstick skillet, sauté onion, garlic, and zucchini until tender-crisp. Add mushroom, tomato, broth, wine, and Italian seasoning. Add salt. Bring to a boil; reduce heat to medium-low and continue to cook about 3-4 minutes. Arrange linguine in a serving bowl, pour vegetables over the pasta, and add freshly ground pepper and Parmesan cheese.

Yield: 2 servings

1 serving contains:

| Cal | Prot | Fat | Carb | Fiber | Chol | Sodium |
|-----|------|-----|------|-------|------|--------|
| 277kc | 10g | 5g | 50g | 2g | 3mg | 195mg |

*To peel tomato: Dip tomato in boiling water for about 10 seconds; slip paring knife under tomato skin and it will slip off very easily.*

MEATLESS

# Penne with Fresh Vegetables and Marinara Sauce

*A quick, easy entrée which is not only colorful, but also delicious.*

¼ lb. penne pasta

1 teaspoon olive oil

¼ cup chopped onion

1 clove garlic, minced

½ sliced zucchini

½ sliced yellow squash

¼ cup sliced mushrooms

2 cups marinara sauce*

dash freshly ground black pepper

1 tablespoon freshly grated Parmesan cheese, made
   with skim milk

Cook penne according to package directions, without added salt or fat. While penne is cooking, add oil to a medium nonstick skillet; sauté onion, garlic, zucchini, squash, and mushrooms until tender-crisp. Add marinara sauce, then heat. Arrange penne on a platter, pour vegetables over the pasta, add freshly ground pepper and Parmesan cheese.

Yield: 2 servings

1 serving contains:

| Cal | Prot | Fat | Carb | Fiber | Chol | Sodium |
|-----|------|-----|------|-------|------|--------|
| 272kc | 14g | 4g | 69g | 4g | 0mg | 633mg |

*When in a hurry, I use a light commercial sauce, i.e. Classico Tomato and Basil.

MEATLESS

# Macaroni and Cheese

*A Southwestern version of an old favorite*

*vegetable spray*

*¾ cup uncooked elbow macaroni*

*1 teaspoon olive oil*

*1 clove garlic, minced*

*1 tablespoon minced onion*

*1 ½ tablespoons all-purpose flour*

*1 ⅓ cups skim milk, heated*

*¼ teaspoon salt*

*½ teaspoon dry mustard*

*dash freshly ground black pepper*

*dash cayenne pepper*

*dash turmeric (optional)*

*2 teaspoons finely chopped fresh parsley*

*½ cup shredded nonfat sharp cheddar cheese*

*½ cup shredded low-fat cheddar cheese*

Preheat oven to 350 degrees. Spray a 2-quart baking dish with vegetable spray. Cook macaroni according to package directions, without added salt or fat. While macaroni is cooking: Heat oil in a medium saucepan over medium-high heat; add garlic and onion, sauté slightly. While constantly stirring with a wire whisk, add flour, slowly add milk, then salt, dry mustard, peppers, turmeric, and parsley; continue to stir until thoroughly blended. Reduce heat to medium-low and continue to cook, stirring frequently for about 5 minutes or until milk thickens slightly. Remove from heat and add cheeses, stirring until melted; add macaroni, stir. Pour into prepared baking dish, bake in 350-degree oven for about 10 minutes or until bubbly. Serve immediately.

Yield: 2 large servings

1 serving contains:

| Cal | Prot | Fat | Carb | Fiber | Chol | Sodium |
|-----|------|-----|------|-------|------|--------|
| 284kc | 26g | 7g | 30g | 1g | 0mg | 1,009mg |

## M E A T L E S S

# Broccoli/Cheese-Stuffed Manicotti

*Broccoli adds color to the impressive manicotti.*

vegetable spray

4 manicotti shells

1 tablespoon chopped green onion

¼ cup coarsely chopped mushrooms

1 cup coarsely chopped broccoli

⅓ cup shredded part-skim mozzarella cheese

⅓ cup fat-free cottage cheese

2 tablespoons grated Parmesan cheese, made with skim milk

dash marjoram

dash freshly ground black pepper

½ cup low-fat, low-sodium marinara sauce

Preheat oven to 350 degrees. Spray a 1-quart, shallow baking dish with vegetable spray. Cook manicotti shells according to directions, using no added salt or fat. While the shells are cooking: Combine green onion, mushrooms, and broccoli in a microwave-safe dish, cover with plastic wrap and microwave on high for 3 minutes. Take 4 tablespoons of the mozzarella cheese and set aside for later. In a medium bowl, combine cottage cheese, remaining mozzarella and Parmesan cheese; add marjoram and pepper. Blend well, then add vegetables. Using a small spoon, stuff filling into shells. Pour about 2 tablespoons of marinara sauce into the bottom of the prepared baking dish. Place stuffed shells in sauce, then pour the remaining sauce over top. Bake 350 degrees for 20 minutes; sprinkle remaining cheese over top and continue to bake 4-5 minutes or until cheese melts. Serve immediately.

Yield: 2 servings

1 serving contains:

| Cal | Prot | Fat | Carb | Fiber | Chol | Sodium |
|------|------|-----|------|-------|------|--------|
| 156kc | 15g | 7g | 19g | 4g | 14mg | 331mg |

Serving Suggestion: Serve with Citrus Salad with Orange Vinaigrette.*

*This recipe can be found in the Salads section of this book.

MEATLESS

# No-Crust Broccoli Quiche

*A simple, nutritious entrée, great for a busy day*

vegetable spray

2 cups broccoli flowerettes

2 tablespoons chopped onion

1 cup shredded low-fat Swiss cheese

1 tablespoon flour

3 egg whites

½ cup egg substitute

1 cup evaporated skimmed milk

dash freshly ground black pepper

⅛ teaspoon salt

½ teaspoon dry mustard

1 tablespoon chopped pimiento

Preheat oven to 350 degrees. Spray an 8" glass pie pan with vegetable spray. Place broccoli and onion in pan, cover with plastic wrap and microwave on high for 2 minutes; drain well.

Sprinkle cheese over broccoli. In a medium mixing bowl, whisk the flour into the egg whites and egg substitute; add milk, pepper, salt, dry mustard, and pimiento; pour over broccoli. Bake in 350-degree oven for about 35 minutes or until knife comes out clean.

Yield: 4 servings

1 serving contains:

| Cal | Prot | Fat | Carb | Fiber | Chol | Sodium |
|------|------|-----|------|-------|------|--------|
| 168kc | 20g | 3g | 7g | 1g | 29mg | 302mg |

Serving Suggestions: Serve with a tossed salad for a light supper. Serve the remaining portion with a fruit cup or cup of soup for lunch a day or two later.

MEATLESS

# Magic Vegetable Quiche

*The crust seems to appear magically in this one-dish meal.*

vegetable spray

¼ cup sliced onion

1 cup sliced yellow or green summer squash

1 large fresh mushroom, sliced (approx. ⅛ lb.)

1 medium fresh tomato, sliced (approx. 4 oz.)

1 teaspoon chopped fresh basil or ¼ tsp. dried

⅛ teaspoon dried oregano

⅛ teaspoon salt

dash freshly ground black pepper

2 egg whites

1 cup egg substitute

1 cup skim milk

1 cup commercial low-fat baking mix

½ cup shredded low-fat white cheese (Swiss, Jarlsburg, etc.)

Preheat oven to 400 degrees. Lightly spray an 8" round baking dish with vegetable spray. Layer onion, squash, mushroom, and tomatoes in baking dish; sprinkle with herbs, salt, and pepper. In a small mixing bowl, whisk together egg whites and egg substitute. Add milk and baking mix; continue to whisk until blended well. Pour egg mixture over vegetables. Bake in a 400-degree oven for 30 minutes. Reduce heat to 350 degrees, sprinkle cheese over top and continue to bake for 10-15 minutes, just until vegetables are tender and cheese is melted.

Yield: 4 servings

1 serving contains:

| Cal | Prot | Fat | Carb | Fiber | Chol | Sodium |
|------|------|-----|------|-------|------|--------|
| 200kc | 17g | 5g | 28g | 1g | 3mg | 580mg |

Serving Suggestion: Serve with spinach salad and raspberry vinaigrette.

*To serve the remainder another day, simply cover with plastic wrap and heat in microwave for about 40-60 seconds on high.*

MEATLESS

# Mom's Mushroom-Stuffed Green Peppers

*The mushroom sauce makes this extra tasty.*

vegetable spray

2 green peppers

1 cup coarse, lightly toasted bread crumbs

1 tablespoon chopped onion

2 tablespoons chopped celery

¼ cup shredded cabbage

¼ cup shredded carrots

¼ teaspoon dried thyme

¼ teaspoon dried ground sage

½ teaspoon dried parsley

¼ teaspoon salt

dash black pepper

2 teaspoons low-fat margarine

½ cup sliced fresh mushrooms or 1 (4 oz.) can

⅛ teaspoon paprika

1 tablespoon unbleached or all-purpose flour

1 cup evaporated skimmed milk

1 teaspoon low-sodium soy sauce

Preheat oven to 350 degrees. Spray a 3x5 baking dish with vegetable spray. Cut tops off peppers; remove and discard seeds. Place in a small microwave-safe dish; add 1 tablespoon water, cover with plastic wrap and microwave on high for 90 seconds. Invert peppers on paper towel to drain well. While peppers are cooking, using a medium mixing bowl, combine bread crumbs, onion, celery, cabbage, carrots, thyme, sage, parsley, salt, and pepper. Set aside. In a medium, heavy saucepan, melt margarine over medium-high heat. Add mushrooms and sauté until tender. Reduce heat to medium. In a jar with a lid, combine flour and milk; shake until completely dissolved. Slowly add to

mushrooms, stirring constantly. Cook 2 minutes, stirring constantly. Add soy sauce and pepper. Continue to stir constantly until sauce thickens. Pour about ¾ of the sauce into the bread and vegetable mixture, or enough to moisten well. Spoon stuffing into peppers, place upright in prepared baking dish, spoon remaining sauce over peppers, and sprinkle with paprika. Cover and bake in a 350-degree oven for 45 minutes. Serve immediately.

Yield: 2 servings

1 serving contains:

| Cal | Prot | Fat | Carb | Fiber | Chol | Sodium |
|-----|------|-----|------|-------|------|--------|
| 230kc | 14g | 8g | 37g | 3g | 6mg | 664mg |

Serving Suggestion: Serve with rice and Waldorf salad.

M E A T L E S S

# S p a n i s h   O m e l e t t e

*A fast, easy, and delicious supper*

1 medium baking potato, baked

½ cup egg substitute plus 4 egg whites or enough
  to equal 1 cup

vegetable spray

2 teaspoons olive oil

2 tablespoons chopped onion

2 tablespoons chopped green or red pepper

⅛ teaspoon salt

freshly ground black pepper to taste

¼ cup fresh salsa

Peel and cube baked potato; set aside. In a small mixing bowl, combine egg substitute and egg whites; beat slightly with a fork; set aside. Spray a 10" nonstick skillet with vegetable spray; heat on medium-high; add 1 teaspoon olive oil. When hot, add onion and green pepper; cook about 3-4 minutes or until tender. Add remaining oil, then cubed potatoes. Continue to cook until slightly browned. Reduce heat to low. Pour egg mixture over potatoes, tilting the skillet to spread. As it cooks, gently lift the edge of the omelette with a spatula and tilt the skillet to permit the uncooked eggs to run to the bottom of the pan. When done, sprinkle with salt and pepper, fold in half and slide onto the serving plate. Serve with salsa.

Yield: 2 servings

1 serving contains:

| Cal | Prot | Fat | Carb | Fiber | Chol | Sodium |
|-----|------|-----|------|-------|------|--------|
| 172kc | 11g | 5g | 21g | 2g | 0mg | 287mg |

Serving Suggestion: Serve with a mixed green salad.

MEATLESS

# Vegetable and Rice Pie

*A light, nutritious main dish*

1 cup broccoli, cut into chunks

1 cup cauliflower, cut into chunks

2 egg whites, divided

1 cup cooked brown rice (cooked without added fat and salt)

3 tablespoons green onions, cut into 1" pieces

1 medium tomato, cut into chunks

2 tablespoons chopped green chilies

¼ cup shredded low-fat provolone cheese

½ cup egg substitute

¼ cup evaporated skimmed milk

⅛ teaspoon garlic powder

¼ teaspoon dried dill weed

Preheat oven to 350 degrees. Spray an 8" pie pan with vegetable spray. In a covered glass dish, microwave broccoli and cauliflower 3 minutes. In a small bowl, combine 1 egg white and brown rice; press into prepared pie pan. Arrange broccoli, cauliflower, onions, and tomatoes over rice; spoon green chilies over all, then sprinkle cheese over all. In a small bowl, combine remaining egg white, egg substitute, milk, garlic powder, and dill weed; pour over vegetables. Bake in a 350-degree oven for 30 minutes or until filling is set.

Yield: 4 servings

1 serving contains:

| Cal | Prot | Fat | Carb | Fiber | Chol | Sodium |
|-----|------|-----|------|-------|------|--------|
| 140kc | 13g | 2g | 20g | 3g | 10mg | 204mg |

Serving Suggestion: Serve with soup and a fresh fruit cup.

MEATLESS

# Zucchini-Barley Mexicali

*Chili adds extra flavor; barley adds fiber.*

vegetable spray

½ teaspoon olive oil

½ cup cubed onion

1 small clove garlic, minced

½ cup cubed tomatoes

1 cup cubed zucchini (approx. ½ lb.)

⅛ teaspoon chili powder

½ tablespoon fresh, chopped parsley

½ cup cooked barley

⅓ cup shredded fat-free sharp cheddar cheese

Preheat oven to 350 degrees. Spray a 1-quart baking dish with vegetable spray. Spray a medium nonstick skillet with vegetable spray; heat on medium; add oil to skillet. When hot add onion and garlic; sauté quickly for 1 minute. Stir in tomatoes and zucchini; continue to cook until tender-crisp. Add chili powder, parsley, and barley. Spoon into prepared dish; sprinkle with cheese. Bake in 350-degree oven for 10-15 minutes or until cheese melts.

Microwave Directions:

Place onion, garlic, and 1 tablespoon water in a microwave-safe dish. Cook on high for 1 minute. Add tomatoes and zucchini; cook on high for 2 minutes or until tender-crisp. Add chili powder, parsley, and barley. Spoon into prepared dish. Cook on 80 percent power for about 90 seconds or until cheese melts. (Times will vary according to your microwave.)

Yield: 2 servings

1 serving contains:

| Cal | Prot | Fat | Carb | Fiber | Chol | Sodium |
|-----|------|-----|------|-------|------|--------|
| 159kc | 9g | 2g | 32g | 5g | 2mg | 263mg |

Variation: Substitute Italian seasoning for chili powder and parsley.

Serving Suggestion: Serve with fruit salad and hot rolls.

MEATLESS

# Zucchini Parmesan

*Use garden-fresh vegetables in this easy, quick entrée.*

½ cup chopped onion

1 clove garlic, minced

1 tablespoon water

2 cups chopped tomatoes

1 sliced, medium zucchini (approx. ½ lb.)

⅛ teaspoon salt

1 tablespoon chopped, fresh basil

½ tablespoon chopped, fresh oregano

2 tablespoons grated Parmesan cheese, made with skim milk, divided

¼ cup shredded part-skim mozzarella cheese

2 tablespoons dry, fine bread crumbs

Use a 1-quart, shallow baking dish that is also safe for range-top cooking. Place onion, garlic, and water in dish. Using medium-high heat, cook for 3-4 minutes. Stir in tomatoes, reduce heat to low and continue to cook about 10 minutes. Remove most of the tomatoes to a bowl, leaving the juices. Arrange zucchini slices in baking dish with juices; sprinkle with salt, basil, oregano, and 1 tablespoon Parmesan cheese. Spoon tomatoes back into baking dish, covering zucchini; cover and continue to cook about 20 minutes over low heat until vegetables are tender. Preheat oven to broil. Sprinkle mozzarella cheese over vegetables. In a small bowl, combine remaining 1 tablespoon Parmesan cheese and bread crumbs; sprinkle over cheese. Place under broiler until crumbs brown and cheese is melted.

Microwave Directions:

Place onion, garlic, and water in a microwave-safe dish. Cook on high for 1 minute. Add tomatoes. Cook on high for 3 minutes. Following the directions on the previous page, remove tomatoes; add zucchini slices, herbs, and 1 tablespoon Parmesan cheese. Return tomatoes to dish. Cook on high for 3 minutes or until vegetables are tender. Proceed with recipe as above, sprinkling remaining cheese and bread crumbs over all and placing under the broiler to brown bread crumbs and melt cheese.

Yield: 2 servings

1 serving contains:

| Cal | Prot | Fat | Carb | Fiber | Chol | Sodium |
|------|------|-----|------|-------|------|--------|
| 154kc | 10g | 5g | 21g | 4g | 12mg | 373mg |

Serving Suggestions: Serve with cooked brown rice. Serve with "yolk-free" noodles.

# VEGETABLES

**V**egetables are naturally low in fat, and they provide fiber, vitamins, and minerals to your diet. Include dark green leafy vegetables as well as deep yellow vegetables several times a week in addition to other vegetables. I prefer to shop for vegetables and fruits every few days in order to always have a fresh supply.

After shopping, carefully prepare and store vegetables to maintain their freshness and nutritional value. I usually don't wash vegetables until I start my meal preparations. However, you can wash broccoli and cauliflower ahead of time: rinse in cold water, drain carefully, and store in a Zip-loc type plastic bag.

To conserve more nutrients, I microwave most of my vegetables, using minimal water and cooking just until barely tender. To cook fresh vegetables for two servings, I normally cook the vegetables, covered, on high for about three minutes.

When ready to serve, be careful you don't add extra fat such as butter or fatty sauces; instead, try the sauce recipes I have included or butter substitute powders and herbs. When using herbs and a butter substitute, you can totally eliminate the salt from most vegetables. Citrus juice or citrus zest adds a sparkle to ordinary vegetables, also.

Include three to five servings of vegetables daily.

VEGETABLES

# Make-Ahead Potatoes

*These are nice to rely on for a busy day.*

1 large baking potato (approx. ¾ lb.)

3 thin slices onion

2 tablespoons skim milk

1 teaspoon low-fat margarine

dash salt

dash freshly ground black pepper

1 teaspoon grated Parmesan cheese, made with
   skim milk

dash paprika

Scrub potato, wipe dry, cut in ½ lengthwise. Divide onions along the 2 halves, put the 2 halves together and wrap loosely in plastic wrap; pierce plastic. Place in microwave oven and cook on high for 7 minutes or until soft. (Or wrap in foil and bake in 400-degree oven for 1 hour or until tender.) When done, scoop onion and potato pulp into small mixing bowl (being careful not to pierce the skin). Add milk, margarine, salt, and pepper; mash until smooth. Divide potato-onion mixture evenly between 2 potato shells. To bake immediately: Sprinkle with Parmesan cheese and paprika, place under broiler until warm and slightly brown. To bake later: Wrap in foil and refrigerate until 25 minutes before serving, sprinkle with Parmesan cheese and paprika, let set at room temperature 15 minutes, then place under the broiler and broil until warm and slightly brown.

Yield: 2 servings

1 serving contains:

| Cal | Prot | Fat | Carb | Fiber | Chol | Sodium |
|-----|------|-----|------|-------|------|--------|
| 91kc | 2g | 1g | 18g | 1g | 1mg | 43mg |

VEGETABLES

# Twice-Baked Potatoes

*Yogurt gives this a tangy flavor.*

1 large baking potato (approx. ¾ lb.)

2 tablespoons onion, chopped

1 tablespoon fat-free plain yogurt

2 tablespoons fat-free cottage cheese

⅛ teaspoon salt

dash black pepper

2 tablespoons chopped, fresh chives or green onion

2 teaspoons imitation nonfat bacon bits

Scrub potato; pierce skin in several places. Place on a paper towel in microwave oven; cook on high for about 5 minutes or until soft to the touch. Cool slightly. Holding potato with a hot pad, cut in half; remove pulp from the potato, being careful not to pierce skin. Place the pulp in a small bowl; set the potato shells aside. While the potato is baking, place the onion in a nonstick skillet with about 2 tablespoons water; cook over medium heat until tender. Add the yogurt and cottage cheese to the potato, mash until fairly smooth; add onion, salt, pepper, and chives. Mix well. Spoon the potato mixture into the 2 potato shells. (The potatoes can be prepared up to this point ahead of time.) Preheat oven to 350 degrees. Place potatoes on a baking pan, heat for about 10 minutes, or if they have been refrigerated cover with foil and heat about 25 minutes or until heated through. Sprinkle with bacon bits.

Yield: 2 servings

1 serving contains:

| Cal | Prot | Fat | Carb | Fiber | Chol | Sodium |
|------|------|-----|------|-------|------|--------|
| 92kc | 4g | 0g | 18g | 1g | 1mg | 197mg |

VEGETABLES

# Baked Tomatoes Dijon

*Dijon adds an extra zing to an old favorite.*

vegetable spray

1 ripe tomato, cut in half (approx. ½ lb.)

1 teaspoon finely chopped fresh chives

½ teaspoon Dijon mustard

1 tablespoon fresh bread crumbs

½ teaspoon minced, fresh basil

Preheat oven to 350 degrees. Spray shallow baking dish with vegetable spray. Place tomato halves, cut side up, in prepared dish. In a small dish, combine chives and mustard; spread over tomatoes. Sprinkle with bread crumbs and minced basil. Baked in 350-degree oven for 10-12 minutes until tomatoes are tender and bread crumbs are brown.

Yield: 2 servings

1 serving contains:

| Cal | Prot | Fat | Carb | Fiber | Chol | Sodium |
|-----|------|-----|------|-------|------|--------|
| 27kc | 1g | 0g | 5g | 1g | 0mg | 66mg |

VEGETABLES

# Broccoli Cheese-Stuffed Potato

*A low-fat version of a favorite treat*

1 medium baking potato (approx. ½ lb.)

¾ cup chopped broccoli, flowerettes only

2 teaspoons low-fat margarine

2 teaspoons fat-free plain yogurt

⅛ teaspoon salt

dash black pepper

1 slice nonfat cheddar cheese

Scrub potato; pierce skin in several places. Place on a paper towel in microwave oven; cook on high for about 5 minutes or until soft to the touch; set aside. Put chopped broccoli in a small bowl, cover and microwave for 3 minutes; drain well; set aside. Cut potato in half lengthwise. Using a spoon, gently scoop out the potato pulp, being careful not to pierce the potato skin. Put potato pulp in a small bowl; add margarine, yogurt, salt, and pepper; mash until fairly smooth. Add broccoli; mix thoroughly. Spoon broccoli-potato mixture into potato skins. Put ½ slice of cheese on each potato half. Put under broiler for about 2 minutes or until cheese melts and browns.

Yields: 2 servings

1 serving contains:

| Cal | Prot | Fat | Carb | Fiber | Chol | Sodium |
|-----|------|-----|------|-------|------|--------|
| 165kc | 5g | 2g | 30g | 3g | 0mg | 344mg |

VEGETABLES

# California Carrots

*Delightfully easy, yet interesting flavor*

3 small carrots, peeled and sliced (approx. ⅓ lb. or more)

1 tablespoon water

1 teaspoon low-fat margarine

1 teaspoon orange zest

1 tablespoon thinly sliced green onion

Place carrots and water in a small microwave-safe dish. Microwave on high for 3½ minutes, drain well. Add margarine; toss gently, then add orange zest and onion; toss again. When ready to serve, return to microwave and cook on high for 1 minute more.

Yield: 2 servings

1 serving contains:

| Cal | Prot | Fat | Carb | Fiber | Chol | Sodium |
|------|------|-----|------|-------|------|--------|
| 57kc | 1g | 1g | 11g | 4g | 0mg | 62mg |

Stove top directions: Steam carrots until just tender. Place in serving dish. Add margarine, orange peel, and onion. Toss to combine.

VEGETABLES

# Carrot Zucchini Sauté

*Fennel adds a distinct flavor.*

vegetable spray

1 zucchini, shredded (approx. ¼ lb.)

1 carrot, shredded (approx. ¼ lb.)

1 tablespoon fresh lemon juice

¼ teaspoon minced fresh fennel

freshly ground white pepper to taste

Spray a medium nonstick skillet with vegetable spray. Heat skillet on medium-high heat. Add vegetables; sauté quickly until just tender. Add lemon juice, fennel, and pepper; toss gently. Serve immediately.

Yield: 2 servings

1 serving contains:

| Cal | Prot | Fat | Carb | Fiber | Chol | Sodium |
|------|------|-----|------|-------|------|--------|
| 13kc | 1g | 0g | 3g | 1g | 0mg | 4mg |

VEGETABLES

# Cauliflower 'n' Cheese

*Cheese develops into a nice sauce after baking.*

*1 ½ cups cauliflower flowerettes*

*dash freshly ground white pepper*

*¼ cup fat-free sour cream*

*¼ cup fat-free shredded cheddar cheese*

*¼ cup fresh, coarse bread crumbs*

Preheat oven to 350 degrees. Place cauliflower in microwave in an oven-proof dish; add 1 tablespoon water. Microwave on high for 3 minutes. Drain very well. Return to dish; sprinkle with pepper. In a small bowl, combine sour cream and cheddar cheese; spoon over cauliflower. Sprinkle with crumbs. Place in 350-degree oven and bake for 10-15 minutes or until cheese is melted and bubbly.

Yield: 2 servings

1 serving contains:

| Cal | Prot | Fat | Carb | Fiber | Chol | Sodium |
|-----|------|-----|------|-------|------|--------|
| 115kc | 11g | 1g | 16g | 1g | 43mg | 428mg |

VEGETABLES

# Chestnut Brown Rice

*Chestnuts add crunch to the nutty flavor of brown rice.*

½ cup brown rice

⅓ cup coarsely chopped water chestnuts

¾ cup water

½ cup apple juice or cider

Preheat oven to 350 degrees. Place rice in a 1-quart, stove-top-safe baking dish. Using medium-high heat, cook rice for about 1 minute, stirring constantly. Add chestnuts, water, and juice. Bring to a boil, cover and bake for 40-45 minutes in 350-degree oven. Bake until liquid is absorbed and rice is tender.

Yield: 2 (¾ cup) servings

1 serving contains:

| Cal | Prot | Fat | Carb | Fiber | Chol | Sodium |
|-----|------|-----|------|-------|------|--------|
| 212kc | 4g | 1g | 46g | 2g | 0mg | 5mg |

VEGETABLES

# Moroccan Couscous

*A welcome change from potatoes*

1 cup low-fat, low-sodium chicken broth

1 tablespoon finely sliced green onion

½ cup couscous, uncooked

2 tablespoons raisins

dash of turmeric

⅛ teaspoon ginger

Put ¼ cup broth in a medium-sized saucepan, add onion and cook over medium heat until tender. Add remaining broth; bring to a boil. Stir in couscous, raisins, turmeric, and ginger. Cover and set aside for 5 minutes. When ready to serve, fluff with a fork.

Yield: 2 generous servings

1 serving contains:

| Cal | Prot | Fat | Carb | Fiber | Chol | Sodium |
|-----|------|-----|------|-------|------|--------|
| 211kc | 8g | 1g | 44g | 1g | 0mg | 7mg |

VEGETABLES

# Chinese Fried Rice with Vegetables

*The sherry/soy sauce combination is interesting.*

*vegetable spray*

*1 teaspoon olive oil*

*½ teaspoon minced, fresh ginger*

*1 clove garlic, minced*

*¼ cup sliced onion*

*½ cup sliced carrot*

*½ cup broccoli flowerettes*

*2 tablespoons water*

*¼ cup sliced green onions, divided*

*1 ½ cups cooked white rice (cooked without added fat or salt)*

*2 tablespoons low-sodium soy sauce*

*2 tablespoons sherry*

*¼ cup low-fat, low-sodium chicken broth*

*¼ cup egg substitute*

Using medium-high heat, spray a wok or non-stick skillet with vegetable spray, then add oil. When hot, add ginger and garlic, stirring quickly (don't let garlic brown). Reduce heat to medium. Add onions and carrots, stirring frequently. Let cook about 3-4 minutes. Add broccoli, continuing to stir. Add water if necessary (1 tablespoon at a time). Cook until vegetables are slightly tender. Add 3 tablespoons green onions; stir. Add rice; stir. In a small bowl, combine soy sauce, sherry, and broth. Add to rice and vegetables; cook until heated through, stirring occasionally. Make an indentation in rice mixture, pour egg substitute into indentation, let cook for about 90 seconds, then stir egg into rice mixture. Continue to cook for about 1 minute more or until it barely cooks. Spoon into serving dish, garnish with remaining 1 tablespoon green onions.

Yield: 2 (1½ cups) servings

1 serving contains:

| Cal | Prot | Fat | Carb | Fiber | Chol | Sodium |
|------|------|-----|------|-------|------|--------|
| 294kc | 10g | 3g | 52g | 3g | 0mg | 550mg |

VEGETABLES

# Creamed Potatoes

*These are as good as Mom's, with less fat.*

1 ½ cups potatoes, peeled and cut into ½" cubes

¼ cup evaporated skimmed milk

1 tablespoon unbleached or all-purpose flour

1 teaspoon fat-free powdered milk

½ teaspoon low-fat margarine

dash salt

dash freshly ground black pepper

Put the potatoes in a small saucepan. Cover with water and cook over medium heat until tender. In a jar with a lid, combine milk, flour, and powdered milk; shake until dissolved. While stirring, slowly pour into potatoes. Cook over medium heat, stirring constantly until thickens. Add seasonings and margarine. Serve.

Yield: 2 (½ cup) servings

1 serving contains:

| Cal | Prot | Fat | Carb | Fiber | Chol | Sodium |
|------|------|-----|------|-------|------|--------|
| 144kc | 5g | 1g | 30g | 2g | 1mg | 54mg |

VEGETABLES

# D i r t y   R i c e

*A spicy variation without all the cholesterol and fat*

vegetable spray

½ teaspoon olive oil

¼ cup chopped onion

1 clove garlic, minced

½ cup long grain white rice

½ cup water

½ cup low-fat, low-sodium chicken broth

⅛ teaspoon dry mustard

⅛ teaspoon black pepper

⅛ teaspoon red pepper

1 teaspoon fresh, minced basil

1 teaspoon fresh, minced parsley

¼ cup chopped red or green pepper

Preheat oven to 350 degrees. Spray a 1-quart oven-proof casserole with vegetable spray. Heat oil in a medium nonstick skillet over medium heat. Add onion and garlic, stirring quickly. Add rice, stirring quickly. Add water, broth, mustard, peppers, basil, parsley, and green/red pepper; stir. Cover and bring to a boil. Pour into prepared casserole. Bake covered in 350-degree oven for 20 minutes or until all liquid is absorbed.

Yield: 2 (¾ cup) servings

1 serving contains:

| Cal | Prot | Fat | Carb | Fiber | Chol | Sodium |
|-----|------|-----|------|-------|------|--------|
| 95kc | 3g | 1g | 13g | 2g | 0mg | 5mg |

VEGETABLES

# Garlicky Green Beans

*The liquid smoke gives it a great flavor.*

1 ½ cups fresh green beans, broken

1 clove garlic, minced

2 teaspoons low-fat margarine

dash Liquid Smoke

¼ teaspoon salt

Wash and drain green beans. Place in saucepan with enough water to just barely cover. Add garlic, margarine, and liquid smoke. Cook about 30 minutes. Add salt before serving.

Microwave directions: Place beans in a microwave-safe, 1-quart casserole. Add ¼ cup water, cover and cook on high 5 minutes. Add garlic, margarine, and Liquid Smoke. Cook on 50 percent power for about 8 minutes or until desired tenderness. Add salt and serve.

Yield: 2 servings

1 serving contains:

| Cal | Prot | Fat | Carb | Fiber | Chol | Sodium |
|------|------|-----|------|-------|------|--------|
| 42kc | 2g | 2g | 6g | 2g | 0mg | 344mg |

VEGETABLES

# Glorified Acorn Squash

*An excellent way to give acorn squash a special flavor*

*vegetable spray*

*1 medium acorn squash (approx. 1 lb.)*

*1 teaspoon low-fat margarine*

*2 teaspoons brown sugar*

*dash ground ginger*

*¼ cup crushed, drained pineapple (packed in its own juice)*

*1 tablespoon raisins*

Preheat broiler. Spray a small, shallow baking dish with vegetable spray. Rinse, dry, then pierce the skin of the squash. Place in a microwave-safe dish. Microwave on high about 6 minutes or until tender. Cut in half. Remove and discard seeds. Scoop out pulp, leaving the shell in tact. Mash pulp. Add remaining ingredients. Place the 2 shells in a shallow baking dish. Spoon the mixture into shells. Place under broiler and broil until slightly browned and bubbly. Serve immediately.

Yield: 2 servings

1 serving contains:

| Cal | Prot | Fat | Carb | Fiber | Chol | Sodium |
|-----|------|-----|------|-------|------|--------|
| 143kc | 2g | 1g | 35g | 3g | 0mg | 32mg |

VEGETABLES

# Golden Risotto

*A dash of saffron adds a lovely gold color plus flavor.*

*2 cups low-fat, low-sodium chicken broth*

*vegetable spray*

*⅓ cup chopped onion*

*½ cup arborio rice*

*dash powdered saffron*

Pour broth in a small saucepan. Place on medium heat. Bring to a gentle boil, reduce heat to low and maintain a low simmer. Spray a medium nonstick skillet with vegetable spray; heat over medium-high. Add chopped onion; sauté until limp. Add rice and cook about 2 minutes. Reduce heat to low. (Correct heat is important: You want the liquids to be lively, but not evaporate too quickly. This entire process should take about 15-20 minutes.) Add ½ cup simmering broth and stir constantly until the liquid has been absorbed. Add another ½ cup broth, repeating the same process until there is about ¼ cup broth left. Test the rice. It should be tender but al dente. If more cooking is needed, add the remaining broth and continue to cook until tender. Sprinkle just a dash of saffron over rice; stir. Serve immediately.

Yield: 2 (¾ cup) servings

1 serving contains:

| Cal | Prot | Fat | Carb | Fiber | Chol | Sodium |
|-----|------|-----|------|-------|------|--------|
| 87kc | 3g | 1g | 18g | 1g | 0mg | 200mg |

VEGETABLES

# Hash Brown Casserole

*A popular, high-fat recipe now drastically reduced in fat, calories and sodium*

vegetable spray

½ package (15 oz.) frozen hash brown potatoes, thawed

¼ cup chopped onion

½ cup fat-free sour cream alternative

1 (10¾ oz.) can low-fat, low-sodium cream of chicken soup

¾ cup shredded fat-free cheddar cheese

dash cayenne pepper

dash black pepper

dash paprika

Preheat oven to 350 degrees. Spray a 2-quart baking dish with vegetable spray. In a medium mixing bowl, toss potatoes and onions to mix. In a small bowl, combine sour cream, soup, grated cheese, cayenne, and black pepper; pour over potatoes. Toss again. Spoon into prepared dish. Sprinkle with paprika. Cover and bake in 350-degree oven for 30 minutes; uncover and continue to bake for 30 minutes more.

Yield: 4 servings

1 serving contains:

| Cal | Prot | Fat | Carb | Fiber | Chol | Sodium |
|-----|------|-----|------|-------|------|--------|
| 89kc | 7g | 3g | 9g | 0g | 23mg | 226mg |

*This is just as good 2-3 days later; simply cover and reheat.*

VEGETABLES

# Herbs 'n' Green Beans

*This is especially good with fresh green beans.*

*1 tablespoon chopped green pepper*

*1 tablespoon thinly sliced green onion*

*½ lb. fresh green beans (or use 2 cups frozen)*

*¼ teaspoon fresh, chopped rosemary*

*¼ teaspoon fresh, chopped basil*

*1 teaspoon low-fat margarine*

Wash and drain green beans; break into 2" pieces. Place pepper, onion, green beans, and rosemary in a medium saucepan. Bring to a boil, reduce heat and cook for 15 minutes. Add basil and margarine. Serve.

Microwave directions: Wash and drain green beans; break into 2" pieces; set aside. Place pepper and onion in a 2-quart microwave-safe dish. Add 1 tablespoon water; cover and microwave on high for 30 seconds. Add beans, 2 tablespoons water, and rosemary; cover and microwave on 50 percent power for 8 minutes, stirring occasionally. Add basil and margarine; cover. Let set for 3-4 minutes before serving.

Yield: 2 servings

1 serving contains:

| Cal | Prot | Fat | Carb | Fiber | Chol | Sodium |
|------|------|-----|------|-------|------|--------|
| 46kc | 2g | 1g | 9g | 3g | 0mg | 31mg |

VEGETABLES

# International Oven Fries

*Different spices give the potatoes different personalities.*

vegetable spray

3 medium potatoes (approx. 1 ½ lb.)

½ tablespoon olive oil

¼ teaspoon garlic powder

¼ teaspoon Italian seasoning

dash seasoned salt

Preheat oven to 450 degrees. Spray a small baking sheet with vegetable spray. Scrub potatoes, (peel if desired). Cut into wedges, about 10 wedges per potato. Lay potatoes on paper towel and dry. Spread potatoes on baking sheet. Carefully drizzle oil over all the potatoes. Using a spatula, toss potatoes around to coat well. Sprinkle garlic powder, Italian seasoning, and salt over the potatoes. Bake in 450-degree oven for about 20 minutes, turn. Continue cooking about 5 minutes more or until potatoes are tender. Serve immediately.

Yield: 2 servings

1 serving contains:

| Cal | Prot | Fat | Carb | Fiber | Chol | Sodium |
|------|------|-----|------|-------|------|--------|
| 250kc | 5g | 4g | 49g | 3g | 0mg | 11mg |

Variations: Omit Italian seasoning and add ⅛ teaspoon chili powder.
Omit Italian seasoning and add ¼ teaspoon oregano and ⅛ teaspoon paprika.
Omit Italian seasoning and add ¼ teaspoon dried dill weed.

VEGETABLES

# L i m a   B e a n   -   T o m a t o   T r e a t

*Great with fresh tomatoes, or you can use canned.*

1 cup fresh or frozen lima beans

1 fresh tomato (approx. ¼ lb.) or ¾ cup canned

¼ cup thinly sliced onion rings

⅛ teaspoon salt

dash freshly ground black pepper

½ tablespoon chopped, fresh basil

Combine beans, tomato, and onion in a saucepan and simmer for about 25 minutes. Add seasonings and continue to cook until beans are tender.

Microwave directions: Place beans in a microwave-safe bowl. Cover with plastic. Cook on high for 3 minutes; stir. Add tomatoes and onion, cook 1 minute on high; stir. Cook on 50 percent power for an additional 5 minutes, stirring after 2 minutes. Add salt, pepper, and basil. Cover and let set about 3 minutes.

Yield: 2 servings

1 serving contains:

| Cal | Prot | Fat | Carb | Fiber | Chol | Sodium |
|-----|------|-----|------|-------|------|--------|
| 113kc | 7g | 1g | 21g | 9g | 0mg | 177mg |

V E G E T A B L E S

# M o m ' s   M a s h e d   P o t a t o e s

*These are creamy without all the fat.*

3 medium potatoes, peeled and cubed
  (about 1 ¼ lb.)

3 tablespoons evaporated skimmed milk

½ tablespoon low-fat margarine

¼ teaspoon salt

Place potatoes in a small saucepan; add enough water to cover. Bring to a boil. Reduce heat to low and continue to cook about 15 minutes or until very tender; drain. Using either a handheld potato masher or electric mixer, mash or beat until creamy and smooth. Add evaporated milk, margarine, and salt, beating until well blended.

Yield: 4 (½ cup) servings

1 serving contains:

| Cal | Prot | Fat | Carb | Fiber | Chol | Sodium |
|------|------|-----|------|-------|------|--------|
| 103kc | 3g | 1g | 22g | 2g | 0mg | 180mg |

*I make extra and use the leftovers for potato cakes.*

VEGETABLES

# Mashed Potatoes with Buttermilk

*A great change in taste for mashed potatoes*

2 medium potatoes, peeled and cubed
  (approx. ¾ lb.)

½ cup low-fat buttermilk

1 tablespoon fat-free plain yogurt

1 teaspoon low-fat margarine

¼ teaspoon salt

dash black pepper

2 tablespoons chopped, fresh chives

Place potatoes in a small saucepan; add enough water to cover. Bring to a boil. Reduce heat to low and continue to cook for about 15 minutes or until very tender; drain. Using a handheld potato masher or electric mixer, beat until just chunky. Remove ½ cup chunks and set aside. Add buttermilk, yogurt, margarine, salt, and pepper; continue to beat until fairly smooth. Add chunks and chives. Stir with spoon to blend.

Yield: 2 servings

1 serving contains:

| Cal | Prot | Fat | Carb | Fiber | Chol | Sodium |
|-----|------|-----|------|-------|------|--------|
| 158kc | 5g | 2g | 31g | 2g | 0mg | 359mg |

V E G E T A B L E S

# F r i e d   O k r a   -   S o r t   o f

*Added crispness comes from the egg beaters and corn meal.*

½ lb. fresh okra pods

1 tablespoon egg substitute

2 tablespoons cornmeal

¼ teaspoon seasoned salt

vegetable cooking spray

2 teaspoons olive oil

Wash okra. Remove ends; cut into ½" slices. Put okra in a medium bowl; add egg substitute, tossing with a fork to coat. Add cornmeal and salt, tossing gently to coat well. Spray a nonstick skillet with vegetable spray. Add olive oil. Heat on high. Add okra; reduce to medium-high. Cook about 5 minutes; reduce heat to low. Continue to cook for about 10-15 minutes or until tender. (The freshness of okra determines length of time to get it tender.)

Yield: 2 servings

1 serving contains:

| Cal | Prot | Fat | Carb | Fiber | Chol | Sodium |
|-----|------|-----|------|-------|------|--------|
| 110kc | 4g | 5g | 15g | 1g | 0mg | 310mg |

VEGETABLES

# Okra and Tomatoes

*A delicious low-fat recipe for your end-of-summer veggies*

½ lb. fresh okra

1 teaspoon olive oil

¼ cup chopped onion

1 clove garlic, minced

1 large ripe tomato, peeled and chunked (approx.
½ lb.)

¼ teaspoon salt

dash black pepper

Wash okra. Cut off tips and stem ends. Slice into about ⅓" slices; set aside. In a large, non-stick skillet, heat oil over medium heat. Add onion; cook about 2 minutes. Add garlic, stirring constantly for a few seconds. Adjust heat to medium-high. Add okra and tomato; bring to a boil. Reduce heat to simmer. Cover and simmer for about 20 minutes. Add salt and pepper.

Yield: 4 (½ cup) servings

1 serving contains:

| Cal | Prot | Fat | Carb | Fiber | Chol | Sodium |
|-----|------|-----|------|-------|------|--------|
| 39kc | 1g | 1g | 6g | 1g | 0mg | 152mg |

VEGETABLES

# Sweet Onion Casserole

*A delightful treat with spring-sweet onions*

vegetable spray

2 cups sweet onions, sliced and separated into rings

½ cup evaporated skimmed milk

½ tablespoon cornstarch

¼ cup egg substitute

dash salt

dash freshly ground black pepper

½ cup shredded fat-free cheddar cheese

dash paprika

Preheat oven to 350 degrees. Spray a 1-quart baking dish with vegetable spray. Place onions in a small, microwave-safe bowl. Add ¼ cup water. Microwave on high for 4 minutes; drain well. Spoon into a 1-quart baking dish. In a small mixing bowl, combine evaporated milk, cornstarch, egg substitute, salt, and pepper. Pour over onion rings; sprinkle with cheese; top with paprika. Place in 350-degree oven and bake uncovered 30 minutes. Serve immediately.

Stove-top directions: Place onions and water in a small saucepan. Bring to a boil, reduce heat, boil for 10 minutes; drain and proceed as above.

Yield: 4 (½ cup) servings

1 serving contains:

| Cal | Prot | Fat | Carb | Fiber | Chol | Sodium |
|-----|------|-----|------|-------|------|--------|
| 71kc | 7g | 0g | 12g | 1g | 4mg | 186mg |

# Parsley and Rice

*A colorful, attractive addition to your menu*

*vegetable spray*

*1 cup white long grain rice*

*1 tablespoon minced onion*

*2 cups hot low-fat, low-sodium chicken broth*

*2 tablespoons minced, fresh parsley*

Preheat oven to 350 degrees. Spray a 2-quart oven-proof casserole with vegetable spray. Spray a medium skillet with vegetable spray. Add rice, onion, and broth. Cover. Bring to a boil. Pour into prepared casserole. Bake in 350-degree oven for about 20 minutes or until rice is tender and all liquid is absorbed. Remove from oven, add parsley and fluff with a fork.

Yield: 6 (½ cup) servings

1 serving contains:

| Cal | Prot | Fat | Carb | Fiber | Chol | Sodium |
|------|------|-----|------|-------|------|--------|
| 51kc | 2g | 0g | 10g | 0g | 0mg | 2mg |

*Package the remaining rice in small zip-lock plastic bags and freeze. When ready to use, remove from freezer, pierce plastic 3-4 times with a fork, place in microwave and heat on high for about 90 seconds or until hot to the touch.*

VEGETABLES

# Peas and Carrots

*Add color and flavor to your meal.*

¾ *cup carrots, peeled and sliced*

*1 cup frozen peas*

*dash freshly ground black pepper*

*dash nutmeg*

*pinch sugar*

Place carrots in a small microwave-safe dish. Add 1 tablespoon water. Cover. Cook on high for 1 minute. Add peas and cook just until barely tender, about 2 minutes. Sprinkle with pepper, nutmeg, and sugar. Cover and let set a few minutes before serving.

Yield: 2 (½ cup) servings

1 serving contains:

| Cal | Prot | Fat | Carb | Fiber | Chol | Sodium |
|------|------|-----|------|-------|------|--------|
| 77kc | 4g | 0g | 14g | 4g | 0mg | 107mg |

VEGETABLES

# New Potatoes with Parsley

*These are a sure sign of spring.*

4-5 small new red potatoes (about ½ lb.)

1 teaspoon low-fat margarine

½ tablespoon chopped, fresh parsley

dash salt

freshly ground black pepper to taste

Scrub potatoes well. Put into a medium saucepan with steaming basket. Bring to a boil and cook on medium heat until just barely tender. Lift basket out, discard water; return potatoes to the warm pan. Melt margarine, pour over potatoes, add parsley, salt, and pepper. Cover and set aside for a few minutes before serving.

Microwave directions: Place potatoes in a small microwave-safe dish. Add 1 tablespoon water. Cover. Cook on high for 4-5 minutes or until tender when pierced. Drain well. Add margarine, parsley, salt, and pepper.

Yield: Approximately 2 (½ cup) servings

1 serving contains:

| Cal | Prot | Fat | Carb | Fiber | Chol | Sodium |
|---|---|---|---|---|---|---|
| 241kc | 5g | 1g | 54g | 4g | 0mg | 37mg |

Variations: Omit parsley and add 1 teaspoon of lemon pepper.
Omit parsley and add ½ teaspoon dill weed.
Omit parsley and add 1 teaspoon fresh, minced fennel weed.

VEGETABLES

# Rice with Fresh Herbs

*Rosemary will get your attention with this rice dish.*

1 cup low-fat, low-sodium chicken broth

2 tablespoons chopped onion

½ cup white long grain rice

¼ teaspoon fresh rosemary

¼ teaspoon fresh thyme

dash turmeric

In a medium saucepan, using medium-high heat, bring broth to a boil. Add onions. Cook about 2 minutes. Add rice, rosemary, thyme, and turmeric; bring to a boil. Reduce heat, cover and simmer for about 17-20 minutes, or until rice is tender and all liquid is absorbed.

Yield: 2 (¾ cup) servings

1 serving contains:

| Cal | Prot | Fat | Carb | Fiber | Chol | Sodium |
|------|------|-----|------|-------|------|--------|
| 95kc | 3g | 1g | 14g | 2g | 0mg | 5mg |

VEGETABLES

# White-Wild Rice Pilaf

*The wild rice gives this a nice crunchiness plus attractive appearance.*

*vegetable spray*

*¼ cup wild rice*

*1 teaspoon olive oil*

*¼ cup chopped onion*

*¾ cup white long grain rice*

*2 cups hot low-fat, low-sodium chicken broth*

*1 tablespoon minced, fresh parsley*

*1 bay leaf*

Preheat oven to 350 degrees. Spray a 2-quart oven-proof casserole with vegetable spray. Place wild rice in a small dish with just enough water to cover rice; cover with plastic wrap. Place in microwave; cook 1 minute on high and 2 minutes on 25 percent power; set aside. Heat oil in a medium skillet over medium heat. Add onions, cooking until tender. Add white rice, stirring quickly to coat grains. Add broth, wild rice, parsley, and bay leaf; stir; cover and bring to a boil. Pour into prepared casserole. Bake covered in 350-degree oven for 20 minutes, or until all the liquid is absorbed.

Yield: 6 (½ cup) servings

1 serving contains:

| Cal | Prot | Fat | Carb | Fiber | Chol | Sodium |
|-----|------|-----|------|-------|------|--------|
| 131kc | 2g | 1g | 28g | 1g | 1mg | 5mg |

Stove-top directions: Cook on top of the stove by simmering for 18-20 minutes, or until all the liquid is absorbed.

*Package the remaining rice in small zip-lock plastic bags and freeze. When ready to use, remove from freezer, pierce plastic 3-4 times with a fork, place in microwave and heat on high for about 90 seconds or until hot to the touch.*

VEGETABLES

# Scalloped Cauliflower

*A nice change from plain cauliflower*

*vegetable spray*

*2 cups cauliflower, flowerettes and stems*

*2 tablespoons onion*

*1 cup skim milk*

*1 tablespoon all-purpose flour*

*½ teaspoon low-fat margarine*

*¼ teaspoon Butter Buds*

*⅛ teaspoon salt*

*dash white pepper*

Preheat oven to 350 degrees. Spray a 1-quart baking dish with vegetable spray. Steam cauliflower and onion until barely tender. Drain; place in prepared dish. Combine milk and flour and blend well. Place in small saucepan and cook on medium heat until it starts to thicken. Add margarine, Butter Buds, salt, and pepper; pour over cauliflower. Bake in 350-degree oven for 30 minutes.

Microwave directions:

Place cauliflower in a small, microwave-safe bowl. Cover and microwave for 2½ minutes on high; set aside. In a small bowl, combine milk and flour, and blend well. Add margarine, cover and microwave for 2 minutes on high, then 1 minute on medium heat or until it just starts to thicken. Be careful the sauce doesn't boil over. Pour sauce over cauliflower. Add Butter Buds, salt, and pepper. Cover and microwave 2 minutes on high (watch constantly to prevent it boiling over). Vent the cover; continue to cook 5 minutes on 25 percent power.

Yield: 2 servings

1 serving contains:

| Cal | Prot | Fat | Carb | Fiber | Chol | Sodium |
|------|------|-----|------|-------|------|--------|
| 99kc | 7g | 1g | 17g | 1g | 2mg | 263mg |

VEGETABLES

# Scalloped Zucchini

*A cheesy, custard-like casserole*

*vegetable spray*

*1 medium zucchini, shredded (approx. ½ lbs.)*

*½ cup shredded fat-free sharp cheddar cheese*

*½ cup egg substitute*

*2 tablespoons minced onion*

*dash freshly ground black pepper*

Preheat oven to 350 degrees. Spray a 1-quart casserole with vegetable spray. Place zucchini in a medium mixing bowl, add cheese, egg substitute, onion, and pepper; stir. Transfer to prepared casserole and cover. Bake in 350-degree oven for 30 minutes.

Yield: 2 servings

1 serving contains:

| Cal | Prot | Fat | Carb | Fiber | Chol | Sodium |
|-----|------|-----|------|-------|------|--------|
| 96kc | 16g | 0g | 9g | 1g | 0mg | 548mg |

VEGETABLES

# Somebody's Carrots

*A special recipe from my dear friend Joyce, who loves to cook*

vegetable spray

2 carrots (approx. ½ lb.) cut into 2" lengths

1 tablespoon minced onion

2 tablespoons prepared horseradish

2 tablespoons fat-free mayonnaise

2 tablespoons fine, dry bread crumbs

1 teaspoon low-fat margarine, melted

1 teaspoon grated Parmesan cheese, made with skim milk

3 tablespoons water

Preheat oven to 350 degrees. Spray a 1-quart baking dish with vegetable spray. Place carrots in microwave-safe dish. Add water, cook on high for 2½ minutes or until tender. Drain, reserving liquid. Place carrots in baking dish. In a small bowl, combine 2 tablespoons cooking liquid, onion, horseradish, and mayonnaise; spoon over carrots. In small bowl, combine bread crumbs and margarine; sprinkle over carrots. Sprinkle Parmesan cheese over bread crumbs. Place in 350-degree oven and bake for 20 minutes.

Yield: 2 servings

1 serving contains:

| Cal | Prot | Fat | Carb | Fiber | Chol | Sodium |
|------|------|-----|------|-------|------|--------|
| 83kc | 2g | 5g | 17g | 3g | 1mg | 245mg |

V E G E T A B L E S

# S p i c e d   C a r r o t s

*I found this in one of my mom's old, old recipe books.*

1 ½ cups carrots, peeled and cut into cubes

1 teaspoon balsamic vinegar

dash ground cloves

½ teaspoon sugar

1 teaspoon low-fat margarine

Steam carrots. While they are cooking, combine vinegar, cloves, sugar, and margarine. When carrots are tender, gently place in serving dish and drizzle sauce over them. Serve immediately.

Microwave directions: Place carrots in a small microwave-safe dish. Add 1 tablespoon water. Cook on high for 2½ minutes or until tender. Proceed as above.

Yield: 2 servings

1 serving contains:

| Cal | Prot | Fat | Carb | Fiber | Chol | Sodium |
|------|------|-----|------|-------|------|--------|
| 61kc | 1g | 1g | 12g | 2g | 0mg | 95mg |

VEGETABLES

# Stuffed Cheyote Squash

*This makes an interesting change and is very good.*

vegetable spray

1 medium cheyote squash (approx. ¾ lb.)

¼ cup low-fat, low-sodium chicken broth

1 tablespoon finely chopped green onion

1 tablespoon chopped pimiento

2 tablespoons fine, dry bread crumbs

¼ teaspoon minced, fresh rosemary, or ⅛ tsp. dried

Preheat oven to 350 degrees. Spray small baking dish with vegetable spray. Rinse and dry squash; cut in half from stem end to bottom. Leaving about ¼" around shell, scoop out centers and finely chop pulp. Spray a small nonstick skillet with vegetable spray; heat on medium. Add chopped pulp, green onion, and broth; reduce heat to medium-low and continue to cook until limp. Remove from heat. Add pimiento, bread crumbs, and rosemary; toss well. (It may be necessary to adjust bread crumbs to make stuffing stick together.) Fill squash shells with stuffing, place in prepared dish, cover and bake 50-60 minutes or until squash shell is tender.

Yield: 2 servings

1 serving contains:

| Cal | Prot | Fat | Carb | Fiber | Chol | Sodium |
|-----|------|-----|------|-------|------|--------|
| 100kc | 3g | 1g | 23g | 3g | 0mg | 54mg |

VEGETABLES

# Sweet Potato Strudel

*The apples give this dish a new twist.*

vegetable spray

1 large sweet potato (approx. ½ lb.)

1 cup peeled, sliced apple

¼ teaspoon cinnamon

⅛ teaspoon nutmeg

¼ cup apple juice

2 tablespoons unbleached or all-purpose flour

¼ cup brown sugar

1 teaspoon low-fat margarine

Preheat oven to 350 degrees. Spray a 1-quart baking dish with vegetable spray. Peel and slice potato about ¼" slices. Place potato and apple slices in prepared baking dish. Sprinkle cinnamon and nutmeg over vegetables; pour juice over all. Cover and bake 30 minutes. In a small bowl, combine flour, sugar, and margarine.

Sprinkle over casserole. Bake 15 minutes or until potatoes are soft.

Microwave directions: Prepare the same method using microwave-safe baking dish. Microwave on high for 5 minutes, sprinkle flour mixture over potatoes and continue to microwave for 3 minutes.

Yield: 2 servings

1 serving contains:

| Cal | Prot | Fat | Carb | Fiber | Chol | Sodium |
|-----|------|-----|------|-------|------|--------|
| 229kc | 2g | 1g | 53g | 3g | 0mg | 34mg |

V E G E T A B L E S

# Judy's Southwestern Vegetables

*An unusual combination, you'll be pleased with the flavor.*

*1 cup cooked black beans\**

*½ cup frozen or fresh whole kernel corn*

*1 medium tomato, peeled and quartered (approx. ½ lb.)*

*dash salt*

*dash freshly ground black pepper*

*1 teaspoon chopped, fresh cilantro or parsley (optional)*

Combine all ingredients in a microwave-safe bowl. Cover; cook 4 minutes on high; stir, then cook 4 minutes on 25 percent power.

Yield: 2 cups

1 serving contains:

| Cal | Prot | Fat | Carb | Fiber | Chol | Sodium |
|-----|------|-----|------|-------|------|--------|
| 183kc | 10g | 1g | 36g | 4g | 0mg | 40mg |

*\*May use canned.*

V E G E T A B L E S

# T w i c e   N i c e   R i c e

*This is a good recipe for that leftover rice you never know what to do with.*

1 cup cooked rice (cooked without added fat or
   salt)

½ cup peas,* cooked

1 tablespoon water

Combine the rice, peas, and water; place in a small Ziploc plastic bag. Barely pierce 3-4 holes in bag with a fork. Heat in microwave on high for 1 minute.

Yield: 2 (¾ cup) servings

1 serving contains:

| Cal | Prot | Fat | Carb | Fiber | Chol | Sodium |
|------|------|-----|------|-------|------|--------|
| 162kc | 5g | 0g | 34g | 2g | 0mg | 2mg |

*Use any leftover vegetable: corn, green beans, etc.*

VEGETABLES

# Vegetable Medley

*A simple, but good combination*

½ cup broccoli, flowerettes and stems

½ cup cauliflower, flowerettes and stems

¼ cup carrots, scraped and sliced

½ tablespoon fresh-snipped basil or ½ teaspoon dried

½ teaspoon Butter Buds

In a medium saucepan with steamer, cook the vegetables on low heat until just tender. Drain the water from pan and put vegetables directly in pan. Add basil and Butter Buds; toss gently to coat. Cover and let set a few minutes before serving.

Microwave directions: Place vegetables in a small microwave-safe bowl; cover with plastic. Cook on high for 3 minutes. Sprinkle with basil and Butter Buds, cover and let set for about 3 minutes to let flavors blend.

Yield: 2 (½ cup) servings

1 serving contains:

| Cal | Prot | Fat | Carb | Fiber | Chol | Sodium |
|------|------|-----|------|-------|------|--------|
| 41kc | 3g | 0g | 8g | 2g | 0mg | 57mg |

VEGETABLES

# Zucchini-Balsamic Vinegar

*Balsamic vinegar adds a pleasingly distinct flavor.*

1 teaspoon olive oil

1 small zucchini, sliced thin

¼ cup sliced fresh mushrooms

4 slices onion

1 tablespoon water

1 tablespoon balsamic vinegar

Heat oil in a small nonstick skillet, using medium-high heat. Add zucchini, mushrooms, and onion slices; stir-fry just until tender. Add water, cover, and cook 1 more minute; add balsamic vinegar, serve.

Yield: 2 (½ cup) servings

1 serving contains:

| Cal | Prot | Fat | Carb | Fiber | Chol | Sodium |
|------|------|-----|------|-------|------|--------|
| 39kc | 2g | 3g | 61g | 1g | 4mg | 6mg |

VEGETABLES

# Zucchini Sour Cream Bake

*A quick, easy, and delicious variation to an old favorite*

*1 medium zucchini, sliced (approx. ½ lb.)*

*¼ cup fat-free sour cream*

*1 teaspoon low-fat margarine*

*1 tablespoon shredded fat-free cheddar cheese*

*1 teaspoon minced chives*

*dash paprika*

Preheat oven to 350 degrees. Place zucchini in microwave-safe dish. Cover, vent and microwave on high 2 minutes; drain; transfer to baking dish. In a small, microwave-safe bowl, combine sour cream, margarine, and grated cheese. Cover and microwave on 75 percent power, stirring every 20 seconds for 1 minute or until cheese is slightly melted; stir in chives. Spoon over zucchini. Sprinkle with paprika. Bake in 350-degree oven until heated through and bubbly.

Yield: 2 servings

1 serving contains:

| Cal | Prot | Fat | Carb | Fiber | Chol | Sodium |
|-----|------|-----|------|-------|------|--------|
| 37kc | 1g | 1g | 3g | 1g | 0mg | 151mg |

V E G E T A B L E S

# Z u c c h i n i   w i t h   M a r j o r a m

*A nice side dish to serve with your favorite fish*

½ teaspoon olive oil

1 ¼ cups zucchini, sliced thin

¼ cup sliced fresh mushrooms

⅛ teaspoon dried marjoram

dash freshly ground black pepper

½ teaspoon balsamic vinegar

In a small nonstick skillet, using medium-high heat, heat oil. Add zucchini and mushrooms. Stir-fry just until tender. Add marjoram, salt, pepper, and vinegar; cover and let set about 3 minutes for flavors to blend.

Yield: 2 (½ cup) servings

1 serving contains:

| Cal | Prot | Fat | Carb | Fiber | Chol | Sodium |
|-----|------|-----|------|-------|------|--------|
| 24kc | 1g | 1g | 3g | 1g | 0mg | 3mg |

# DESSERTS

While sugars and fats are at the top of the food pyramid and should be used sparingly, I personally do not totally exclude them from our diet. I think when desserts are eliminated from your diet they become that much more appealing; when eaten occasionally and in moderation you don't feel so deprived.

Fruits are a wonderful source for desserts; I use fruits extensively in our meals for desserts and salads. I have included a number of sauces to use sparingly with fresh fruits, or combine nonfat yogurt and fruits. Today there is such a wonderful variety of fat-free frozen desserts and puddings, sugar-free puddings, yogurts, and prepackaged fruits or fruit packed in its own juice. You can now have your dessert and enjoy it without feeling guilty, saving the desserts higher in sugar for special occasions only.

*I do not recommend the "extralight" margarine for baking. I use regular low-fat.*

DESSERTS

# Fresh Fruit 'n' Pudding

*This is our favorite light dessert.*

½ cup pineapple chunks, packed in its own juice

1 tablespoon instant, sugar-free vanilla pudding mix

½ small apple

½ small orange

½ small banana

Drain pineapple. Set aside. In a small bowl, combine pudding mix and about ¼ cup of juice, blend thoroughly. In a small bowl, combine fruit. Gently fold pudding into fruit.

Yield: 2 servings

1 serving contains:

| Cal | Prot | Fat | Carb | Fiber | Chol | Sodium |
|-----|------|-----|------|-------|------|--------|
| 102kc | 1g | 0g | 26g | 2g | 0mg | 6mg |

D E S S E R T S

# Jell-O Bavarian

*Cool, light, and refreshing*

*1 (3 oz.) package sugar-free raspberry Jell-O*

*1 cup boiling water*

*¾ cup cold water*

*½ cup fat-free plain yogurt*

*1 cup fresh fruit \**

In a medium mixing bowl, combine Jell-O and boiling water, stirring until completely dissolved. Add cold water; stir; refrigerate until Jell-O starts to thicken. Add yogurt to thickened Jell-O; beat with an electric mixer on low speed until well blended and fluffy. Fold in fruit and spoon into individual serving dishes or a mold. Refrigerate until set.

Yield: 6 (½ cup) servings

1 serving contains:

| Cal | Prot | Fat | Carb | Fiber | Chol | Sodium |
|-----|------|-----|------|-------|------|--------|
| 27kc | 1g | 0g | 6g | 1g | 0mg | 15mg |

Serving Suggestions:
*1 fresh nectarine
1 peach
½ cup fresh blueberries, strawberries, etc.
Garnish with fresh raspberries. Garnish with thin lemon slice

DESSERTS

# Deep - Dish Apple Crisp

*A great variation to the all-American favorite*

*1 cup unbleached or all-purpose flour*

*½ cup old-fashioned oats, uncooked*

*¼ cup soft low-fat margarine*

*½ cup brown sugar*

*4 cups peeled, sliced, tart, juicy apples*

*½ teaspoon ground cinnamon*

*dash ground nutmeg*

Preheat oven to 375 degrees. In a medium mixing bowl, combine flour, oats, margarine, and sugar; remove ¾ cup for topping; set aside. Press remaining crumbs into an 8" round pie pan or a 2-quart casserole; arrange the apple slices evenly over crumbs. Gently toss spices with remaining crumbs; sprinkle crumbs over apples. Place in 375-degree oven and bake for 35-40 minutes or until apples are tender. (Different apples require different cooking times.)

Yield: 6 servings

1 serving contains:

| Cal | Prot | Fat | Carb | Fiber | Chol | Sodium |
|-----|------|-----|------|-------|------|--------|
| 252kc | 5g | 5g | 49g | 3g | 0mg | 97mg |

Serving Suggestions: Serve with a little skim milk. Serve with nonfat frozen vanilla yogurt or ice milk.

DESSERTS

# Blueberry Mystery Dessert

*What a surprise when you serve this; cake and blueberry sauce, too.*

2 cups fresh or frozen blueberries

1 tablespoon lemon juice

½ tablespoon creme de cassis, liquor

1¼ cups sugar, divided

3 tablespoons soft low-fat margarine

1 teaspoon baking powder

1 cup unbleached or all-purpose flour

½ cup skim milk

1 tablespoon cornstarch

⅛ teaspoon ground nutmeg

1 cup boiling water

Preheat oven to 400 degrees. Put blueberries in an 8x8 pan; sprinkle lemon juice and liquor over berries and toss gently. In a medium mixing bowl, cream ¾ cup sugar and margarine. In a small bowl, combine baking powder and flour; add flour and milk alternately to the margarine mixture, beating well after each addition. Spoon batter over blueberries. Combine ½ cup sugar and cornstarch; sprinkle over batter. (Do not stir.) Sprinkle nutmeg over batter. Pour boiling water over all. (Do not stir.) Bake in a 400-degree oven for 45 minutes.

Yield: 10 servings

1 serving contains:

| Cal | Prot | Fat | Carb | Fiber | Chol | Sodium |
|-----|------|-----|------|-------|------|--------|
| 182kc | 2g | 2g | 40g | 1g | 0mg | 49mg |

## DESSERTS

# Baked Stuffed Pears

*A dollop of yogurt with a dusting of nutmeg makes this special, or simply bake and serve unadorned.*

2 firm pears

1 tablespoon sugar

1 teaspoon lemon juice

2 tablespoons raisins

½ cup apple juice

¼ cup fat-free vanilla yogurt, artificially sweetened

dash freshly ground nutmeg

Preheat oven to 350 degrees. Cut pears in half and remove core; place in a shallow baking dish. In a small bowl, combine sugar, lemon juice, and raisins; stuff the hollow in the pears with this mixture. Pour apple juice in pan, cover and bake in 350-degree oven for about 30 minutes or until tender. Allow to cool before serving. When ready to serve, transfer 2 pear halves onto each individual serving dish, spoon yogurt over this and dust lightly with nutmeg.

Yield: 2 servings

1 serving contains:

| Cal | Prot | Fat | Carb | Fiber | Chol | Sodium |
|-----|------|-----|------|-------|------|--------|
| 170kc | 2g | 1g | 42g | 4g | 1mg | 25mg |

Variation: Substitute apples for pears; substitute light maple syrup for sugar.

DESSERTS

# Brandied Applesauce

*Elegant and easier than anything*

3 cups apples, peeled and sliced (cooking apples)

2 tablespoons water or apple juice

2 tablespoons apple-flavored brandy (or any flavor)

2 teaspoons brown sugar

dash ground cinnamon

dash ground cloves

1 teaspoon low-fat margarine

½ teaspoon cornstarch

Place apples and 1 tablespoon water in a small microwave-safe bowl; cover. Microwave about 5 minutes or until apples are cooked very tender. (Times will vary according to microwave.) Add brandy, sugar, cinnamon, cloves, and margarine; gently combine. In a small bowl, blend cornstarch and remaining 1 tablespoon water; add to apple mixture; stir well. Return to microwave and cook about 1 minute or until start-ing to thicken. Remove; let set a few minutes to cool before serving.

Yield: 5 (½ cup) servings

1 serving contains:

| Cal | Prot | Fat | Carb | Fiber | Chol | Sodium |
|-----|------|-----|------|-------|------|--------|
| 91kc | 3g | 1g | 14g | 2g | 1mg | 44mg |

The yield will vary slightly according to type of apples used.

Serving Suggestions: Serve over frozen fat-free vanilla yogurt, ice milk, angel food cake, or vanilla pudding.

DESSERTS

# Festive Broiled Grapefruit

*A simple yet colorful dessert; serve with dinner or brunch.*

*1 grapefruit, halved*

*1 teaspoon maraschino cherry juice or grenadine syrup*

*2 fresh strawberries*

Preheat oven to broil. Place grapefruit halves cut side up on a baking dish. Spoon syrup over each half. Place under broiler for about 2-3 minutes or until bubbly. Garnish with strawberry halves. Serve warm.

Yield: 2 servings

1 serving contains:

| Cal | Prot | Fat | Carb | Fiber | Chol | Sodium |
|------|------|-----|------|-------|------|--------|
| 40kc | 0g | 0g | 10g | 1g | 0mg | 0mg |

D E S S E R T S

# B r a n d i e d   Y o g u r t

*A very satisfying dessert*

*1 cup fat-free vanilla yogurt, sweetened with
    artificial sweetener*

*1 teaspoon apricot brandy (or other flavor)*

*1 cup peach slices (pears, nectarines, bananas, etc.)*

In a small bowl, combine yogurt and brandy; cover and refrigerate 10-20 minutes to allow flavors to blend. Gently fold in sliced peaches. Serve immediately.

Yield: 2 servings

1 serving contains:

| Cal | Prot | Fat | Carb | Fiber | Chol | Sodium |
|-----|------|-----|------|-------|------|--------|
| 141kc | 7g | 1g | 26g | 1g | 3mg | 76mg |

## HEALTHY COOKING FOR TWO

D E S S E R T S

# E l e g a n t   F r o s t e d   P e a c h e s

*A light dessert, elegant enough for guests*

1 cup fat-free vanilla yogurt, artificially sweetened

½ tablespoon honey

1 tablespoon minced crystallized ginger

1 cup fresh sliced peaches (nectarines, strawberries)

Chill 2 champagne or wine glasses. In a small bowl, combine yogurt, honey, and ginger; cover and refrigerate 10-20 minutes to let flavors blend. When ready to serve, gently fold in fresh fruit. Rub the rims of glasses with a touch of low-fat margarine, dip into granulated sugar, then carefully spoon yogurt and fruit into glasses. Serve immediately.

Yield: 2 servings

1 serving contains:

| Cal | Prot | Fat | Carb | Fiber | Chol | Sodium |
|------|------|-----|------|-------|------|--------|
| 102kc | 7g | 1g | 18g | 2g | 2mg | 87mg |

DESSERTS

# Fresh Fruit with Ginger Sauce

*Ginger adds an interesting flavor.*

*2 teaspoons cornstarch*

*½ tablespoon sugar*

*dash ground ginger*

*½ cup orange juice*

*2 cups assorted fresh fruit*

Combine cornstarch, sugar, and ginger in a small, microwave-safe bowl; gradually add juice, stirring until smooth. Cover and cook on high 1 minute and 15 seconds, stirring every 15 seconds; remove and set aside to cool completely. In a small bowl, combine fruit; pour sauce over and toss gently.

Yield: 4 servings

1 serving contains:

| Cal | Prot | Fat | Carb | Fiber | Chol | Sodium |
|------|------|-----|------|-------|------|--------|
| 56kc | 0g | 0g | 14g | 2g | 0mg | 0mg |

D E S S E R T S

# F r u i t   a n d   Y o g u r t   C u p

*Easy, surprisingly smooth dessert*

*1 envelope unflavored gelatin*

*¼ cup water*

*1 cup fat-free cottage cheese*

*1 cup fat-free vanilla yogurt, artificially sweetened*

*2 tablespoons sugar\**

*½ teaspoon coconut flavoring*

*dash ground allspice*

*½ cup sliced mango*

*½ banana, sliced*

In a small bowl, sprinkle gelatin over water; let stand 1 minute to soften. Heat in microwave on high for 30 seconds. Stir until gelatin is completely dissolved. Cool completely. Place cottage cheese and yogurt in a blender; process until smooth; add sugar and flavoring. With blender on low, gradually add gelatin, blending well. Place fruit in small, individual dessert dishes; pour gelatin mixture over fruit; sprinkle with allspice; cover and chill until set.

Yield: 4 servings

1 serving contains:

| Cal | Prot | Fat | Carb | Fiber | Chol | Sodium |
|---|---|---|---|---|---|---|
| 139kc | 10g | 0g | 24g | 1g | 4mg | 70mg |

*\*Substitute 3 packets of artificial sweetener for sugar.*

Serving Suggestion: Garnish with mint leaves.

DESSERTS

# Mandarin Orange Dessert

*A delicious tart, sweet, "light" dessert*

1 (3 oz.) package sugar-free orange Jell-O

1 cup boiling water

¾ cup cold water

1 (11 oz.) can mandarin orange slices, drained

dash ground ginger

4 sprigs of fresh spearmint (optional)

In a medium mixing bowl, combine Jell-O and boiling water, stirring until completely dissolved; add cold water; stir. Refrigerate until Jell-O starts to thicken. Add orange slices and ginger; stir gently to blend. Pour into 4 custard cups; chill until set. Serve with a sprig of mint.

Yield: 4 servings

1 serving contains:

| Cal | Prot | Fat | Carb | Fiber | Chol | Sodium |
|-----|------|-----|------|-------|------|--------|
| 35kc | 10g | 0g | 9g | 0g | 0mg | 4mg |

Serving Suggestion: Serve in champagne glasses garnished with mint.

DESSERTS

# Mom's Bread Pudding

*This was a favorite of John's childhood years; I simply added apples and reduced the fat and cholesterol.*

*½ cup egg substitute*

*½ cup skim milk*

*½ cup evaporated skimmed milk*

*1 tablespoon powdered milk*

*¼ cup + 1 tablespoon sugar*

*1 teaspoon vanilla*

*1 cup bread crumbs (large crumbs)*

*⅓ cup raisins*

*1 cup cooking apple slices*

*Dash nutmeg*

Preheat oven to 350 degrees. Spray a 2-quart baking dish with vegetable spray. Pour egg substitute into a medium mixing bowl; beat slightly with a fork. Add the 3 kinds of milk, sugar, and vanilla; mix well. Fold bread crumbs into milk mixture. Add raisins and apple slices.

Pour into prepared baking dish; sprinkle with nutmeg. Bake in a 350-degree oven for 35 minutes or until a knife comes out clean.

Yield: 4 servings

1 serving contains:

| Cal | Prot | Fat | Carb | Fiber | Chol | Sodium |
|-----|------|-----|------|-------|------|--------|
| 253kc | 11g | 1g | 50g | 2g | 4mg | 293mg |

Serving Suggestions: Top with a dollop of Cinnamon Sauce.* Serve in a small bowl with skim milk.

*This recipe can be found in the Sauces section of this book.*

D E S S E R T S

# P e a c h   P u d d i n g

*A delightful dessert when fresh peaches are in season.*

*vegetable spray*

*1 ½ cups sugar, divided*

*1 tablespoon soft low-fat margarine*

*½ cup skim milk*

*1 teaspoon vanilla*

*1 teaspoon baking powder*

*1 cup unbleached or all-purpose flour*

*2 cups peaches, peeled and sliced*

*1 cup water*

Preheat oven to 350 degrees. Spray a 9x9 baking dish with vegetable spray. In a medium mixing bowl, cream ½ cup sugar and margarine until smooth. Add milk, vanilla, baking powder, and flour; mix well. Spoon into prepared baking dish. Arrange peaches on top of batter, sprinkle 1 cup sugar over peaches, then pour 1 cup water over all. Bake in a 350-degree oven for 45 minutes.

Yield: 12 servings

1 serving contains:

| Cal | Prot | Fat | Carb | Fiber | Chol | Sodium |
|-----|------|-----|------|-------|------|--------|
| 154kc | 2g | 1g | 36g | 1g | 0mg | 54mg |

Variation: Substitute blueberries for peaches.

DESSERTS

# Pear Melba

*A simple summer favorite*

1 cup fat-free vanilla frozen yogurt or ice milk

4 spiced pear halves*

¼ cup low-fat chocolate sauce**

Place ½ cup frozen yogurt in sherbet dish; lay 2 pear halves on top; spoon 2 tablespoons chocolate sauce over all. Serve immediately.

## *Spiced Pears

¼ cup sugar

½ cup water

1 cinnamon stick

2 whole cloves

2 pears, peeled, cored, and halved

In a small saucepan, stir together sugar, water, cinnamon, and cloves; bring to a boil; add pear halves. Simmer for about 20 minutes or until tender. Remove cinnamon and cloves.

Yield: 2 servings

1 serving contains:

| Cal | Prot | Fat | Carb | Fiber | Chol | Sodium |
|-----|------|-----|------|-------|------|--------|
| 357kc | 4g | 2g | 87g | 7g | 1mg | 91mg |

**Low-fat chocolate sauce can be found in the grocery store with other chocolate sauces.*

Variation: Substitute fresh peaches for pears.

DESSERTS

# Mom's Pumpkin Pie

*This was one of my childhood favorites; now our son's favorite*

1½ cups pumpkin, cooked and mashed, or canned

¾ cup sugar

¼ teaspoon ground nutmeg

¼ teaspoon ground cinnamon

1 cup evaporated skimmed milk

3 egg whites, slightly beaten

2 teaspoons low-fat margarine, melted

1 (9") pastry shell, unbaked, made with canola oil

Preheat oven to 425 degrees. In a medium mixing bowl, combine the pumpkin, sugar, and spices; blend in the milk, egg whites, and then margarine. Pour into pastry shell. Bake in a 425-degree oven for 45 minutes, or until a knife inserted in the center comes out clean.

Yield: 8 servings

1 serving contains:

| Cal | Prot | Fat | Carb | Fiber | Chol | Sodium |
|-----|------|-----|------|-------|------|--------|
| 252kc | 5g | 8g | 42g | 1g | 1mg | 194mg |

D E S S E R T S

# R a s p b e r r y   P a r f a i t s

*An easy yet elegant dessert*

⅓ cup fat-free cottage cheese

⅓ cup fat-free cream cheese

3 tablespoons sugar

1 cup fresh raspberries

2 tablespoons all-fruit raspberry jelly, melted

¼ cup graham cracker crumbs

2 tablespoons low-fat frozen whipped topping

Process cottage cheese in blender until smooth; add cream cheese and sugar, process slightly, just until smooth. In a small bowl, combine raspberries and jelly; spoon ½ of the fruit into the bottom of 2 parfait or wine glasses and top with ½ the cheese mixture. Sprinkle with the cracker crumbs; top with remaining cheese mixture. Spoon remaining fruit mixture over all and top with the whipped topping. Chill well before serving.

Yield: 2 servings

1 serving contains:

| Cal | Prot | Fat | Carb | Fiber | Chol | Sodium |
|------|------|-----|------|-------|------|--------|
| 263kc | 30g | 2g | 51g | 3g | 37mg | 209mg |

DESSERTS

# Creamy Rice Pudding

*This tastes like the creamy rice pudding Mom used to make.*

*vegetable spray*

*2 cups cooked white rice (cooked without added fat or salt)*

*½ cup water*

*1 cup skim milk*

*1 cup evaporated skimmed milk*

*2 egg whites*

*¼ cup egg substitute*

*¼ cup + 2 tablespoons sugar*

*1 teaspoon vanilla*

*dash nutmeg*

*dash ground cinnamon*

*1 cup raisins*

*1 cup skim milk (optional)*

Preheat oven to 350 degrees. Spray a 2-quart baking dish with vegetable spray. In a medium saucepan, combine rice and water; simmer 2-3 minutes to absorb all the water. Add both kinds of milk. Bring to a gentle boil, reduce heat to low and continue to cook 5 minutes, stirring frequently. Remove from heat. In a small bowl, combine egg white, egg substitute, sugar, vanilla, nutmeg, cinnamon, and raisins. Pour a small amount of hot rice into egg mixture, stir, then pour the egg mixture into pan of hot rice. Pour into prepared baking dish. Place in a pan containing 1" hot water. Bake in a 350-degree oven for 30-35 minutes or until knife comes out clean.

Yield: 4 (½ cup) servings

1 serving contains:

| Cal | Prot | Fat | Carb | Fiber | Chol | Sodium |
|-----|------|-----|------|-------|------|--------|
| 376kc | 14g | 1g | 80g | 2g | 4mg | 110mg |

Serving Suggestions: Spoon into dessert dishes and pour a small amount of skim milk over all. Top with meringue and brown slightly.

DESSERTS

# Sugar-Free Strawberry Mousse

*Simple to prepare, low in calories*

½ tablespoon cornstarch

⅓ cup low-calorie cranberry juice

½ cup egg substitute

1 envelope unflavored gelatin

½ tablespoon cold water

½ cup boiling water

1 cup fresh or frozen strawberries

½ cup fat-free vanilla yogurt, sweetened with
   artificial sweetener

4 packages sugar substitute

Combine cornstarch and juice in a small bowl; put in blender container; add egg substitute, gelatin, and cold water. Process to blend; add boiling water; blend again. Add strawberries; blend until pureed; add yogurt and sweetener; blend until smooth. Pour into individual serving bowls and refrigerate for 2-4 hours until set.

Yield: 4 (½ cup) servings

1 serving contains:

| Cal | Prot | Fat | Carb | Fiber | Chol | Sodium |
|------|------|-----|------|-------|------|--------|
| 63kc | 7g | 0g | 9g | 1g | 0mg | 66mg |

D E S S E R T S

# Strawberry Romanoff

*Elegant dessert; serve with sparkling champagne.*

1 pint fresh ripe strawberries, washed; leave stem on

½ cup fat-free sour cream

½ cup brown sugar

Arrange strawberries in an attractive serving dish. Put sour cream in a small serving bowl, and brown sugar in another small serving bowl. This is a "finger food"; each person takes 1 strawberry, holding it by the green stem, dips it into the sour cream, then into the brown sugar. Pop it into the mouth—you can hardly keep them supplied with strawberries.

Yield: 4 servings

1 serving contains:

| Cal | Prot | Fat | Carb | Fiber | Chol | Sodium |
|-----|------|-----|------|-------|------|--------|
| 90kc | 1g | 0g | 23g | 2g | 0mg | 6mg |

DESSERTS

# Strawberries and Rhubarb

*If fresh fruit is not available, use frozen.*

*1 cup chopped rhubarb*

*1 cup whole strawberries*

*1 tablespoon orange-flavored brandy (optional)*

*½ cup sugar, divided*

*½ teaspoon cornstarch*

*¼ cup unbleached or all-purpose flour*

*2 tablespoons soft low-fat margarine*

Preheat oven to 375 degrees. In a medium mixing bowl, combine rhubarb and strawberries. (Sprinkle with brandy if desired.) In a small mixing bowl, combine ¼ cup sugar and cornstarch. Pour sugar mixture over the fruit and gently mix; spoon into a 10" pie plate. In a small bowl, combine ¼ cup sugar, flour, and margarine; blend with a pastry blender until crumbly; spoon over fruit. Bake in a 375-degree oven for 30 minutes or until fruit is bubbly.

Yield: 4 servings

1 serving contains:

| Cal | Prot | Fat | Carb | Fiber | Chol | Sodium |
|------|------|-----|------|-------|------|--------|
| 184kc | 1g | 3g | 35g | 1g | 0mg | 72mg |

Variations: Substitute 4 packages artificial sweetener for sugar; substitute 2 tablespoons oat bran for 2 tablespoons flour.

D E S S E R T S

# Y o g u r t   a   l' O r a n g e

*Keep this simple yet delicious dessert on hand for all occasions.*

¼ gallon fat-free vanilla frozen yogurt, softened

6 oz. frozen orange juice concentrate, partially
  thawed

2 tablespoons Cointreau or apricot brandy

Stir all ingredients together; pour into freezer
container, cover tightly and refreeze.

Yield: 6 (½ cup) servings

1 serving contains:

| Cal | Prot | Fat | Carb | Fiber | Chol | Sodium |
|-----|------|-----|------|-------|------|--------|
| 138kc | 2g | 0g | 28g | 0g | 0mg | 80mg |

D E S S E R T S

# Old - Fashioned Apricot Cookies

*These taste just like Grandma used to make.*

vegetable spray

1 ¼ cups sugar

¾ cup soft low-fat margarine

3 egg whites, slightly beaten

3 cups unbleached or all-purpose flour

½ teaspoon baking soda

2 teaspoons baking powder

⅓ cup sour skim milk*

½ teaspoon vanilla

½ cup dried apricots, chopped fine

½ cup apricot jam

Preheat oven to 375 degrees. Lightly spray cookie sheets with vegetable spray. In a large mixing bowl, cream sugar and margarine; add egg whites. In a medium bowl, combine flour, baking soda, and baking powder. Add dry ingredients and sour milk alternately to the sugar mixture; mix well. Add vanilla and chopped apricots; stir until just blended. Drop by the teaspoon onto prepared cookie sheet. Using a teaspoon, drop about ⅛ teaspoon of jam onto top of cookie, making an indentation with the back of the spoon. Bake in a 375-degree oven for 12-14 minutes, or until set.

Yield: 50 cookies

*Place ½ tablespoon lemon juice in a ⅓ measuring cup and fill with skim milk; let set for a few minutes.

1 serving contains:

| Cal | Prot | Fat | Carb | Fiber | Chol | Sodium |
|------|------|-----|------|-------|------|--------|
| 72kc | 1g | 1g | 14g | 0g | 0mg | 64mg |

D E S S E R T S

# B a n a n a   C o o k i e s

*Wonderfully moist and flavorful, they taste like banana cake.*

vegetable spray

¾ cup + 1 tablespoon soft low-fat margarine,
   divided

¾ cup sugar

2 egg whites, slightly beaten

2 teaspoons vanilla extract, divided

1 cup mashed bananas (approx. 2 bananas)

2 cups unbleached or all-purpose flour

1 teaspoon baking soda

¼ cup skim milk

½ cup firmly packed brown sugar

2 cups sifted powdered sugar

Preheat oven to 350 degrees. Lightly spray cookie sheet with vegetable spray. In a large mixing bowl, cream ¾ cup margarine and sugar; add egg whites, 1 teaspoon vanilla, and mashed bananas. In a small bowl, combine flour and soda; add to banana mixture, ½ cup at a time, mixing well. Drop by the teaspoon onto prepared cookie sheet. Bake in a 350-degree oven for 8 minutes or until just browned around edge; remove to wire rack to cool.

Frosting:

In a small saucepan, combine 1 tablespoon margarine, milk, and brown sugar; over medium-high heat, bring to a boil. Reduce heat to medium and continue to boil for 2 minutes. Remove from heat, add powdered sugar and remaining vanilla, beating until smooth. (It may be necessary to adjust milk or sugar to get the desired spreading consistency.) Spread a thin layer of frosting on each cookie. Let icing harden before storing cookies.

Yield: 60 cookies

1 serving contains:

| Cal | Prot | Fat | Carb | Fiber | Chol | Sodium |
|------|------|-----|------|-------|------|--------|
| 59kc | 1g | 1g | 12g | 0g | 0mg | 15mg |

DESSERTS

# Jenny's Dainty Cinnamon Gems

*These tiny little morsels will melt in your mouth.*

*vegetable spray*

*1 cup soft low-fat margarine*

*1 cup sifted powdered sugar*

*½ cup + 2 tablespoons granulated sugar, divided*

*¼ cup sweetened applesauce*

*1 teaspoon vanilla*

*2½ cups unbleached or all-purpose flour*

*2 teaspoons ground cinnamon, divided*

Preheat oven to 350 degrees. Lightly spray cookie sheets with vegetable spray. In a medium mixing bowl, cream margarine, powdered sugar, and ½ cup granulated sugar; add applesauce and vanilla. In a small bowl, combine flour and 1½ teaspoons cinnamon; gradually add to margarine mixture ½ cup at a time, mixing well. In a small, shallow bowl, combine 2 tablespoons sugar and remaining ½ teaspoon cinnamon. Using about 1 teaspoon of dough, shape small balls, place on prepared cookie sheets. Grease the bottom of a glass with margarine, dip glass in sugar-cinnamon mixture and flatten cookies slightly. Bake in a 350-degree oven for 13-15 minutes or until slightly brown; dust with sugar-cinnamon mixture. Let cool about 30 seconds before removing to a wire rack to cool.

Yield: 45 cookies

1 serving contains:

| Cal | Prot | Fat | Carb | Fiber | Chol | Sodium |
|-----|------|-----|------|-------|------|--------|
| 62kc | 1g | 2g | 10g | 0g | 0mg | 50mg |

D E S S E R T S

# C o c o n u t   M a c a r o o n s

*These are so much like the real thing, you could never guess what is in them.*

½ cup soft low-fat margarine

1 cup sugar

2 egg whites, slightly beaten

1½ cups dehydrated potato flakes*

2 teaspoons coconut flavoring

1 cup low-fat baking mix**

vegetable spray

In a medium mixing bowl, cream margarine and sugar; add egg whites, potato flakes, and flavoring; mix well; add baking mix and mix well. Chill for at least 2 hours. Preheat oven to 350 degrees. Lightly spray cookie sheet with vegetable spray. Shape dough into small balls about quarter size; place on prepared cookie sheet. Gently press balls with a fork dusted with flour. Bake in a 350-degree oven for 6-8 minutes; gently remove to wire rack to cool.

Yield: 45 cookies

1 serving contains:

| Cal | Prot | Fat | Carb | Fiber | Chol | Sodium |
|------|------|-----|------|-------|------|--------|
| 40kc | 1g | 1g | 8g | 0g | 0mg | 42mg |

*Use potato flakes, not buds.
**I use a popular low-fat baking mix.

DESSERTS

# Grandma's Cherry Winks

*These are a colorful treat any time, especially at Christmas.*

vegetable spray

2¼ cups unbleached or all-purpose flour

1 teaspoon baking powder

½ teaspoon baking soda

¾ cup soft low-fat margarine

1 cup sugar

3 egg whites, slightly beaten

2 tablespoons skim milk

1 teaspoon vanilla

¾ cup chopped maraschino cherries, drained

1 cup chopped dates

Preheat oven to 350 degrees. Lightly spray cookie sheets with vegetable spray. In a medium bowl, combine flour, baking powder, and baking soda; set aside. In a large mixing bowl, cream margarine and sugar together. Add egg whites, milk, and vanilla to the creamed mixture. Gradually add flour mixture; mix well. Stir in cherries and dates. Drop by the teaspoon onto prepared cookie sheet; bake in 350-degree oven for 10-12 minutes.

Yield: 50 cookies.

1 serving contains:

| Cal | Prot | Fat | Carb | Fiber | Chol | Sodium |
|-----|------|-----|------|-------|------|--------|
| 64kc | 1g | 1g | 12g | 1g | 0mg | 55mg |

DESSERTS

# Down-Home Raisin-Oatmeal Cookies

*A friend's grandmother used to make these deliciously moist cookies.*

vegetable spray

1 ½ cups raisins

water

1 cup sugar

¾ cup canola oil or oil of choice

3 egg whites, slightly beaten

1 teaspoon ground cinnamon

1 teaspoon baking soda

2 cups unbleached or all-purpose flour

2 cups old-fashioned oats, uncooked

Preheat oven to 375 degrees. Lightly spray cookie sheets with vegetable spray. Place the raisins in a small saucepan, pour water over them until just covered, bring to a boil, then set aside. In a large mixing bowl, combine sugar and oil; add egg whites and cinnamon. Drain raisins, reserving ½ cup liquid. Stir baking soda into the ½ cup of liquid; add to sugar mixture. Gradually add flour, ½ cup at a time; stir in oats and raisins; blend well. Drop by the teaspoon onto prepared cookie sheet. Bake in a 375-degree oven for 10-12 minutes.

Yield: 55 cookies

1 serving contains:

| Cal | Prot | Fat | Carb | Fiber | Chol | Sodium |
|-----|------|-----|------|-------|------|--------|
| 81kc | 1g | 3g | 12g | 1g | 0mg | 18mg |

DESSERTS

# Johnny's Gingerbread Cookies

*Our son loved to come home from school to this special treat.*

⅓ cup soft low-fat margarine

1 cup brown sugar

1½ cups molasses

6 cups unbleached or all-purpose flour

2 teaspoons baking soda

1 teaspoon cinnamon

1 teaspoon ground allspice

1⅛ teaspoons ground ginger

1⅛ teaspoons cloves

⅔ cup cold water

vegetable spray

In a large mixing bowl, cream margarine and sugar; add molasses; mix well. In a medium bowl, combine flour, baking soda, cinnamon, allspice, ginger, and cloves. Gradually add flour mixture and water alternately to the margarine, mixing well. Cover and chill dough for at least one hour. Preheat oven to 350 degrees. Lightly spray cookie sheets with vegetable spray. Roll dough out on a lightly floured surface, until it is about ⅜" thick. Cut with a 2¼" round cookie cutter, or gingerbread cookie cutter; place on prepared cookie sheet. Bake in a 350-degree oven for 12-14 minutes or until slightly firm to the touch. Gently remove to wire rack to cool.

Yield: 40 cookies

1 serving contains:

| Cal | Prot | Fat | Carb | Fiber | Chol | Sodium |
|-----|------|-----|------|-------|------|--------|
| 114kc | 2g | 1g | 25g | 1g | 0mg | 45mg |

D E S S E R T S

# A n d y ' s   H o n e y   C o o k i e s

*Slightly dense texture, delicious taste, and very easy to make*

vegetable spray

⅓ cup soft low-fat margarine

1 ¼ cups honey

3 egg whites, slightly beaten

½ cup skim milk

3 ½ cups unbleached or all-purpose flour

2 teaspoons baking powder

½ teaspoon baking soda

1 teaspoon ground cinnamon

1 teaspoon ground cloves

½ teaspoon ground nutmeg

1 ¼ cups apple, peeled and chopped fine

1 cup raisins

Preheat oven to 350 degrees. Lightly spray cookie sheets with vegetable spray. In a large mixing bowl, blend margarine and honey; add egg whites and milk. In a medium bowl, combine flour, baking powder, baking soda, cinnamon, cloves, and nutmeg; add to the margarine mixture ½ cup at a time; mix well. Fold in apples and raisins. Drop by the teaspoon onto prepared cookie sheet. Bake in a 350-degree oven for about 12-15 minutes.

Yield: 75 cookies

1 serving contains:

| Cal | Prot | Fat | Carb | Fiber | Chol | Sodium |
|-----|------|-----|------|-------|------|--------|
| 51kc | 1g | 1g | 11g | 0g | 0mg | 37mg |

Variation: Substitute ¼ cup oat bran for ¼ cup flour.

DESSERTS

# Joe's Magic Chocolate Cookies

*These are so yummy they will melt in your mouth.*

*2 cups sugar*

*¾ cup cocoa powder*

*½ cup + 2 teaspoons canola oil or oil of choice*

*6 egg whites, slightly beaten*

*2 teaspoons vanilla*

*2 cups unbleached or all-purpose flour*

*2 teaspoons baking powder*

*vegetable spray*

*¾ cup powdered sugar*

In a large mixing bowl, combine sugar, cocoa, and oil; mix until well blended. Add egg whites and vanilla. In a separate bowl, combine flour and baking powder; add to sugar mixture about ½ cup at a time, mixing well. Cover and refrigerate dough for 3 hours or overnight (until firm enough to handle). Preheat oven to 350 degrees. Lightly spray cookie sheet with vegetable spray. Put powdered sugar in a small shallow bowl. Shape dough into 1" balls; roll in powdered sugar; place on prepared cookie sheet. Bake in a 350-degree oven for about 10 minutes. Cool and store.

Yield: 70 cookies

1 serving contains:

| Cal | Prot | Fat | Carb | Fiber | Chol | Sodium |
|------|------|-----|------|-------|------|--------|
| 54kc | 1g | 2g | 10g | 0g | 0mg | 15mg |

D E S S E R T S

# M o l a s s e s   C r i n k l e s

*A rich, gingery cookie; you will love them.*

½ cup soft low-fat margarine

1 cup brown sugar

2 egg whites, slightly beaten

¼ cup molasses

2⅓ cups unbleached or all-purpose flour

2 teaspoons baking soda

½ teaspoon ground cloves

¾ teaspoon ground cinnamon

1 teaspoon ground ginger

⅛ teaspoon allspice

vegetable spray

1 tablespoon white sugar

Remove ½ teaspoon margarine; set aside. Put the remainder of margarine and sugar in a large mixing bowl and cream until smooth; add egg whites and molasses. In a medium bowl, com-bine flour, baking soda, cloves, cinnamon, ginger, and allspice; gradually add to the marga-rine mixture, mixing well. Cover and chill for at least 1 hour. Preheat oven to 350 degrees. Spray cookie sheet with vegetable spray. Roll a teaspoon of dough into a ball; place on prepared cookie sheet. Grease the bottom of a flat-bottomed glass with reserved margarine, dip the glass in sugar, then slightly flatten the ball of dough with the glass. Bake in a 350-degree oven for 10-12 minutes.

Yield: 55 cookies

1 serving contains:

| Cal | Prot | Fat | Carb | Fiber | Chol | Sodium |
|-----|------|-----|------|-------|------|--------|
| 41kc | 0g | 1g | 9g | 0g | 0mg | 55mg |

D E S S E R T S

# J o h n ' s   O a t m e a l   D o o d l e s

*These cookies have a unique flavor, similar to Snicker Doodles.*

vegetable spray

¾ cup soft low-fat margarine

1½ cups sugar

2 egg whites, slightly beaten

1 teaspoon vanilla

2 cups unbleached or all-purpose flour

2 teaspoons baking soda

1 cup old-fashioned oats, uncooked

1 cup raisins

Preheat oven to 375 degrees. Lightly spray cookie sheets with vegetable spray. In a large mixing bowl, cream margarine and sugar together; add egg whites and vanilla. Stir in flour, baking soda, and oats, stirring just until mixed; stir in raisins. Roll into 1" balls and place on prepared cookie sheet. Bake in a 375-degree oven for about 10 minutes or until slightly brown. Let cool about 30 seconds before removing to a rack to cool.

Yield: 55 cookies

1 serving contains:

| Cal | Prot | Fat | Carb | Fiber | Chol | Sodium |
|-----|------|-----|------|-------|------|--------|
| 63kc | 1g | 1g | 12g | 1g | 0mg | 65mg |

D E S S E R T S

# N a n a ' s   S u g a r   C o o k i e s

*A favorite of our children; now a favorite of our grandchildren, especially when they help make them*

¾ cup soft low-fat margarine

1½ cups powdered sugar

2 egg whites, slightly beaten

1 teaspoon vanilla

2½ cups unbleached or all-purpose flour

1 teaspoon baking powder

1 teaspoon cream of tartar

vegetable spray

colored sugar (optional)

In a large mixing bowl, cream margarine and sugar; add egg whites and vanilla. In a medium bowl, combine flour, baking powder, and cream of tartar; gradually add to margarine mixture. Cover bowl and chill 1 hour. Preheat oven to 400 degrees. Lightly spray cookie sheet with vegetable spray. Roll dough on a lightly floured surface; cut into desired shapes with cookie cutters. Decorate with colored sugar if desired. Bake in a 400-degree oven for 7-8 minutes or until slightly golden.

Yield: 45 cookies

1 serving contains:

| Cal | Prot | Fat | Carb | Fiber | Chol | Sodium |
|-----|------|-----|------|-------|------|--------|
| 55kc | 1g | 2g | 9g | 0g | 0mg | 49mg |

*You may decorate with frosting after cookies are cooled.*

D E S S E R T S

# S t r a w b e r r y   C a k e

*A delightfully easy, moist, tender and colorful cake*

vegetable spray

1 (18 oz.) box low-fat white cake mix

1 teaspoon sugar-free strawberry Jell-O powder

3 egg whites

½ cup water

1 tablespoon canola oil or oil of choice

1 cup very ripe strawberries or frozen, drained (reserve liquid)

½ cup powdered sugar

Preheat oven to 350 degrees. Spray a 9x13 baking pan with vegetable spray. In a large mixing bowl, combine cake mix, Jell-O, egg whites, water, oil, and strawberries; blend on low speed of electric mixer until well mixed. Beat at medium speed for 2 minutes. Scrape sides of bowl; spoon batter into prepared pan. Bake in 350-degree oven for 30 minutes or until wooden pick comes out clean. Combine 2 tablespoons reserved strawberry juice and powdered sugar, blending well (add enough liquid to be able to pour). Pour over slightly warm cake. Cool.

Yield: 16 servings

1 serving contains:

| Cal | Prot | Fat | Carb | Fiber | Chol | Sodium |
|------|------|-----|------|-------|------|--------|
| 162kc | 1g | 2g | 32g | 0g | 0mg | 247mg |

D E S S E R T S

# S u m m e r ' s   S p e c i a l   J e l l - O   C a k e

*A wonderfully cool, refreshing summer dessert*

*1 (18 oz.) low-fat white cake mix*

*1 (3 oz.) package sugar-free strawberry Jell-O*

*¾ cup boiling water*

*½ cup cold water*

*1 pint fresh strawberries, sliced*

*2 tablespoons powdered sugar*

Bake cake according to package directions in a 9x13 pan. While cake is baking, dissolve Jell-O in boiling water, add cold water, stir well and set aside at room temperature. Cool cake 20-30 minutes. Poke deep holes in cake with a meat fork. Using a cup, slowly pour gelatin mixture over the cake. Refrigerate until cold. When ready to serve, put a few strawberry slices on top of each piece of cake; sprinkle lightly with powdered sugar.

Yield: 12 servings

1 serving contains:

| Cal | Prot | Fat | Carb | Fiber | Chol | Sodium |
|-----|------|-----|------|-------|------|--------|
| 166kc | 3g | 0g | 39g | 1g | 0mg | 296mg |

Variation: Frost lightly with a fluffy, white, powdered sugar frosting.

*You can use any combination of Jell-O and fruit for this cake. How about a chocolate cake and cherry Jell-O?*

DESSERTS

# David's Hot Fudge Cake

*A great combination; chocolate cake and chocolate sauce*

*vegetable spray*

*1 ¼ cups sugar, divided*

*1 cup unbleached or all-purpose flour*

*2 teaspoons baking powder*

*3 tablespoons + ¼ cup cocoa, divided*

*½ cup skim milk*

*2 tablespoons canola oil or oil of choice*

*1 teaspoon vanilla*

*½ cup brown sugar*

*1 ¾ cups hot water*

Preheat oven to 350 degrees. Spray 9x9 pan with vegetable spray. In a medium mixing bowl, combine ¾ cup sugar, flour, baking powder, and 3 tablespoons cocoa. In a small bowl, combine milk, oil, and vanilla. Stir into the flour mixture; blend well. Pour into a 9x9" pan.

Combine ½ cup white sugar, ½ cup brown sugar, ¼ cup cocoa; sprinkle over the top of the batter, then pour hot water over entire mixture. (Do not stir.) Bake in a 350-degree oven for 45 minutes.

Yield: 12 servings

1 serving contains:

| Cal | Prot | Fat | Carb | Fiber | Chol | Sodium |
|-----|------|-----|------|-------|------|--------|
| 171kc | 2g | 3g | 36g | 0g | 0mg | 78mg |

Serving Suggestion: We love this served with a scoop of nonfat frozen vanilla yogurt.

D E S S E R T S

# C h o c o l a t e / A p p l e s a u c e   C a k e

*Moistness from the applesauce with the surprising flavor of chocolate makes for a refreshingly different cake.*

2 cups unbleached or all-purpose flour

1 teaspoon baking soda

1 teaspoon baking powder

1 teaspoon ground cinnamon

½ teaspoon ground nutmeg

1 tablespoon cornstarch

6 tablespoons soft low-fat margarine

1 cup sugar

3 tablespoons cocoa

2 cups unsweetened applesauce

1 cup raisins

¼ cup powdered sugar

Preheat oven to 350 degrees. Spray bundt or angel food cake pan with vegetable spray. In a medium mixing bowl, combine flour, baking soda, baking powder, cinnamon, nutmeg, and cornstarch. Set aside. In a large mixing bowl, cream margarine and sugar until creamy; add cocoa and blend thoroughly. Stir in applesauce. Gradually add flour mixture, beating well after each addition. Fold in raisins. Pour into prepared pan. Bake in 350-degree oven for 1 hour or until wooden pick comes out clean; invert onto wire rack. Let cool slightly, then dust with powdered sugar.

Yield: 16 servings

1 serving contains:

| Cal | Prot | Fat | Carb | Fiber | Chol | Sodium |
|-----|------|-----|------|-------|------|--------|
| 176kc | 2g | 2g | 38g | 1g | 0mg | 136mg |

*You can freeze half or the entire cake; it freezes wonderfully.*

# Banana Fruitcake

*At last, a low-fat and low-cholesterol fruitcake*

vegetable spray

½ cup low-fat margarine

2 cups sugar

2 egg whites

3 ripe, mashed bananas

1 teaspoon baking soda

⅓ cup boiling water

1 ¾ cups unbleached or all-purpose flour

1 teaspoon baking powder

½ teaspoon ground cinnamon

½ teaspoon ground cloves

½ cup gold raisins

½ cup dark raisins

½ cup chopped, candied fruit

½ cup chopped, candied cherries

½ cup chopped dates

Preheat oven to 350 degrees. Spray a 9x5 loaf pan with vegetable spray. In a large mixing bowl, beat the margarine and sugar until fluffy. Add egg whites; beat until smooth. Add bananas, beating until smooth. Dissolve soda in hot water; add to batter. In a small bowl, combine flour, baking powder, cinnamon, and cloves. Gradually add dry ingredients to the margarine mixture; blend well. Fold in raisins, fruit, and dates. Pour into prepared pan. Bake in a 350-degree oven for 1½ hours or until a pick inserted in center comes out clean. Invert onto wire rack and cool completely. For a more moist cake, wrap securely and let set overnight or longer.

Yield: 12 servings

1 serving contains:

| Cal | Prot | Fat | Carb | Fiber | Chol | Sodium |
|------|------|-----|------|-------|------|--------|
| 345kc | 3g | 4g | 77g | 2g | 0mg | 230mg |

D E S S E R T S

# Glazed Applesauce Spice Cake

*A gently spiced, moist cake*

vegetable spray

1¾ cups unbleached or all-purpose flour

1 teaspoon baking soda

1 teaspoon ground cinnamon

½ teaspoon ground cloves

¼ cup canola oil or oil of choice

¾ cup firmly packed brown sugar

1 cup unsweetened applesauce

¼ cup + 1 tablespoon unsweetened apple juice or water, divided

1 egg white

¼ cup egg substitute

½ cup sifted powdered sugar

dash ground cinnamon

Preheat oven to 350 degrees. Lightly spray angel food or bundt cake pan with vegetable spray. In a medium mixing bowl, combine flour, soda, cinnamon, and cloves; set aside. In a larger mixing bowl, combine oil and sugar. Add applesauce, ¼ cup apple juice, egg white, and egg substitute, beating until well blended. Gradually add flour mixture, beating until well blended. Pour into prepared cake pan. Bake in a 350-degree oven 40 minutes or until wooden pick comes out clean. Cool in pan 5 minutes; invert onto wire rack until cool. In a small bowl, mix 1 tablespoon apple juice, powdered sugar, and cinnamon; beat until smooth. Drizzle over cake. Let set until glaze is firm before cutting.

Yield: 16 servings

1 serving contains:

| Cal | Prot | Fat | Carb | Fiber | Chol | Sodium |
|-----|------|-----|------|-------|------|--------|
| 129kc | 2g | 4g | 23g | 0g | 0mg | 63mg |

*This freezes beautifully!*

# SAUCES

lways keep in mind sauces are used to enhance food, not disguise it. They are wonderful to perk up an otherwise plain dish by giving the food color, taste, and texture contrast. Sauces do wonders for leftover foods; they will turn leftovers into a special treat.

By using fat-free or reduced-fat products, you greatly reduce fat and cholesterol in the sauces. Bear in mind, however, these products don't require as much cooking time and should be stirred frequently; otherwise they may tend to separate. If you choose to serve the sauce separate, serve it in a small interesting container, such as a small cream pitcher, an interesting small bowl, or a pretty demitasse cup.

SAUCES

# Blueberry Sauce

*Serve over fresh fruit, fat-free pound cake, or fat-free frozen yogurt.*

¼ cup water

1 teaspoon cornstarch

2 tablespoons red currant jelly

½ cup fresh or frozen blueberries

In a small dish, combine 2 tablespoons water and cornstarch; set aside. In a small saucepan, combine 2 tablespoons water and jelly; heat until dissolved, stirring constantly. Add blueberries and cook over low heat until blueberries are soft. Stir cornstarch mixture into blueberries; cook over medium-low heat, stirring constantly, until mixture thickens. Cool before serving.

Yield: 4 servings

1 serving contains:

| Cal | Prot | Fat | Carb | Fiber | Chol | Sodium |
|------|------|-----|------|-------|------|--------|
| 38kc | 0g | 0g | 10g | 2g | 0mg | 3mg |

SAUCES

# Cinnamon Sauce

*Serve over fat-free vanilla frozen yogurt or apple pie.*

½ tablespoon cornstarch

2 tablespoons sugar

½ cup water

2 teaspoons low-fat margarine

½ teaspoon vanilla flavoring

⅛ teaspoon cinnamon*

In a small saucepan, combine cornstarch and sugar; stir in water. Using medium heat, cook slowly, stirring constantly until mixture begins to boil. Boil for 1 minute, continuing to stir constantly. Remove from heat; stir in margarine, flavoring, and cinnamon. Cool before serving.

Yield: 4 (2 tablespoons) servings

1 serving contains:

| Cal | Prot | Fat | Carb | Fiber | Chol | Sodium |
|------|------|-----|------|-------|------|--------|
| 36kc | 0g | 1g | 7g | 0g | 0mg | 23mg |

*Omit the cinnamon for vanilla sauce, or substitute your choice of ginger, nutmeg, or cloves for a different flavor.

S A U C E S

# Cranberry-Pear Compote

*A nice addition for poultry, French toast, or pancakes*

⅓ cup sugar

⅓ cup water

½ teaspoon lemon juice

½ cinnamon stick

2 whole cloves

2 pears, peeled, cut into large chunks

1 cup washed, fresh cranberries

Combine sugar, water, and lemon juice in a medium saucepan. Tie cinnamon stick and cloves in a small piece of cheesecloth; add spices and pears to the pan. Bring to a gentle boil, reduce heat to low and cook for about 15 minutes or until pears are almost tender; add cranberries and continue to cook about 15 minutes or until the skin bursts on the berries. Remove spices and discard.

Yield: 6 servings

1 serving contains:

| Cal | Prot | Fat | Carb | Fiber | Chol | Sodium |
|------|------|-----|------|-------|------|--------|
| 72kc | 0g | 0g | 19g | 1g | 0mg | 0mg |

S A U C E S

# C r e a m y   Y o g u r t   S a u c e

*This adds the finishing touch to garden-fresh fruit.*

½ cup fat-free vanilla yogurt, artificially sweet-ened

2 tablespoons fat-free cream cheese

1 tablespoon brown sugar

Combine all the ingredients in a small bowl; stir briskly to blend; cover and chill for at least 30 minutes.

Yield: 4 servings

1 serving contains:

| Cal | Prot | Fat | Carb | Fiber | Chol | Sodium |
|-----|------|-----|------|-------|------|--------|
| 24kc | 2g | 0g | 4g | 0g | 1mg | 22mg |

SAUCES

# Custard Sauce

*Serve with angel food cake or fresh fruit.*

½ teaspoon cornstarch

2 tablespoons sugar

½ cup skim milk

2 tablespoons egg substitute

¼ teaspoon vanilla flavoring (or your choice of
   flavoring)

In a small saucepan, combine cornstarch and sugar; stir in milk and egg substitute. Using medium heat, cook slowly, stirring constantly until mixture begins to boil. Boil for 1 minute, continuing to stir constantly. Remove from heat; stir in flavoring. Cool before serving.

Yield: 2 (¼ cup) servings

1 serving contains:

| Cal | Prot | Fat | Carb | Fiber | Chol | Sodium |
|-----|------|-----|------|-------|------|--------|
| 80kc | 4g | 0g | 16g | 0g | 1mg | 55mg |

S A U C E S

# Dijon Mustard Sauce

*A tart, sweet flavor adds interest to most meats or vegetables.*

1 teaspoon cornstarch

¼ cup evaporated skimmed milk

2 teaspoons honey

4 teaspoons Dijon mustard

⅛ teaspoon dried basil

1 teaspoon low-fat margarine

Using a whisk, combine cornstarch and evaporated milk in a small saucepan; add honey. Cook over medium-low heat until thickened. Add mustard, basil, and margarine.

Yield: 6 (1 tablespoon) servings

1 serving contains:

| Cal | Prot | Fat | Carb | Fiber | Chol | Sodium |
|------|------|-----|------|-------|------|--------|
| 24kc | 1g | 1g | 4g | 0g | 0mg | 119mg |

S A U C E S

# Gingerbread Sauce

*A rich, mellow-tasting sauce*

¼ cup granulated sugar

¼ cup brown sugar, packed

1 tablespoon cornstarch

¾ cup boiling water

1 teaspoon low-fat margarine

dash nutmeg

In a small saucepan, blend sugars and cornstarch well. Using medium heat, add water gradually, stirring constantly until it comes to a boil. Boil for 1 minute; remove from heat. Add margarine and nutmeg; stir until dissolved. Serve warm over gingerbread.

Yield: 6 (2 tablespoons) servings

1 serving contains:

| Cal | Prot | Fat | Carb | Fiber | Chol | Sodium |
|-----|------|-----|------|-------|------|--------|
| 62kc | 0g | 0g | 15g | 0g | 0mg | 10mg |

Variation: May add ½ cup of raisins if desired.

SAUCES

# Evelena's Italian Meat Sauce

*A wonderful, mildly spiced sauce for now, or freeze for later*

vegetable spray

1 lb. ground chicken breast or turkey, no skin

1 egg white

⅔ cup fresh bread crumbs

2 teaspoons chopped, fresh parsley

¼ teaspoon salt

½ lb. Italian turkey sausage

1 cup chopped onion

3 cloves garlic, minced

4 cups water

1 (28 oz.) can stewed tomatoes

1 (29 oz.) can tomato sauce

1 (12 oz.) can tomato paste

1 tablespoon Italian seasoning

2 tablespoons chopped, fresh parsley

1 tablespoon chopped, fresh basil

1 teaspoon thyme

1 tablespoon sugar

Preheat oven to broil; spray broiler pan with vegetable spray. In a medium mixing bowl, combine ground poultry, egg white, bread crumbs, parsley, and salt. Shape into 20 meatballs; place on broiler pan. Cook under broiler about 5 minutes or until browned and juices are no longer pink. Squeeze the meat from sausage casings into a shallow, microwave-safe bowl; microwave on high for about 3 minutes, stirring after each minute. Spread sausage on paper towel to drain. Using about an 8-quart pan, cook onion in a small amount of water on medium-high for about 2 minutes, stirring frequently; add garlic, stirring constantly for about 30 seconds. Add ½ cup water, reduce heat and continue to cook for about 3 minutes, adding more water if needed. Adjust heat to high. Add tomatoes, sauce, paste, remaining water, and all the seasonings. Bring to a boil; add cooked sausage. Reduce heat to low

and cook about 2 hours, stirring occasionally. Add meatballs.* Continue to cook for 1 hour or longer until sauce is the desired thickness.

Yield: 10 servings (11 cups of sauce, 20 meatballs)

1 serving contains:

| Cal | Prot | Fat | Carb | Fiber | Chol | Sodium |
|------|------|-----|------|-------|------|--------|
| 186kc | 16g | 3g | 24g | 3g | 20mg | 952mg |

*You can add 2 chicken breast halves at this time along with the meatballs and let it all cook for one hour. When done, I place the chicken along with some of the sauce in a small freezer dish, seal well and freeze for an extra meal. Divide sauce and meatballs into freezer containers, seal well and freeze. I get 5 meals from this recipe.

## SAUCES

# Orange Sauce

*Serve over plain cake or vanilla pudding.*

½ cup sugar

1 tablespoon cornstarch

½ cup orange juice

2 tablespoons lemon juice

¼ cup + 2 tablespoons boiling water

1 teaspoon grated orange zest

In a small saucepan over medium-low heat, combine sugar and cornstarch; stir well. Stir in orange juice, lemon juice, and boiling water. Boil 1 minute, stirring constantly. Remove from heat. Stir in orange zest. Cool before serving.

Yield: 1 cup or 8 (⅛ cup) servings

1 serving contains:

| Cal | Prot | Fat | Carb | Fiber | Chol | Sodium |
|-----|------|-----|------|-------|------|--------|
| 60kc | 0g | 0g | 15g | 0g | 0mg | 0mg |

S A U C E S

# Peppermint Candy Sauce

*Wonderful served over fat-free vanilla frozen yogurt or ice milk*

1 ¾ cups coarsely crushed hard peppermint
   candy*, divided

½ cup water

In a small saucepan, mix 1½ cups candy and water; cover and bring to a boil. Reduce heat to low and cook until candy is melted, about 20 minutes. Remove from heat, cover and chill until mixture thickens. Stir in remaining crushed candy before serving.

Yield: 8 (1 tablespoon) servings

1 serving contains:

| Cal | Prot | Fat | Carb | Fiber | Chol | Sodium |
|-----|------|-----|------|-------|------|--------|
| 82kc | 0g | 0g | 21g | 0g | 0mg | 8mg |

*Use only stick peppermint, not the round star mints.*

HEALTHY
COOKING
FOR TWO

SAUCES

# Pineapple Sauce

*Serve over angel food cake or fat-free vanilla frozen yogurt.*

½ cup pineapple tidbits (packed in its own juice)

2 tablespoons fresh orange juice

½ tablespoon cornstarch

dash allspice

Drain pineapple; reserve juice. In a small saucepan, combine ¼ cup pineapple juice, orange juice, and cornstarch. Using medium heat, cook until mixture boils and thickens; add pineapple and allspice; stir. Cool before serving.

Yield: 8 (2 tablespoons) servings

1 serving contains:

| Cal | Prot | Fat | Carb | Fiber | Chol | Sodium |
|------|------|-----|------|-------|------|--------|
| 13kc | 0g | 0g | 3g | 0g | 0mg | 0mg |

S A U C E S

# P i q u a n t   S a u c e

*Use this on meat loaf, turkey loaf, baked chicken, or fish.*

¼ cup catsup

1 tablespoon brown sugar

¼ teaspoon nutmeg

1 teaspoon dry mustard

Combine all the ingredients in a small bowl; mix well. Spoon over meat loaf before baking; spoon over baked chicken or fish 10 minutes before removing from oven.

Yield: 4 (1 tablespoon) servings

1 serving contains:

| Cal | Prot | Fat | Carb | Fiber | Chol | Sodium |
|-----|------|-----|------|-------|------|--------|
| 29kc | 1g | 0g | 7g | 0g | 0mg | 179mg |

S A U C E S

# S a l s a

*Fresh salsa tops off your favorite Mexican dish.*

½ cup cooked, drained black beans

1 medium ripe tomato (approx. ½ lb.)

2 tablespoons chopped cilantro

¼ cup chopped green onion

2 tablespoons lime juice

3 tablespoons chopped green chilies

Combine all the ingredients in a small bowl, cover and chill for at least 30 minutes.

Yield: 4 (⅓ cup) servings

1 serving contains:

| Cal | Prot | Fat | Carb | Fiber | Chol | Sodium |
|------|------|-----|------|-------|------|--------|
| 40kc | 2g | 1g | 11g | 1g | 0mg | 14mg |

S A U C E S

# Sour Cream-Caramel Sauce

*Serve with apples, grapes, or bananas.*

¼ *cup fat-free sour cream*

*3 tablespoons brown sugar*

In a small bowl, combine the sour cream and sugar; cover and refrigerate for about 30 minutes to let flavors blend.

Yield: 2 servings

1 serving contains:

| Cal | Prot | Fat | Carb | Fiber | Chol | Sodium |
|-----|------|-----|------|-------|------|--------|
| 58kc | 1g | 0g | 14g | 0g | 0mg | 19mg |

Serving Suggestion: Serve fruit in bite-sized chunks with wooden picks to dip fruit into sauce.

S A U C E S

# White Sauce

*The base for many other sauces*

¾ cup skim milk

1 tablespoon fat-free powdered milk

1 tablespoon unbleached or all-purpose flour

⅛ teaspoon salt

dash white pepper

1 teaspoon low-fat margarine

In a jar, combine milk, powdered milk, and flour; cover and shake until smooth. Pour into a medium saucepan and cook over medium heat until it begins to thicken, stirring constantly. Remove from heat; stir in salt, pepper, and margarine.

Yield: 1 cup

1 serving contains:

| Cal | Prot | Fat | Carb | Fiber | Chol | Sodium |
|-----|------|-----|------|-------|------|--------|
| 137kc | 10g | 2g | 19g | 0g | 5mg | 182mg |

Variations:

Curry Sauce: Add ½ teaspoon curry powder.

Cucumber Sauce: Add ½ cup thinly sliced cucumber and a dash of dill weed.

Dill Sauce: Add 1 teaspoon fresh minced dill or ½ teaspoon dried and a dash of nutmeg.

Seafood Sauce: Add ½ cup chopped, cooked shrimp or crabmeat.

Lemon Sauce: Add 1 teaspoon fresh lemon juice and ½ teaspoon lemon zest.

## H e r b s

An herb lover's instinctive inclination toward the cultivation and use of herbs, and our goal of a year-round supply, conforms to the same desires of Charlemagne's, whose definition of an herb was, "The friend of the physician and the pride of cooks."

I grow and harvest many of my herbs. This is one of the constant joys in my gardening and culinary endeavors. They should be grown in full sun and in a location protected from any chemical sprays. I clip my herbs constantly to prevent them from reaching the blooming stage. Before harvesting, hose them off gently, let dry, then clip. I secure each handful of herbs with a rubber band, then a piece of string, which I then attach to a wire hanger. Hang the hanger in a safe place away from direct sun to dry, and make sure there is adequate space for air to circulate around the bundles.

The drying can take up to four to eight days, according to the herb and the size of bundle. After the herbs are completely dry, store them in glass jars with lids for later use. I always harvest enough to hang over my kitchen sink for a nice decorative touch.

Herbs are very beneficial for all foods, but especially in salt-free diets. They may be used fresh or dried. When using fresh, they are not as potent, so you will need to use more. A general rule of thumb is one tablespoon of fresh herbs equals 1 teaspoon dried. While I use herbs constantly, I am careful to not use too much of any one herb in a recipe, and never to use too many kinds in any one dish.

Following are some suggestions on what herbs to combine with what foods. Notice I said "suggestions"; experiment on your own. Cooking with herbs is an exciting and fun adventure.

**Anise-***(Licorice flavored seeds)-Can be used in casseroles, vegetables, cookies, or cakes. Make flavored sugar by storing in an airtight container overnight with anise seeds, then use the sugar on sugar cookies, pancakes, or hot toast. If you don't want the anise seeds in your food, use anisette, an anise-flavored liqueur.*

**Basil-***A most versatile herb and exceptionally easy to grow. It can be used with fish, Italian dishes, chicken, fresh tomatoes, squash, peas, carrots, cauliflower, salads, tomatoes, or make your own basil vinegar. (See Salads)*

**Bay Leaf-***Gives a pleasant flavor to beans, soups, chicken, rice, cooked red cabbage. Always remove the leaf before serving because it is unpalatable.*

**Burnet-***The flavor is similar to cucumber. Use the new inner leaves in salads, salad dressings.*

**Chervil-***Use in soup, salads, and sauces. Similar flavor to anise.*

**Chives-***A member of the onion family, it is another herb which is so easy to use and as a perennial will come back in your garden year after year. Using only the green leaves, try it in chowder, chicken, tuna, salads, mashed potatoes, soups, zucchini, bread dough, vegetable dips, or sprinkled over fresh tomatoes.*

**Cilantro-***Great in Mexican foods, salsa, soups, or chopped in a salad. A word of caution: Cilantro has a distinctive and strong flavor, so use with caution.*

**Coriander-***Use with apple pie, or other apple dishes, sugar cookies.*

**Dill-***A pungent and unique flavor. Gives a distinct taste to biscuits, rolls or any homemade bread, salads, freshly sliced cucumbers, fresh tomatoes, vegetable dip, asparagus, green beans, cooked potatoes, potato salad, beets, fish, or make your own dill vinegar. (See Salads)*

**Fennel-***Use fresh leaves or seeds in potatoes, rice, lentils, or fish.*

**Garlic-**A member of the onion family. When cooking garlic, never allow it to brown. Use it in vegetable dips, chicken, Italian dishes, Mexican dishes, fish, soup. I much prefer fresh to powdered.

**Horseradish-** An overpowering flavor, use with caution. It is wonderful with beef, fish, seafood cocktail sauces, or dips.

**Leeks-**Another type of onion which is wonderful for seasoning and the very best for use in soups. Use only the white portion and wash carefully before using.

**Marjoram-**Use with discretion because it has a pungent flavor. Use to flavor zucchini, soup, chicken, biscuits, or sprinkle over fresh tomatoes, a basic in Italian dishes.

**Mints-**Chop fine to use in peas, pea soup, fruit, or leave the leaf whole to use as a garnish. Various mints are wonderful for teas.

**Mustard-**Whether using powdered, seeds, or prepared mustard, it can be used advantageously in small quantities. Seeds are a must for pickles and sauces for cabbage salads; powdered mustard enhances sauces, chicken, cheese dishes. Prepared has much less strength then powdered; it is a favorite on sandwiches, cold meats, salads, chicken, and fish.

**Oregano-**Sometimes confused with marjoram because of similar flavor. It can be used in bread dough, Italian dishes, Mexican dishes, zucchini.

**Parsley-**Use in salads, bread dough, new potatoes, creamed potatoes, vegetable dips, soup, rice, fish, meatballs, chicken.

**Peppers-**Black or white; when freshly ground is very pungent. Use in meats, sauces, stews, vegetables, and salads. Green or Red; can be used fresh or roasted; also freezes very well when chopped and placed in an airtight bag. Whole peppers are used in vegetable dishes, salads, appetizers, meats, chili, and stews,

but our favorite is stuffed. Cayenne, or chili peppers, come in any colors and many degrees of hot. Use cautiously, but use in meat, soups, stews, dips, and appetizers.

**Rosemary-**Another pungent herb; use the lightly crushed leaves sparsely in chicken, biscuits, stuffing, green beans, rice.

**Saffron-**A very powerful flavor, use sparingly in breads, dressings, chicken, rice, risotto, and cakes. Used to color and flavor foods.

**Sage-**A favorite herb for meats and stews. Use in chicken, meat loaf, rice, stuffing, gravy.

**Scallions-**Sometimes referred to as green onion. They can be used in cooking or eaten raw in salads, etc.

**Shallots-**While similar to onion or garlic, it's flavor is much more delicate. When cooking with shallots, never let them brown. Use in sauces, soups, chicken.

**Tarragon-**Try to use fresh, it loses some of its flavor when dried. Use with caution, because this herb is quite pungent. It gives a distinct flavor to fish, chicken, sauces, vegetable dips, salads, green beans, or make your own tarragon vinegar.

**Thyme-**Whether you use fresh leaves or dried powder, be sure to use it in chicken, stuffing, rice, beets, carrots, green beans.

**Bouquet garni-**_If you prefer not to have little bits of herbs floating in your soups or sauces, simply tie herbs in a piece of cheesecloth, and add to the food. When cooking is complete, remove bag and discard. You can use any combination of herbs for a Bouquet garni, or keep on hand a supply of the traditional combination which calls for bay leaf, parsley, marjoram, or thyme._

Using fresh herbs:
   ½ bay leaf
   2-3 sprigs parsley
   2 sprigs marjoram or thyme
Using dried herbs:
   1 bay leaf
   2 tablespoons parsley
   1 teaspoon marjoram or thyme

**fines Herbes-**_This is a classic phrase which means a delicate blend of fresh herbs. Use equal parts of parsley, tarragon, chives, and chervil. You may add any mild herb you like. Add the finely minced herbs at the last minute to the food to take advantage of their flavors yet retain their fresh color._

**Citrus Zests-**_"Zest" is the name for gratings of the colorful outer coatings of citrus fruits otherwise known as grated rind. The zest adds a rich, fruity flavor and aroma as well as color. It is to be used sparingly for a subtle seasoning. Use only the colored portion of the citrus skins; the white is bitter. I use a "zester" purchased in a kitchen shop, or you can use a regular grater. If you don't have the fresh fruit to zest, substitute 2 tablespoons fresh juice for one teaspoon zest._

# Spices

**Allspice**-*A combination of nutmeg, clove, and cinnamon flavors, use in soups, sauces, chicken, fruit, puddings, dips, French toast, or pancakes.*

**Cardamon**-*Use as you would for cinnamon or cloves.*

**Cinnamon**-*Whether in stick form or powder, it is a warm, sweet, aromatic spice. Use with any fruit, whether fresh, in pies, dips, salads, or cakes. It is a must in gingerbread, cookies, pies, puddings, and on toast.*

**Cloves**-*Use either whole or powder. When using whole, always remove them before serving. A fairly strong sweet spice, use with fruits, fruit pies, pumpkin pie, puddings, salads, red cabbage.*

**Curry**-*A special blend of pungent spices. Use in curries, chicken, seafood, rice, cocktail sauce, stewed fruits, chutneys, pickles, marinades, stews, and dips.*

**Ginger**-*A bold, pungent flavor found in fresh or powdered form. Peel and slice fresh ginger before adding to stews, stir-frys, chicken. Powdered ginger is a favorite in baking items, cookies, gingerbread, fruit pies, pumpkin, pudding, carrots. Fresh ginger can be substituted for ground ginger; use about 1 tablespoon raw for ⅛ teaspoon powder.*

**Nutmeg**-*A full-flavored spice similar to mace. Use in sweet potatoes, pumpkin, quiche, peas, carrots, sauces, fruit pies, or puddings.*

**Paprika**-*Actually made from peppers, can range from mild to sharp. Use in Hungarian dishes, fish, chicken, or vegetables. A great way to add a hint of color also.*

**Turmeric**-*A slightly bitter taste to be used sparingly. It gives a golden color and can be used in place of saffron. Use in salads, coleslaw, chicken, pickles, or curry powder.*

**Vanilla**-*Found in either bean or extracts. Use in vanilla-flavored ice cream, cakes, frostings, or cookies; the uses are many and varied.*

# Equivalents and Substitutions
## for Common Ingredients

| | |
|---|---|
| Apples, 1 pound | 3 cups peeled and sliced |
| Arrowroot, 2 teaspoons | 1 tablespoon cornstarch |
| Baking powder, 1 teaspoon | ¼ teaspoon baking soda plus ½ teaspoon cream of tartar |
| Baking powder, 1 teaspoon | ¼ teaspoon baking soda plus ½ cup buttermilk or yogurt |
| Bananas, 3 medium mashed | 1 cup or one pound |
| Beans, fresh green, 1 pound | 3 cups raw or 2½ cups cooked |
| Beans, lima, dry 1 pound | 2½ cups or 6 cups cooked |
| Beans, kidney, dry 1 pound | 2½ cups or 6 cups cooked |
| Beans, navy, dry ½ pound | 1 cup or 2½ cups cooked |
| Bread, 4 slices, dry | 1 cup crumbs |
| Bread, soft, 2 slices | 1 cup crumbs |
| Cabbage, 1 pound | 4½ cups shredded |
| Carrots, fresh, 1 pound | 3 cups shredded or 2½ cups diced |
| Cheese, ¼ pound | 1 cup freshly shredded |
| Chocolate, 1 square | 3 tablespoons cocoa plus 1 teaspoon shortening |
| Cornflakes, 3 cups, dry | 1 cup crushed |

| Crackers, saltine, 28 | 1 cup crumbs |
| Crackers, graham, 14 squares | 1 cup crumbs |
| Whole egg | 2 egg whites or ¼ cup egg substitute |
| Egg whites, large, 8 | 1 cup |
| Flour, 1 tablespoon | 1½ teaspoons cornstarch |
| Flour, 1 tablespoon | 1 tablespoon tapioca |
| Flour, 1 tablespoon | 1½ teaspoons arrowroot |
| Flour, cake, 1 cup | 1 cup minus 2 tablespoons sifted all-purpose flour plus 2 tablespoons cornstarch |
| Garlic powder, ⅛ teaspoon | 1 small clove garlic |
| Gelatin, one 4-ounce package | 1 tablespoon |
| Ginger, powdered, ⅛ teaspoon | 1 tablespoon raw |
| Herbs, dried herbs 1 teaspoon | 1 tablespoon fresh herbs |
| Lemon, 1 medium | 3 tablespoons juice |
| Lentils, dry, 1 pound | 2¼ cups or 5 cups cooked |
| Lime, 1 medium | 1½ - 2 tablespoons juice |
| Marshmallows, 10 miniature | 1 large marshmallow |
| Milk, instant nonfat, 1 cup | ⅓ cup plus ¾ cup water |

| Milk, sour, 1 cup | 1 cup milk minus 1 tablespoon plus 1 tablespoon lemon juice or vinegar |
| Mushrooms, fresh, 8 ounces | 3 cups or 1 cup sliced, cooked |
| Mustard, prepared, 1 tablespoon | 1 teaspoon dry mustard |
| Noodles, uncooked, 1 pound | 6-8 cups cooked |
| Orange, 1 medium | 6-8 tablespoons juice |
| Peas, dried, split, 1 pound | 2¼ cups or 5 cups cooked |
| Potatoes, 1 pound | 3-4 cups raw, diced |
| Raisins, 1 pound | 2 ¾ cups |
| Rice, 1 pound | 2 cups raw or 6 cups cooked |
| Spaghetti, dry, 1 pound | 6 ½ cups cooked |
| Strawberries, fresh, 1 quart | 4 cups sliced |
| Vanilla wafers, 22 | 1 cup crumbs |
| Yeast, dry, 1 package | 1 tablespoon |
| Yeast, 2 ounces, compressed | 3 packets of dry yeast |
| Yogurt, 1 cup | 1 cup buttermilk |

# Measurement  Equivalent  Chart

a few grains ............................................................. less than ⅛ teaspoon

60 drops ................................................................. 1 teaspoon

1 tablespoon ........................................................... 3 teaspoons

2 tablespoons .......................................................... ⅛ cup

4 tablespoons .......................................................... ¼ cup

5 tablespoons + 1 teaspoon .................................... ⅓ cup

8 tablespoons. ......................................................... ½ cup

12 tablespoons ........................................................ ¾ cup

16 tablespoons ........................................................ 1 cup

⅜ cup ..................................................................... ¼ cup plus 2 tablespoons

⅝ cup ..................................................................... ½ cup plus 2 tablespoons

⅞ cup ..................................................................... ¾ cup plus 2 tablespoons

4 fluid ounces ......................................................... ½ cup

8 fluid ounces ......................................................... 1 cup

16 fluid ounces ....................................................... 1 pound

2 cups .................................................................... 1 pint

2 pints ................................................................... 1 quart

4 cups .................................................................... 1 quart

Linear Measures:

1 centimeter ........................................................... 0.394 inch

1 inch .................................................................... 2.54 centimeters

1 meter ................................................................... 39.37 inches

# Healthy Menus for Any Occasion

## Breakfast for Hearty Eaters
*Freshly Squeezed Orange Juice*
*Scrambled Eggs*

*Oatmeal Cakes* ...................................... 75

*Applesauce*
*Toast*
*Beverage of Choice*

## Easy Workday Breakfast

*Blueberry Sauce with Fresh Fruit* ............... 365

*Fresh Bagels with Nonfat Cream Cheese*
*Beverage of Choice*

## Midweek Breakfast

*Fresh Orange Slices with Orange Sauce* ........ 374

*Vanilla Yogurt*

*Raspberry Muffins* ................................... 81

*Beverage of Choice*

## Breakfast for a Rushed Weekday
*Chilled Fruit Juice of Choice*
*Dry Cereal of Choice*
*1/2 Banana Sliced over Cereal*
*Skim Milk*

*Refrigerator Bran Muffin* .......................... 82

## Breakfast to Warm You and Your Heart

*Baked Stuffed Pears* ............................... 325

*Hot Cream of Wheat*

*Banana Bran Muffins* ............................. 64

*Skim Milk*

## Lazy Weekend Breakfast
*Chilled Cranberry Juice*

*Pancakes 'n' Fruit* ................................... 77

*Warm Maple Syrup*
*Beverage of Choice*

# HEALTHY COOKING FOR TWO

### Lazy Holiday Breakfast

*Chilled Grapefruit Juice*
*Raisin French Toast* ................................. 80
*Warm Maple Syrup*
*Beverage of Choice*

### Easy Warming Weekday Breakfast

*Chilled Orange Juice*
*Rice Pancakes* ....................................... 83
*Blueberry Sauce* .................................... 365
*Beverage of Choice*

### Holiday Brunch

*Assorted Fruit Juices*
*Vegetable and Rice Pie* ........................... 269
*Citrus Salad with Orange Vinaigrette* .......... 102
*California Bran Bread* ............................. 66
*Pumpkin-Cranberry Tea Bread* .................... 78
*Coffee or Tea*

### Brunch for Weekend Guest

*Festive Broiled Grapefruit* ....................... 327
*Fresh Fruit with Ginger Sauce* ................... 330
*Scrambled Eggs (Egg Substitute)*
*Grits Casserole* ..................................... 71
*Toasted Mixed Grains Bread*
*Glazed Applesauce Spice Cake* ................... 361
*Coffee or Tea*

### Cool Summer Lunch

*Smoked Turkey Rice Salad* ....................... 122
*Pumpkin-Cranberry Tea Bread* .................... 78
*Jell-O Bavarian* ..................................... 322
*Iced Mint Tea*

### Lunch for a Cold Winter Day

*Pear-Raspberry Salad* ............................. 118
*Italian Vegetarian Soup* ........................... 50
*Assorted Nonfat Crackers*
*Johnny's Gingerbread Cookies* ................. 350
*Warm Cider*

# HEALTHY COOKING FOR TWO

## Small Intimate Lunch for Guest

Cream of Potato Soup .............................. 40
Crab Salad ......................................... 105
Assorted Crackers
Yogurt a l'Orange ................................. 342
Iced Raspberry Tea

## Lunch for The Ladies

Smoked Chicken with Cantaloupe .............. 121
Couscous with Marinated Vegetables ............ 104
Variety of Miniature Lemon,
Pumpkin, and Raspberry Muffins ........... 79/81
Strawberry Cake ................................... 356
Iced Tea served with Mint Sprigs

## Vegetarian Lunch

Summer Fruit Salad with
Raspberry Vinaigrette ............................. 140
Spanish Omelette ................................. 268
Multigrain Banana-Lemon Bread ............... 74
Old-Fashioned Apricot Cookies ................. 343
Bottled Water

## Lunch for a Busy Day

(Prepare the entire meal early in the morning)
Leafy Green Salad with
Herb Vinaigrette Dressing ....................... 136
Judy's Chalupa Soupa ............................. 32
Baked Tortilla Chips
Salsa ................................................ 378
Choice of Fresh Fruit
Beverage of Choice

# HEALTHY COOKING FOR TWO

## Intimate Lunch for Two

Fresh Vegetable and Crab Quiche ............... 239
Pear-Raspberry Salad ........................... 118
Frozen Yogurt
Apple Mint Iced Tea

## Garden Fresh Lunch

Chicken-Stuffed Tomatoes ........................ 101
Assorted Nonfat Crackers
Zucchini-Lemon Bread ........................... 84
Pear Melba ........................................ 335
Iced Mint Tea

## Card Club Lunch

Tuna Macaroni Salad .......................... 128
Summer's Special Jell-O Cake ................... 357
Hot Dinner Rolls
Beverage of Choice

## Plan Ahead Dinner

Deviled Eggs ..................................... 19
Green Salad-Basil Buttermilk Dressing ........ 129
Hearty Lentil Soup .............................. 34
Herbs and Corny Corn Bread ..................... 72
Brandied Applesauce over Angel Food Cake .... 326
Beverage of Choice

## Intimate Dinner for Two

Smoked Salmon Cheese Spread with Crackers ... 22
Fruit Salad with Lemon-Honey Dressing ...... 112
Savory Roast Beef
Cooked White Rice
Somebody's Carrots ............................. 309
Brandied Yogurt ................................. 328
White Wine

# HEALTHY COOKING FOR TWO

## Italian Dinner

*Green Salad-Raspberry Vinaigrette Dressing* .. 140
*Pasta Seafood Italiano* ........................... 230
*Crusty Italian Loaf*
*Fresh Fruit with Nonfat Cheese*
*Chilled Wine of Choice*

## Dinner for a Cold Winter Night

*Nonfat Cheese and Assorted Nonfat Crackers*
*Cajun Seafood Gumbo* ............................. 42
*White Steamed Rice*
*Crusty French Rolls* ............................. 86
*Deep-Dish Apple Crisp* .......................... 323
*Beverage of Choice*

## Dinner For the Boss

*Garlic Herb Cheese Spread and*
*Nonfat Crackers*
*Caesar Salad* ....................................... 99
*Creamy Chicken and Dumplings.* .............. 190
*Green Peas*
*Yogurt a l'Orange* ................................ 342
*Nana's Sugar Cookies* ........................... 355
*Beverage of Choice*

## Weeknight Dinner

*Triple Lemon Filets.* ............................. 223
*Cauliflower 'n' Cheese* .......................... 283
*Garlicky Green Beans* ........................... 290
*Mary's Oatmeal Molasses Bread* ................. 90
*Assorted Fresh Fruit*
*Beverage of Choice*

# HEALTHY COOKING FOR TWO

## Another Weeknight Dinner

Oven-Fried Chicken ............................... 155
Creamed Potatoes .................................. 288
Fried Okra-Sort Of ............................... 299
Dinner Rolls
Fruit and Yogurt Cup ............................ 331
Skim Milk

## Stir-Fry Dinner

Judy's Napa Cabbage-Chicken ................. 198
Cooked White Rice
Cornmeal Sugar-Coated Muffins ................ 69
Fresh Fruit with Ginger Sauce .................. 330
Hot Tea

## Dinner on the Grill

Citrus Salad with Orange Vinaigrette .......... 102
Grilled Fish with Vegetable Kabobs. ............. 217
Cooked Brown Rice
Glazed Applesauce Spice Cake .................. 361
Wine Coolers

## Impressive But Simple Dinner

Baked Crabmeat Dip and Crackers. ............... 5
Green Salad with Herb Vinaigrette Dressing .. 136
Broccoli / Cheese-Stuffed Manicotti ............ 262
Crusty French Bread
Fat-Free Vanilla Frozen Yogurt
Jenny's Dainty Cinnamon Gems ................. 346
Wine

## Special Company Dinner

Smoked Salmon Cheese Spread and
Nonfat Crackers
Asparagus-Raspberry Salad ....................... 95
Cornish Hens Baked in Wine .................... 149
White-Wild Rice Pilaf ............................ 306
Carrot Zucchini Sauté ............................ 282
Dinner Rolls
Brandied Yogurt .................................. 328
White Wine

# HEALTHY COOKING FOR TWO

## Casual Company Dinner

*Curry Dip with Veggies*
*Spinach Salad and No-Oil Italian Dressing*
*Scallops and Asparagus with Linguine* ......... 233
*Crusty Rolls*
*Strawberry Romanoff* ............................ 340
*Beverage of Choice*

## Down-home Meal

*Navy Bean Soup* ................................. 38
*Marinated Cucumbers and Tomatoes* ............ 116
*Mom's Mashed Potatoes* ........................ 297
*Corn Bread*
*Mandarin Orange Dessert* ...................... 332
*Iced Tea*

## Meatless Dinner

*Fresh Fruit with Lemon-Honey Dressing* ....... 112
*Mushroom-Stuffed Green Peppers* .............. 266
*Peas and Carrots* ................................ 303
*Multigrain Banana-Lemon Bread* .............. 74
*Creamy Rice Pudding* ........................... 338
*Beverage of Choice*

## Dinner for the Bridge Group

*Shrimp Dip Olé with Veggies* ...................... 12
*Spicy Beef Stew* ................................... 243
*Assorted Crackers*
*Mom's Bread Pudding* ........................... 333
*Beverage of Choice*

# HEALTHY COOKING FOR TWO

## Buffet for Your Sunday School Class

Spicy Smoked Turkey Dip and Fresh Veggies ..... 13
Baked Crabmeat Dip ................................... 5
Marinated Mushrooms ............................. 20
Caesar Salad ............................................ 99
Audrey's Vegetable Lasagna ...................... 256
Crusty French Rolls ................................. 86
Chocolate / Applesauce Cake ..................... 359
Beverage of Choice

## Holiday Dinner for Four

Salmon Dip and Veggies ........................... 11
Glazed Turkey Breast .............................. 150
Mashed Sweet Potatoes
Cornbread Stuffing
Cranberry-Pear Compote .......................... 367
Broccoli
Dinner Rolls
Mom's Pumpkin Pie .............................. 336
Beverage of Choice

## Summer Cookout

Creme de Cassis-Yogurt Dip and Fresh Fruit ..... 6
Harold's Italian Grilled Chicken ................ 165
Chinese Salad ...................................... 100
Okra and Tomatoes. .............................. 300
Herbed Cheer Bread .............................. 67
Blueberry Mystery Dessert ...................... 324
Iced Mint Tea

## Quick Dinner

Spicy Baked Fish ................................... 238
Moroccan Couscous .............................. 285
Sliced Tomatoes
Dinner Rolls
Fresh Fruit with Orange Sauce ................. 374
Beverage of Choice

# HEALTHY COOKING FOR TWO

## Grilled Dinner for Guest

Curry-Stuffed Tomatoes .............................. 18
Grilled Salmon Filet .............................. 221
Chestnut Brown Rice ........................... 284
Stuffed Cheyote Squash .......................... 311
Pumpernickel Bread
Strawberries and Rhubarb ....................... 341
Wine Coolers

## Summer's Bounty

Audrey's Green Beans and Red Potatoes ........ 196
Coleslaw
Corn Bread
Peach Pudding ..................................... 334
Iced Tea

## Fiesta Dinner

Lisa's Tortilla Rolls .................................... 14
San Carlos Seafood ............................... 232
Rice
Judy's Southwestern Vegetables ................... 313
David's Hot Fudge Cake ......................... 358
Iced Tea

## Last Minute Dinner

Apricot-Cheese Spread and Crackers .............. 16
Shrimp Stir-Fry .................................... 236
Steamed White Rice
Sour Cream-Caramel Sauce
with Fresh Fruit .................................... 379
Beverage of Choice

## Healthy Cooking for Two

### Supper After the Ice Skating Party

Spicy Smoked Turkey Dip .......................... 13
Nonfat Tortilla Chips
Vegetable and Bean Soup........................... 52
Herbs and Corny Corn Bread ..................... 72
Johnny's Gingerbread Cookies ................... 350
Mulled Wine

### Friday Night Fish Fry

Baked Fried Fish ................................. 209
International Oven Fries ......................... 295
Coleslaw
Corn-Tomato Muffins ............................. 70
Jell-O Bavarian ................................. 322
Iced Tea

### Supper After the Board Meeting

Creamy Vegetable Dip and Veggies ................. 7
Sloppy Joes
Barbara's Pasta-Dijon Salad..................... 117
Blueberry Mystery Dessert ...................... 324
Beverage of Choice

### Hearty Soup and Salad Supper

Mixed Greens Salad-Nonfat Salad Dressing
Brunswick Stew ................................... 28
Herbed Cheer Bread .............................. 67
Andy's Honey Cookies ........................... 351
Hot Cider

### Supper in a Hurry

Fruit Salad with Lemon-Honey Dressing ...... 112
Bonnie's Jambalaya ............................... 27
Potato Bread ..................................... 85
Angel Food Cake and Pineapple Sauce ......... 376
Beverage of Choice

# HEALTHY COOKING FOR TWO

## Sunday Supper

Crunchy Oriental Turkey Salad ................. 108
Sliced Tomatoes
Crusty French Bread
Molasses Crinkles ............................... 353
Beverage of Choice

## Hot Summer Supper

Chicken-Stuffed Tomatoes ........................ 101
Zucchini-Lemon Bread ........................... 84
Low-fat Vanilla Frozen Yogurt
with Peppermint Candy Sauce ................... 375
Iced Lemon Tea

## Italian Supper

Green Salad with Nonfat Italian Dressing
Meatballs from Evelena's Italian Meat Sauce . 372
with Crusty French Rolls made into sandwiches
Fresh Fruit 'n' Pudding ......................... 321
Wine of Choice

## Southwest Brunch

Gazpacho .......................................... 59
Fiesta Dip with Assorted Fat-Free Crackers ....... 8
Corn-Pea Salad .................................. 103
Zucchini-Balsamic Vinegar ...................... 316
Tex-Mex Sausage-Chili-Cheese Casserole ...... 179
Beer Muffins. ..................................... 65
Baked Stuffed Pears. ............................. 325

## South of the Border Dinner

Cream of Corn Soup .............................. 31
Turkey-Corn Burritos ............................ 182
Shredded Lettuce and Chopped Tomatoes
Mock Guacamole
with Baked Low-Fat Tortilla Chips. ............... 9
Brandied Applesauce over Frozen
Fat-Free Vanilla Yogurt ......................... 326

## Tex-Mex Buffet for Guests

Chicken Chalupas (Make Your Own) ............ 177

Mexican Turkey in a Pot ......................... 184

Zucchini-Barley Mexicali ........................ 270

Judy's Southwestern Vegetables. .................. 313

Creamy Tomato and Cucumber Salad .......... 107

Shredded Lettuce and Chopped Tomatoes

Salsa ................................................. 378

Fruit and Yogurt Cup ............................. 331

Yogurt a l'Orange ................................. 342

Jenny's Dainty Cinnamon Gems ................. 346

# Index

## A

Acapulco Chicken, 176
American Heart Association
   recommended limits of cholesterol intake, xxi
   recommended limits of fat intake, xxi
   recommended limits of fat intake, xxv, xxvi
Andy's Honey Cookies, 351
Angie's Lemon Basil Chicken, 162
Ann's Zucchini-Macaroni Soup, 55
Another Weeknight Dinner (menu), 400
Appetizer(s)
   about, 1-2
   Apricot-Cheese Spread, 16
   Baked Crabmeat Dip, 5
   Baked Potato Skins, 21
   Betty's Crabmeat Dip, 3
   Creamy Vegetable Dip, 7
   Creme de Cassis-Yogurt Dip, 6
   Cucumber-Stuffed Tomatoes, 17
   Curry-Stuffed Tomatoes, 18
   Deviled Eggs, 19
   Fiesta Dip, 8
   Garlic-Herb Spread, 16
   Indian Dip, 10
   Lisa's Tortilla Rolls, 14
   Marinated Mushrooms, 20
   Mexican Spread, 16
   Mock Guacamole, 9
   Oriental Chicken Nibbles, 15
   Salmon Dip, 11
   Sassy Clam Dip, 4
   Shrimp Dip Olé, 12

   Smoked Salmon Cheese Spread, 22
   Spicy Smoked Turkey Dip, 13
   Trash Nibblers, 23
Apple(s)
   Brandied Applesauce, 326
   Chocolate/Applesauce Cake, 359
   Deep-Dish Apple Crisp, 323
   Glazed Applesauce Spice Cake, 361
Apricot(s)
   Apricot-Cheese Spread, 16
   Old-Fashioned Apricot Cookies, 343
Apricot-Cheese Spread, 16
Artichokes
   Chicken with Artichokes, 146
   Chicken with Lemon Artichokes, 156-157
Asparagus-Raspberry Salad, 95
Asparagus-Tuna Salad, 96
Asparagus/Cheese-Stuffed Chicken Breast, 185
Asparagus
   Asparagus-Raspberry Salad, 95
   Asparagus-Tuna Salad, 96
   Asparagus/Cheese-Stuffed Chicken Breast, 185
   Asparagus and Tomatoes, 97
   Asparagus Chicken Stir-Fry, 186
   Scallops and Asparagus with Linguine, 233
Asparagus and Tomatoes, 97
Asparagus Chicken Stir-Fry, 186
Audrey's Green Beans and Red Potatoes, 196
Audrey's Vegetable Lasagna, 256-257
Avocado, See Mock Guacamole

## B

Bacon, substitute for in fat reduction, xxix
Baked Crabmeat Dip, 5
Baked Eggplant, 255
Baked Fried Fish, 209
Baked Potatoes with Chunky Chicken Topping, 187
Baked Potato Skins, 21
Baked Stuffed Pears, 325
Baked Tomatoes Dijon, 279
Balsamic-Thyme Chicken, 145
Banana(s)
   Banana Bran Muffins, 64
   Banana Cookies, 344-345
   Banana Fruitcake, 360
   Banana Pancakes, 63
   Multigrain Banana-Lemon Bread, 74
Banana Bran Muffins, 64
Banana Cookies, 344-345
Banana Fruitcake, 360
Banana Pancakes, 63
Barb's Beef Stroganoff, 244
Barbara's Pasta-Dijon Salad, 117
Barbecued Catfish, 210
Basil Buttermilk Dressing, 129
Bean(s)
   Audrey's Green Beans and Red Potatoes, 196
   Garlicky Green Beans, 290
   Herbs 'n' Green Beans, 294
   Judy's Southwestern Vegetables, 313
   Lima Bean-Tomato Treat, 296
   Mixed Bean Soup, 37

Navy Bean Soup, 38
Vegetable and Bean Soup, 52
Beef
    Barb's Beef Stroganoff, 244
    Chinese Pepper Steak, 246
    Ground Beef Stew, 33
    Healthier Beef Bourguignonne, 252
    Spicy Beef Stew, 243
    Tom's Fried Rice, 249
Beer Muffins, 65
Berry-Flavored Vinegar, 131
Betty's Crabmeat Dip, 3
Blueberry
    Blueberry Chicken, 188
    Blueberry Mystery Dessert, 324
    Blueberry Sauce, 365
    Blueberry Vinegar, 131
Blueberry Chicken, 188
Blueberry Mystery Dessert, 324
Blueberry Sauce, 365
Blueberry Vinegar, 131
Bonnie's Jambalaya, 27
Bran
    Banana Bran Muffins, 64
    California Bran Bread, 66
    Refrigerator Bran Muffins, 82
Brandied Applesauce, 326
Brandied Yogurt, 328
Bread(s)
    about, 61
    Banana Bran Muffins, 64
    Banana Pancakes, 63
    Beer Muffins, 65
    California Bran Bread, 66
    Corn-Tomato Muffins, 70
    Corn Cakes Tex-Mex, 68
    Cornmeal Sugar-Coated Muffins, 69
    Crusty French Rolls, 86-87
    Grits Casserole, 71
    Herbed Cheer Bread, 67

Herbs and Corny Corn Bread, 72
Honey-Wheat Muffins, 92
Italian Bread Sticks, 88-89
Mary's Oatmeal Molasses Bread, 90-91
Miniature Lemon Muffins, 73
Multigrain Banana-Lemon Bread, 74
Oatmeal Cakes, 75
Orange Pancakes, 76
Pancakes 'n' Fruit, 77
Potato Bread, 85
Pumpkin-Cranberry Tea Bread, 78
Pumpkin Muffins, 79
Raisin French Toast, 80
Raspberry Muffins, 81
Refrigerator Bran Muffins, 82
Rice Pancakes, 83
yeast
    Crusty French Rolls, 86-87
    Italian Bread Sticks, 88-89
    Mary's Oatmeal Molasses Bread, 90-91
    Zucchini-Lemon Bread, 84
Breakfast, menus, 395, 396
Breakfast for a Rushed Weekday (menu), 395
Breakfast for Hearty Eaters (menu), 395
Breakfast to Warm You and Your Heart (menu), 395
Brenda's Grilled Fish, 211
Broccoli/Cheese-Stuffed Manicotti, 262-263
Broccoli
    Broccoli/Cheese-Stuffed Manicotti, 262-263
    Broccoli and Chicken Stir-Fry, 189
    Broccoli Cheese-Stuffed Potato, 280
    No-Crust Broccoli Quiche, 264
    Broccoli and Chicken Stir-Fry, 189
    Broccoli Cheese-Stuffed Potato, 280
    Broiled Scallops in Wine, 234
Brunch
    menus, 396, 405
Brunch for a Weekend Guest (menu), 396
Brunswick Stew, 28-29
Buffet, menus, 402, 406

Buffet for Your Sunday School Class (menu), 402
Burgers, Chicken, 192-193
Busy Day Goulash, 171
Butter, substitute for in fat reduction, xxviii
Buttermilk-Garlic Creamy Dressing, 133
Buttermilk
    Buttermilk-Garlic Creamy Dressing, 133
    Zucchini-Buttermilk Soup, 54

## C

Cabbage
    Cabbage Waldorf, 98
    Chinese Salad, 100
    Judy's Napa-Cabbage Chicken, 198
Cabbage Waldorf, 98
Caesar Salad, 99
Cajun Seafood Gumbo, 42-43
Cake(s)
    Banana Fruitcake, 360
    Chocolate/Applesauce Cake, 359
    David's Hot Fudge Cake, 358
    Glazed Applesauce Spice Cake, 361
    Strawberry Cake, 356
    Summer's Special Jell-o Cake, 357
California Bran Bread, 66
California Carrots, 281
Calories
    foods needed for daily levels of (table), xviii
    suggested daily levels of (table), xvii
Cantaloupe
    Cold Cantaloupe Soup, 56
    Smoked Chicken with Cantaloupe, 121
Card Club Lunch (menu), 398
Caroline's Pineapple-Cranberry Mousse, 119
Carrot(s)
    California Carrots, 281
    Carrot Soup, 57
    Carrot Zucchini Sauté, 282
    Peas and Carrots, 303

# HEALTHY COOKING FOR TWO

Somebody's Carrots, 309
Spiced Carrots, 310
Carrot Soup, 57
Carrot Zucchini Sauté, 282
Casual Company Dinner (menu), 401
Cauliflower 'n' Cheese, 283
Cauliflower, Scalloped Cauliflower, 307
Cereal, Trash Nibblers, 23
Cheese, hard, substitute for in fat reduction, xxix
    Apricot-Cheese Spread, 16
    Broccoli/Cheese-Stuffed Manicotti, 262-263
    Macaroni and Cheese, 260-261
    Smoked Salmon Cheese Spread, 22
    Turkey-Ham and Cheese Omelet, 206
Chestnut Brown Rice, 284
Chicken-Stuffed Tomatoes, 101
Chicken
    Acapulco Chicken, 176
    Angie's Lemon Basil Chicken, 162
    Asparagus/Cheese-Stuffed Chicken Breast, 185
    Asparagus Chicken Stir-Fry, 186
    Baked Potatoes with Chunky Chicken Topping, 187
    Balsamic-Thyme Chicken, 145
    Blueberry Chicken, 188
    Bonnie's Jambalaya, 27
    Broccoli and Chicken Stir-Fry, 189
    Brunswick Stew, 28-29
    Chicken-Stuffed Tomatoes, 101
    Chicken Breast in Orange Sauce, 147
    Chicken Burgers, 192-193
    Chicken Chalupas, 177
    Chicken Dijon, 194-195
    Chicken Dinner in a Pocket, 163
    Chicken Fricassee, 170
    Chicken Sun-Dried Tomato Stir-Fry, 168
    Chicken Tortilla Casserole, 180-181
    Chicken Vegetable Soup, 30
    Chicken with Artichokes, 146
    Chicken with Lemon Artichokes, 156-157

Chicken Zucchini Crisp, 148
Creamy Chicken and Dumplings, 190
Creamy Chicken and Fettuccine, 169
Creamy Chicken and Noodles, 191
Cumin Chicken Bake, 178
Gourmet Chicken, 151
Grecian Chicken, 172
Grilled Lime Chicken Breast, 167
Harold's Italian Grilled Chicken, 165
Hawaiian Chicken, 197
Hungarian Chicken with Dried Tomatoes, 152
Italian Parmesan Baked Chicken, 173
Joyce's Connecticut Chicken, 153
Judy's Napa-Cabbage Chicken, 198
Lemon-Lime Mustard Baked Chicken, 154
Lemony Chicken Stir-Fry, 199
Lisa's Tortilla Rolls, 14
Lou's Spicy Baked Chicken, 160
Mediterranean Chicken with Pasta, 174-175
Mixed Bean Soup, 37
Oriental Chicken Nibbles, 15
Oven-Fried Chicken, 155
Rosemary Lemon Chicken, 158
Salem's Sunshine Chicken, 200
Scallop and Chicken Kabobs, 231
Smoked Chicken with Cantaloupe, 121
Spanish Rice, 159
Spicy Chicken Kabobs, 166
Tortilla Soup, 46-47
White Chili, 53
Chicken Breast in Orange Sauce, 147
Chicken Burgers, 192-193
Chicken Chalupas, 177
Chicken Dijon, 194-195
Chicken Dinner in a Pocket, 163
Chicken Fricassee, 170
Chicken Sun-Dried Tomato Stir-Fry, 168
Chicken Tortilla Casserole, 180-181
Chicken Vegetable Soup, 30
Chicken with Artichokes, 146

Chicken with Lemon Artichokes, 156
Chicken Zucchini Crisp, 148
Chili, White Chili, 53
Chinese Fried Rice with Vegetables, 286-287
Chinese Pepper Steak, 246
Chinese Salad, 100
Chocolate, baking, substitute for in fat reduction, xxix
Chocolate/Applesauce Cake, 359
Chocolate
    Chocolate/Applesauce Cake, 359
    David's Hot Fudge Cake, 358
    Joe's Magic Chocolate Cookies, 352
Cholesterol, xxi
Chowder, See Soup(s)
Cinnamon Sauce, 366
Citrus Salad with Orange Vinaigrette, 102
Clam(s), Sassy Clam Dip, 4
Coconut Macaroons, 347
Cold Cantaloupe Soup, 56
Cookies
    Andy's Honey Cookies, 351
    Banana Cookies, 344-345
    Coconut Macaroons, 347
    Down-Home Raisin-Oatmeal Cookies, 349
    Grandma's Cherry Winks, 348
    Jenny's Dainty Cinnamon Gems, 346
    Joe's Magic Chocolate Cookies, 352
    John's Oatmeal Doodles, 354
    Johnny's Gingerbread Cookies, 350
    Molasses Crinkles, 353
    Nana's Sugar Cookies, 355
    Old-Fashioned Apricot Cookies, 343
Cool Summer Lunch (menu), 396
Corn-Pea Salad, 103
Corn-Tomato Muffins, 70
Corn
    Corn-Pea Salad, 103
    Corn Cakes Tex-Mex, 68
    Cream of Corn Soup, 31

Turkey-Corn Burritos, 182-183
Corn bread(s), See Bread(s)
Corn Cakes Tex-Mex, 68
Cornish Hens/Herbs Grilled, 164
Cornish Hens
    Cornish Hens/Herbs Grilled, 164
    Cornish Hens Baked in Wine, 149
Cornish Hens Baked in Wine, 149
Cornmeal Sugar-Coated Muffins, 69
Couscous
    Couscous with Marinated Vegetables, 104
    Moroccan Couscous, 285
Couscous with Marinated Vegetables, 104
Crab(meat)
    Baked Crabmeat Dip, 5
    Betty's Crabmeat Dip, 3
    Crab-Stuffed Flounder, 214
    Crab Au Gratin, 212-213
    Crab Salad, 105
 Fresh Vegetable and Crab Quiche, 239
Crab-Stuffed Flounder, 214
Crab Au Gratin, 212-213
Crab Salad, 105
Cranberry-Pear Compote, 367
Cranberry
    Caroline's Pineapple-Cranberry Mousse, 119
    Cranberry-Pear Compote, 367
    Cranberry Salad, 106
    Pumpkin-Cranberry Tea Bread, 78
Cranberry Salad, 106
Cream, heavy, substitute for in fat reduction,
    xxviii
Cream, sour, substitute for in fat reduction, xxviii
Creamed Potatoes, 288
Cream of Corn Soup, 31
Cream of Potato Soup, 40-41
Cream of Tomato Soup, 45
Creamy Basil Dressing, 130
Creamy Chicken and Dumplings, 190
Creamy Chicken and Fettuccine, 169

Creamy Chicken and Noodles, 191
Creamy French Dressing, 134
Creamy Rice Pudding, 338
Creamy Tomato and Cucumber Salad, 107
Creamy Vegetable Dip, 7
Creamy Yogurt Sauce, 368
Creme de Cassis-Yogurt Dip, 6
Crispy Baked Fish, 215
Crunchy Oriental Turkey Salad, 108
Crusty French Bread, 86-87
Cucumber(s)
    Creamy Tomato and Cucumber Salad, 107
    Cucumber-Pea Salad, 109
    Cucumber-Stuffed Tomatoes, 17
    Cucumber-Yogurt Soup, 58
    Lemony Cucumber and Onions, 114
    Marinated Cucumbers and Tomatoes, 116
Cucumber-Pea Salad, 109
Cucumber-Stuffed Tomatoes, 17
Cucumber-Yogurt Soup, 58
Cumin Chicken Bake, 178
Curry-Stuffed Tomatoes, 18
Custard Sauce, 369

**D**

David's Hot Fudge Cake, 358
Deep-Dish Apple Crisp, 323
Desserts
    about, 319
    Andy's Honey Cookies, 351
    Baked Stuffed Pears, 325
    Banana Cookies, 344-345
    Banana Fruitcake, 360
    Blueberry Mystery Dessert, 324
    Brandied Applesauce, 326
    Brandied Yogurt, 328
    Chocolate/Applesauce Cake, 359
    Coconut Macaroons, 347
    Creamy Rice Pudding, 338
    David's Hot Fudge Cake, 358

Deep-Dish Apple Crisp, 323
Down-Home Raisin-Oatmeal Cookies, 349
Elegant Frosted Peaches, 329
Festive Broiled Grapefruit, 327
Fresh Fruit 'n' Pudding, 321
Fresh Fruit with Ginger Sauce, 330
Fruit and Yogurt Cup, 331
Glazed Applesauce Spice Cake, 361
Grandma's Cherry Winks, 348
Jell-O Bavarian, 322
Jenny's Dainty Cinnamon Gems, 346
Joe's Magic Chocolate Cookies, 352
John's Oatmeal Doodles, 354
Johnny's Gingerbread Cookies, 350
Mandarin Orange Dessert, 332
Molasses Crinkles, 353
Mom's Bread Pudding, 333
Mom's Pumpkin Pie, 336
Nana's Sugar Cookies, 355
Old-Fashioned Apricot Cookies, 343
Peach Pudding, 334
Pear Melba, 335
Raspberry Parfaits, 337
Strawberries and Rhubarb, 341
Strawberry Cake, 356
Strawberry Romanoff, 340
Sugar-Free Strawberry Mousse, 339
Summer's Special Jell-O Cake, 357
Yogurt a l'Orange, 342
Deviled Eggs, 19
Dijon Mustard Sauce, 370
Dinner, menus, 398-406
Dinner for a Cold Winter Night (menu), 399
Dinner for the Boss (menu), 399
Dinner for the Bridge Group (menu), 401
Dinner on the Grill (menu), 400
Dip(s)
    Baked Crabmeat Dip, 5
    Betty's Crabmeat Dip, 3
    Creamy Vegetable Dip, 7

Creme de Cassis-Yogurt Dip, 6
Fiesta Dip, 8
Indian Dip, 10
Mock Guacamole, 9
Salmon Dip, 11
Sassy Clam Dip, 4
Shrimp Dip Olé, 12
Spicy Smoked Turkey Dip, 13
Dirty Rice, 289
Down-home Meal (menu), 401
Down-Home Raisin-Oatmeal Cookies, 349
Dumplings, See Creamy Chicken and Dumplings

**E**

Easy Warming Weekday Breakfast (menu), 396
Easy Workday Breakfast (menu), 395
Egg(s)
    Deviled Eggs, 19
    Fresh Vegetable and Crab Quiche, 239
    Magic Vegetable Quiche, 265
    No-Crust Broccoli Quiche, 264
    Spanish Omelette, 268
    substitute for in fat reduction, xxviii
    Turkey-Ham and Cheese Omelet, 206
Eggplant, Baked Eggplant, 255
Elegant Frosted Peaches, 329
Endive-Raspberry Salad with Raspberry
    Vinaigrette, 110
Endive, Endive-Raspberry Salad with Raspberry
    Vinaigrette, 110
English Pea Salad, 111
Equivalents
    food (table), 389-391
    food, xxviii-xxix
    measurements (chart), 393
Evelena's Italian Meat Sauce, 372-373

**F**

Fat (dietary)
    recommended daily intake, xxi-xxiii

techniques that reduce intake of, xxvii-xxix
    ways to reduce intake of, xxvi, xxx
Festive Broiled Grapefruit, 327
Festive Italian Vinegar, 135
Fiesta Dinner (menu), 403
Fiesta Dip, 8
Filet Dijon, 216
Fish
    Asparagus-Tuna Salad, 96
    Baked Fried Fish, 209
    Barbecued Catfish, 210
    Brenda's Grilled Fish, 211
    Crispy Baked Fish, 215
    Filet Dijon, 216
    Green-Topped Flounder, 220
    Grilled Fish with Vegetable Kabobs, 217
    Grilled Salmon Filet, 221
    Halibut Italian Style, 222
    Mardi Gras Filet, 226-227
    Marlin in Wine Sauce, 225
    San Carlos Seafood, 232
    Scotty's Lemon Filets, 235
    Spicy Baked Fish, 238
    Triple Lemon Filets, 223
    White Fish Baked in Orange Sauce, 218-219
    White Fish with Lemon Stuffing, 224
    See also Seafood and names of fish
Flounder
    Crab-Stuffed Flounder, 214
    Green-Topped Flounder, 220
Food Guide Pyramid (table), xix
Food Guide Pyramid, xvii
    bread group, xx
    explained, xx
    fruit group, xx
    meat group, xx
    milk group, xx
    vegetable group, xx
French Toast, Raisin, 80
Fresh Fruit 'n' Pudding, 321

Fresh Fruit with Ginger Sauce, 330
Fresh Vegetable and Crab Quiche, 239
Fresh Vegetables and Linguine, 258
Friday Night Fish Fry (menu), 404
Fried Okra-Sort of, 299
Fruit
    Banana Fruitcake, 360
    Citrus Salad with Orange Vinaigrette, 102
    Fresh Fruit 'n' Pudding, 321
    Fresh Fruit with Ginger Sauce, 330
    Fruit and Yogurt Cup, 331
    Fruit Salad with Lemon-Honey Dressing, 112
    Pancakes 'n' Fruit, 77
    See also names of fruit
Fruit and Yogurt Cup, 331
Fruit Salad with Lemon-Honey Dressing, 112

**G**

Garden Fresh Lunch (menu), 398
Garlic-Herb Spread, 16
Garlicky Green Beans, 290
Gazpacho, 59
Gingerbread
    Johnny's Gingerbread Cookies, 350
    sauce, 371
Gingerbread Sauce, 371
Glazed Applesauce Spice Cake, 361
Glazed Turkey Breast, 150
Glorified Acorn Squash, 291
Golden Risotto, 292
Gourmet Chicken, 151
Gourmet Herb Vinegar, 135
Grandma's Cherry Winks, 348
Grapefruit, Festive Broiled Grapefruit, 327
Grecian Chicken, 172
Green-Topped Flounder, 220
Grilled Dinner for Guest (menu), 403
Grilled Fish with Vegetable Kabobs, 217
Grilled Lime Chicken Breast, 167
Grilled Salmon Filet, 221

Grits Casserole, 71
Ground Beef Stew, 33
Gumbo, See Soup(s)

**H**

Halibut, Halibut Italian Style, 222
Halibut Italian Style, 222
Harold's Italian Grilled Chicken, 165
Hash Brown Casserole, 293
Hawaiian Chicken, 197
Healthier Beef Bourguignonne, 252
Hearty Lentil Soup, 34
Hearty Soup and Salad Supper (menu), 404
Heavy cream, substitute for in fat reduction, xxviii
Herb(s)
  about, 381
  anise, 382
  basil, 382
  bay leaf, 382
  Bouquet garni, 385
  burnet, 382
  chervil, 382
  chives, 382
  cilantro, 382
  citrus zests, 385
  coriander, 382
  dill, 382
  fennel, 382
  fines Herbes, 385
  garlic, 383
  horseradish, 383
  leeks, 383
  marjoram, 383
  mints, 383
  mustard, 383
  oregano, 383
  parsley, 383
  peppers, 383
  rosemary, 384
  saffron, 384

sage, 384
scallions, 384
shallots, 384
tarragon, 384
thyme, 384
Herbed Cheer Bread, 67
Herbs 'n' Green Beans, 294
Herbs and Corny Corn Bread, 72
Herb Vinaigrette Dressing, 136
Holiday Brunch (menu), 396
Holiday Dinner for Four (menu), 402
Honey-Mustard Creamy Dressing, 137
Honey-Mustard Vinaigrette, 138
Honey-Wheat Muffins, 92
Hot Summer Supper (menu), 405
Hungarian Chicken with Dried Tomatoes, 152

**I**

Impressive But Simple Dinner (menu), 400
Indian Dip, 10
International Oven Fries, 295
Intimate Dinner for Two (menu), 398
Intimate Lunch for Two (menu), 398
Italian Bread Sticks, 88-89
Italian Dinner (menu), 399
Italian Parmesan Baked Chicken, 173
Italian Potato Salad, 113
Italian Supper (menu), 405
Italian Vegetarian Soup, 50-51

**J**

Jell-O Bavarian, 322
Jenny's Dainty Cinnamon Gems, 346
Joe's Magic Chocolate Cookies, 352
John's Oatmeal Doodles, 354
Johnny's Gingerbread Cookies, 350
Joyce's Connecticut Chicken, 153
Judy's Chalupa Soupa, 32
Judy's Napa-Cabbage Chicken, 198
Judy's Southwestern Vegetables, 313

**L**

Lasagna, Audrey's Vegetable Lasagna, 256-257
Last Minute Dinner (menu), 403
Lazy Holiday Breakfast (menu), 396
Lazy Weekend Breakfast (menu), 395
Lemon(s)
  Lemony Cucumber and Onions, 114
  Miniature Lemon Muffins, 73
  Multigrain Banana-Lemon Bread, 74
  Zucchini-Lemon Bread, 84
Lemon-Lime Mustard Baked Chicken, 154
Lemon/Basil-Stuffed Turkey Tenderloins, 204-205
Lemony Chicken Stir-Fry, 199
Lemony Cucumber and Onions, 114
Lentil(s), Hearty Lentil Soup, 34
Lima Bean-Tomato Treat, 296
Lisa's Tortilla Rolls, 14
Lou's Spicy Baked Chicken, 160
Low-fat cooking, techniques, xxvii
Lunch, menus, 396-398
Lunch for a Busy Day (menu), 397
Lunch for a Cold Winter Day (menu), 396
Lunch for the Ladies (menu), 397

**M**

Macaroni and Cheese, 260-261
Magic Vegetable Quiche, 265
Make-Ahead Potatoes, 277
Mandarin Orange Dessert, 332
Mandarin Orange Salad with
  Raspberry Vinaigrette, 115
Manicotti, Broccoli/Cheese-Stuffed Manicotti,
  262-263
Mardi Gras Filet, 226-227
Marinated Cucumbers and Tomatoes, 116
Marinated Mushrooms, 20
Marlin, Marlin in Wine Sauce, 225
Marlin in Wine Sauce, 225
Mary's Oatmeal Molasses Bread, 90-91

Mashed Potatoes with Buttermilk, 298
Measurement equivalents, (chart), 393
Meat(s)
    about, 141
    Barb's Beef Stroganoff, 244
    Chinese Pepper Steak, 246
    Evelena's Italian Meat Sauce, 372-373
    Healthier Beef Bourguignonne, 252
    Pork Chops with Apples, 248
    Spicy Beef Stew, 243
    Sweet 'n' Sour Pork, 247
    Tom's Fried Rice, 249
    Veal Cutlets, 245
    Venison Sauerbraten, 250-251
    See also names of meats
Meat, Red, about, 241
Meatball Stew, 35
Meatless Dinner (menu), 401
Meatless meals
    about, 253
    Audrey's Vegetable Lasagna, 256-257
    Baked Eggplant, 255
    Broccoli/Cheese-Stuffed Manicotti, 262-263
    Fresh Vegetables and Linguine, 258
    Macaroni and Cheese, 260-261
    Magic Vegetable Quiche, 265
    Mom's Mushroom-Stuffed Green Peppers, 266-267
    No-Crust Broccoli Quiche, 264
    Penne with Fresh Vegetables and Marinara Sauce, 259
    Spanish Omelette, 268
    Vegetable and Rice Pie, 269
    Zucchini-Barley Mexicali, 270-271
    Zucchini Parmesan, 272-273
Mediterranean Chicken with Pasta, 174-175
Menus, healthy, 395-406
Mexican Fiesta Vinegar, 135
Mexican Spread, 16
Mexican Turkey in a Pot, 184

Midweek Breakfast (menu), 395
Milk, whole, substitute for in fat reduction, xxviii
Miniature Lemon Muffins, 73
Mixed Bean Soup, 37
Mock Guacamole, 9
Molasses Crinkles, 353
Mom's Bread Pudding, 333
Mom's Mashed Potatoes, 297
Mom's Mushroom-Stuffed Green Peppers, 266-267
Mom's Pumpkin Pie, 336
Moroccan Couscous, 285
Muffins
    Banana Bran Muffins, 64
    Beer Muffins, 65
    Corn-Tomato Muffins, 70
    Cornmeal Sugar-Coated Muffins, 69
    Honey-Wheat Muffins, 92
    Miniature Lemon Muffins, 73
    Pumpkin Muffins, 79
    Raspberry Muffins, 81
    Refrigerator Bran Muffins, 82
    See also Bread(s)
Multigrain Banana-Lemon Bread, 74
Mushroom(s)
    Marinated Mushrooms, 20
    Mom's Mushroom Stuffed Green Peppers, 266-267
    Mushroom Chowder, 36
Mushroom Chowder, 36

N

Nana's Sugar Cookies, 355
National Academy of Sciences, suggested daily calorie
    levels, xvii
National Cholesterol Education Program, recommended limits of cholesterol intake, xxi
Navy Bean Soup, 38
New Potatoes with Parsley, 304

No-Crust Broccoli Quiche, 264
No Red Meat (Shriver and Tinsley), xv, xxv

O

Oatmeal
    Down-Home Raisin-Oatmeal Cookies, 349
    John's Oatmeal Doodles, 354
    Mary's Oatmeal Molasses Bread, 90-91
    Oatmeal Cakes, 75
Oatmeal Cakes, 75
Okra
    Fried Okra-Sort of, 299
    Okra and Tomatoes, 300
Okra and Tomatoes, 300
Old-Fashioned Apricot Cookies, 343
Onion(s), Sweet Onion Casserole, 301
Orange(s)
    Mandarin Orange Dessert, 332
    Mandarin Orange Salad with Raspberry Vinaigrette, 115
    Orange Pancakes, 76
    Orange Sauce, 374
Yogurt a l'Orange, 342
Orange Pancakes, 76
Orange Sauce, 374
Oregano Vinegar, See Gourmet Herb Vinegar
Oriental Chicken Nibbles, 15
Oriental Scallops, 228-229
Oven-Fried Chicken, 155

P

Pancakes 'n' Fruit, 77
Pancakes
    Banana Pancakes, 63
    Oatmeal Cakes, 75
    Orange Pancakes, 76
    Pancakes 'n' Fruit, 77
    Rice Pancakes, 83
Parsley and Rice, 302
Pasta

Ann's Zucchini-Macaroni Soup, 55
Barbara's Pasta-Dijon Salad, 117
Broccoli / Cheese-Stuffed Manicotti, 262-263
Busy Day Goulash, 171
Creamy Chicken and Fettuccine, 169
Fresh Vegetables and Linguine, 258
Italian Vegetarian Soup, 50-51
Macaroni and Cheese, 260-261
Mediterranean Chicken with Pasta, 174-175
Pasta Seafood Italiano, 230
Penne with Fresh Vegetables and Marinara
Sauce, 259
Ravioli Soup, 39
Salmon-Pasta Salad, 120
Scallops and Asparagus with Linguine, 233
Tuna Macaroni Salad, 128
Pasta Seafood Italiano, 230
Pea(s)
Corn-Pea Salad, 103
Cucumber-Pea Salad, 109
English Pea Salad, 111
Peas and Carrots, 303
Split Pea Soup, 44
Peach(es)
Elegant Frosted Peaches, 329
Peach Pudding, 334
Peach Pudding, 334
Pear(s)
Baked Stuffed Pears, 325
Cranberry-Pear Compote, 367
Pear-Raspberry Salad, 118
Pear Melba, 335
Pear-Raspberry Salad, 118
Pear Melba, 335
Peas and Carrots, 303
Penne with Fresh Vegetables and Marinara Sauce,
259
Pepper(s), Mom's Mushroom-Stuffed Green
Peppers, 266-267
Peppermint Candy Sauce, 375

Pie(s)
Mom's Pumpkin Pie, 336
Vegetable and Rice Pie, 269
See also Quiche
See also Strudel
Pineapple, Caroline's Pineapple-Cranberry
Mousse, 119
Pineapple Sauce, 376
Piquant Sauce, 377
Plan Ahead Dinner (menu), 398
Pork
Pork Chops with Apples, 248
Sweet 'n' Sour Pork, 247
Pork Chops with Apples, 248
Potato(es)
Audrey's Green Beans and Red Potatoes, 196
Baked Potatoes with Chunky Chicken Topping,
187
Baked Potato Skins, 21
Broccoli Cheese-Stuffed Potato, 280
Creamed Potatoes, 288
Cream of Potato Soup, 40-41
Hash Brown Casserole, 293
International Oven Fries, 295
Italian Potato Salad, 113
Make-Ahead Potatoes, 277
Mashed Potatoes with Buttermilk, 298
Mom's Mashed Potatoes, 297
New Potatoes with Parsley, 304
Potato Bread, 85
Twice-Baked Potatoes, 278
Potato Bread, 85
Poultry
about, 143
See names of poultry
Pudding
Creamy Rice Pudding, 338
Fresh Fruit 'n' Pudding, 321
Mom's Bread Pudding, 333
Peach Pudding, 334

Pumpkin-Cranberry Tea Bread, 78
Pumpkin
Mom's Pumpkin Pie, 336
Pumpkin-Cranberry Tea Bread, 78
Pumpkin Muffins, 79
Pumpkin Muffins, 79

Q

Quiche
Fresh Vegetable and Crab Quiche, 239
Magic Vegetable Quiche, 265
No-Crust Broccoli Quiche, 264
Quick Dinner (menu), 402

R

Raisin French Toast, 80
Raspberry
Asparagus-Raspberry Salad, 95
Endive-Raspberry Salad with Raspberry
Vinaigrette, 110
Pear-Raspberry Salad, 118
Raspberry Muffins, 81
Raspberry Parfaits, 337
Raspberry Salad Dressing, 139
Raspberry Vinaigrette, 140
Raspberry Muffins, 81
Raspberry Parfaits, 337
Raspberry Salad Dressing, 139
Raspberry Vinaigrette, 140
Ravioli Soup, 39
Refrigerator Bran Muffins, 82
Rhubarb, Strawberries and Rhubarb, 341
Rice
Chestnut Brown Rice, 284
Chinese Fried Rice with Vegetables, 286-287
Creamy Rice Pudding, 338
Dirty Rice, 289
Golden Risotto, 292
Parsley and Rice, 302
Rice Pancakes, 83

Rice with Fresh Herbs, 305
Smoked Turkey Rice Salad, 122
Spanish Rice, 159
Tom's Fried Rice, 249
Twice Nice Rice, 314
Vegetable and Rice Pie, 269
White-Wild Rice Pilaf, 306
Rice Pancakes, 83
Rice with Fresh Herbs, 305
Rosemary Lemon Chicken, 158

**S**

Salad(s)
    about, 93-94
    Asparagus-Raspberry Salad, 95
    Asparagus-Tuna Salad, 96
    Asparagus and Tomatoes, 97
    Barbara's Pasta-Dijon Salad, 117
    Cabbage Waldorf, 98
    Caesar Salad, 99
    Caroline's Pineapple-Cranberry Mousse, 119
    Chicken-Stuffed Tomatoes, 101
    Chinese Salads, 100
    Citrus Salad with Orange Vinaigrette, 102
    Corn-Pea Salad, 103
    Couscous with Marinated Vegetables, 104
    Crab Salad, 105
    Cranberry Salad, 106
    Creamy Tomato and Cucumber Salad, 107
    Crunchy Oriental Turkey Salad, 108
    Cucumber-Pea Salad, 109
    Endive-Raspberry Salad with Raspberry Vinaigrette, 110
    English Pea Salad, 111
    Fruit Salad with Lemon-Honey Dressing, 112
    Italian Potato Salad, 113
    Lemony Cucumber and Onions, 114
    Mandarin Orange Salad with Raspberry Vinaigrette, 115
    Marinated Cucumbers and Tomatoes, 116

Pear-Raspberry Salad, 118
Salmon-Pasta Salad, 120
Smoked Chicken with Cantaloupe, 121
Smoked Turkey Rice Salad, 122
Spaghetti Squash—Sun-Dried Tomatoes, 123
Sweet-Tart Marinated Vegetables, 124
Tabouli Salad, 125
Tomato Squash Basil, 126
Tropical Salad, 127
Tuna Macaroni Salad, 128
Salad dressings
    Basil Buttermilk Dressing, 129
    Berry-Flavored Vinegar, 131
    Buttermilk-Garlic Creamy Dressing, 133
    Creamy Basil Dressing, 130
    Creamy French Dressing, 134
    Festive Italian Vinegar, 135
    Gourmet Herb Vinegar, 135
    Herb Vinaigrette Dressing, 136
    Honey-Mustard Creamy Dressing, 137
    Honey-Mustard Vinaigrette, 138
    Mexican Fiesta Vinegar, 135
    Raspberry Salad Dressing, 139
    Raspberry Vinaigrette, 140
    Soft Berry Vinegar, 132
Salem's Sunshine Chicken, 200
Salmon-Pasta Salad, 120
Salmon
    Grilled Salmon Filet, 221
    Salmon-Pasta Salad, 120
    Salmon Dip, 11
    Smoked Salmon Cheese Spread, 22
Salmon Dip, 11
Salsa, 378
San Carlos Seafood, 232
Sassy Clam Dip, 4
Sauce(s)
    about, 363
    Blueberry Sauce, 365
    Cinnamon Sauce, 366

Cranberry-Pear Compote, 367
Creamy Yogurt Sauce, 368
Custard Sauce, 369
Dijon Mustard Sauce, 370
Evelena's Italian Meat Sauce, 372-373
Gingerbread Sauce, 371
Orange Sauce, 374
Peppermint Candy Sauce, 375
Pineapple Sauce, 376
Piquant Sauce, 377
Salsa, 378
Sour Cream-Caramel Sauce, 379
White Sauce, 380
Sauerkraut and Sausage Casserole, 201
Sausage-Basil and Wine, 202
Scallop(s)
    Broiled Scallops in Wine, 234
    Oriental Scallops, 228-229
    Scallop and Chicken Kabobs, 231
    Scallops and Asparagus with Linguine, 233
Scallop and Chicken Kabobs, 231
Scalloped Cauliflower, 307
Scalloped Zucchini, 308
Scallops and Asparagus with Linguine, 233
Scotty's Lemon Filets, 235
Seafood
    about, 207
    Asparagus-Tuna Salad, 96
    Baked Crabmeat Dip, 5
    Baked Fried Fish, 209
    Barbecued Catfish, 210
    Betty's Crabmeat Dip, 3
    Brenda's Grilled Fish, 211
    Broiled Scallops in Wine, 234
    Cajun Seafood Gumbo, 42-43
    Crab-Stuffed Flounder, 214
    Crab Au Gratin, 212-213
    Crab Salad, 105
    Crispy Baked Fish, 215
    Filet Dijon, 216

Fresh Vegetable and Crab Quiche, 239
Green-Topped Flounder, 220
Grilled Fish with Vegetable Kabobs, 217
Grilled Salmon Filet, 221
Halibut Italian Style, 222
Mardi Gras Filet, 226-227
Marlin in Wine Sauce, 225
Oriental Scallops, 228-229
Pasta Seafood Italiano, 230
Salmon-Pasta Salad, 120
Salmon Dip, 11
San Carlos Seafood, 232
Sassy Clam Dip, 4
Scallop and Chicken Kabobs, 231
Scallops and Asparagus with Linguine, 233
Scotty's Lemon Filets, 235
Shrimp and Vegetable Kabobs, 240
Shrimp Dip Ole, 12
Shrimp Stir-Fry, 236-237
Smoked Salmon Cheese Spread, 22
Spicy Baked Fish, 238
Triple Lemon Filets, 223
Tuna Macaroni Salad, 128
White Fish Baked in Orange Sauce, 218-219
White Fish with Lemon Stuffing, 224
See also names of various seafood
Serving, what counts as a, xx
Shortening, substitute for in fat reduction, xxviii
Shrimp
    Shrimp and Vegetable Kabobs, 240
    Shrimp Dip Ole, 12
    Shrimp Stir-Fry, 236-237
Shrimp and Vegetable Kabobs, 240
Shrimp Dip Ole, 12
Shrimp Stir-Fry, 236-237
Small Intimate Lunch for a Guest (menu), 397
Smoked Chicken with Cantaloupe, 121
Smoked Salmon Cheese Spread, 22
Smoked Turkey Rice Salad, 122
Snacks

Apricot-Cheese Spread, 16
Baked Potato Skins, 21
Cucumber-Stuffed Tomatoes, 17
Curry-Stuffed Tomatoes, 18
Deviled Eggs, 19
Garlic-Herb Spread, 16
Marinated Mushrooms, 20
Mexican Spread, 16
Smoked Salmon Cheese Spread, 22
Trash Nibblers, 23
See also Appetizer(s)
Soft Berry Vinegar, 132
Somebody's Carrots, 309
Soup(s)
    about, 25
    Ann's Zucchini-Macaroni Soup, 55
    Bonnie's Jambalaya, 27
    Brunswick Stew, 28-29
    Cajun Seafood Gumbo, 42-43
    Carrot Soup, 57
    Chicken Vegetable Soup, 30
    cold, 56, 57, 58, 59
    Cold Cantaloupe Soup, 56
    cream of celery, substitute for in fat reduction, xxix
    cream of chicken, substitute for in fat reduction, xxix
    Cream of Corn Soup, 31
    cream of mushroom, substitute for in fat reduction, xxix
    Cream of Potato Soup, 40-41
    Cream of Tomato Soup, 45
    Cucumber-Yogurt Soup, 58
    Gazpacho, 59
    Ground Beef Stew, 33
    Hearty Lentil Soup, 34
    Italian Vegetarian Soup, 50-51
    Judy's Chalupa Soupa, 32
    Meatball Stew, 35
    Mixed Bean Soup, 37

    Mushroom Chowder, 36
    Navy Bean Soup, 38
    Ravioli Soup, 39
    Split Pea Soup, 44
    Tortilla Soup, 46-47
    Turkey Stew, 48-49
    Vegetable and Bean Soup, 52
    White Chili, 53
    Zucchini-Buttermilk Soup, 54
Sour Cream-Caramel Sauce, 379
Sour cream, substitute for in fat reduction, xxviii
South of the Border Dinner (menu), 405
Southwest Brunch (menu), 405
Spaghetti Squash—Sun-Dried Tomatoes, 123
Spanish Omelette, 268
Spanish Rice, 159
Special Company Dinner (menu), 400
Spice(s)
    about
    allspice, 387
    cardamon, 387
    cinnamon, 387
    cloves, 387
    curry, 387
    ginger, 387
    nutmeg, 387
    paprika, 387
    turmeric, 387
    vanilla, 387
Spiced Carrots, 310
Spicy Baked Fish, 238
Spicy Beef Stew, 243
Spicy Chicken Kabobs, 166
Spicy Smoked Turkey Dip, 13
Split Pea Soup, 44
Spread(s)
    Apricot-Cheese Spread, 16
    Garlic-Herb Spread, 16
    Mexican Spread, 16
    Smoked Salmon Cheese Spread, 22

Squash
    Glorified Acorn Squash, 291
    Spaghetti Squash—Sun-Dried Tomatoes, 123
    Stuffed Cheyote Squash, 311
    Tomato Squash Basil, 126
Stew(s)
    Brunswick Stew, 28-29
    Ground Beef Stew, 33
    Meatball Stew, 35
    Spicy Beef Stew, 243
    Turkey Stew, 48-49
    See also Soup(s)
Stir-Fry Dinner (menu), 400
Strawberries and Rhubarb, 341
Strawberry
    Strawberries and Rhubarb, 341
    Strawberry Cake, 356
    Strawberry Romanoff, 340
    Sugar-Free Strawberry Mousse, 339
Strawberry Cake, 356
Strawberry Romanoff, 340
Strudel, Sweet Potato Strudel, 312
Stuffed Cheyote Squash, 311
Substitutions for common ingredients (table),
    389-391, xxviii-xxix
Sugar-Free Strawberry Mousse, 339
Summer's Bounty (menu), 403
Summer's Special Jell-O Cake, 357
Summer Cookout (menu), 402
Sunday Supper (menu), 405
Supper After the Board Meeting (menu), 404
Supper After the Ice Skating Party (menu), 404
Supper in a Hurry (menu), 404
Sweet 'n' Sour Pork, 247
Sweet-Tart Marinated Vegetables, 124
Sweet Onion Casserole, 301
Sweet Potato(es), Sweet Potato Strudel, 312
Sweet Potato Strudel, 312

T
Tabouli Salad, 125
Tex-Mex Buffet for Guests (menu), 406
Tex-Mex Sausage-Chili-Cheese Casserole, 179
Tom's Fried Rice, 249
Tomato(es)
    Asparagus and Tomatoes, 97
    Baked Tomatoes Dijon, 279
    Chicken-Stuffed Tomatoes, 101
    Chicken Sun-Dried Tomato Stir-Fry, 168
    Corn-Tomato Muffins, 70
    Cream of Tomato Soup, 45
    Creamy Tomato and Cucumber Salad, 107
    Cucumber-Stuffed Tomatoes, 17
    Curry-Stuffed Tomatoes, 18
    Hungarian Chicken with Dried Tomatoes, 152
    Lima Bean-Tomato Treat, 296
    Marinated Cucumbers and Tomatoes, 116
    Okra and Tomatoes, 300
    Salsa, 378
    Spaghetti Squash—Sun-Dried Tomatoes, 123
    Tomato Squash Basil, 126
Tomato Squash Basil, 126
Tortilla(s)
    Chicken Chalupas, 177
    Chicken Tortilla Casserole, 180-181
    Judy's Chalupa Soupa, 32
    Lisa's Tortilla Rolls, 14
    Tortilla Soup, 46-47
    Turkey-Corn Burritos, 182-183
Tortilla Soup, 46-47
Trans-fatty acids, xxii
Trash Nibblers, 23
Triple Lemon Filets, 223
Tropical Salad, 127
Tuna
    Asparagus-Tuna Salad, 96
    Tuna Macaroni Salad, 128
Turkey-Corn Burritos, 182-183

Turkey-Ham and Cheese Omelet, 206
Turkey
    Audrey's Green Beans and Red Potatoes, 196
    Busy Day Goulash, 171
    Crunchy Oriental Turkey Salad, 108
    Glazed Turkey Breast, 150
    Hearty Lentil Soup, 34
    Judy's Chalupa Soupa, 32
    Lemon/Basil-Stuffed Turkey Tenderloins, 204-
    205
    Meatball Stew, 35
    Mexican Turkey in a Pot, 184
    Sauerkraut and Sausage Casserole, 201
    Sausage-Basil and Wine, 202
    Smoked Turkey Rice Salad, 122
    Spicy Smoked Turkey Dip, 13
    Tex-Mex Sausage-Chili-Cheese Casserole, 179
    Turkey-Corn Burritos, 182-183
    Turkey-Ham and Cheese Omelet, 206
    Turkey Cutlets in Mushroom Sauce, 203
    Turkey Cutlets in Tomato-Wine Sauce, 161
    Turkey Stew, 48-49
Turkey Cutlets in Mushroom Sauce, 203
Turkey Cutlets in Tomato-Wine Sauce, 161
Turkey Stew, 48-49
Twice-Baked Potatoes, 278
Twice Nice Rice, 314

U

United States Department of Agriculture, See
    USDA
USDA
    developed Food Guide Pyramid, xvii
    study of trans-fatty acids, xxii

V

Veal, Veal Cutlets, 245
Veal Cutlets, 245
Vegetable and Bean Soup, 52
Vegetable and Rice Pie, 269

Vegetable Medley, 315
Vegetables
    about, 275
    Baked Tomatoes Dijon, 279
    Broccoli Cheese-Stuffed Potato, 280
    California Carrots, 281
    Carrot Zucchini Sauté, 282
    Cauliflower 'n' Cheese, 283
    Chestnut Brown Rice, 284
    Chinese Fried Rice with Vegetables, 286-287
    Creamed Potatoes, 288
    Dirty Rice, 289
    Fried Okra-Sort of, 299
    Garlicky Green Beans, 290
    Glorified Acorn Squash, 291
    Golden Risotto, 292
    Hash Brown Casserole, 293
    Herbs 'n' Green Beans, 294
    International Oven Fries, 295
    Judy's Southwestern Vegetables, 313
    Lima Bean-Tomato Treat, 296
    Make-Ahead Potatoes, 277
    Mashed Potatoes with Buttermilk, 298
    Mom's Mashed Potatoes, 297
    Moroccan Couscous, 285
    New Potatoes with Parsley, 304
    Okra and Tomatoes, 300
    Parsley and Rice, 302
    Peas and Carrots, 303
    Rice with Fresh Herbs, 305
    Scalloped Cauliflower, 307
    Scalloped Zucchini, 308
    Somebody's Carrots, 309
    Spiced Carrots, 310
    Stuffed Cheyote Squash, 311
    Sweet Onion Casserole, 301
    Sweet Potato Strudel, 312
    Twice-Baked Potatoes, 278
    Twice Nice Rice, 314

Vegetable Medley, 315
    White-Wild Rice Pilaf, 306
    Zucchini-Balsamic Vinegar, 316
    Zucchini Sour Cream Bake, 317
    Zucchini with Marjoram, 318
    See also names of vegetables
Vegetarian Lunch (menu), 397
Venison, Venison Sauerbraten, 250-251
Venison Sauerbraten, 250-251

## W

Weeknight Dinner (menu), 399
White-Wild Rice Pilaf, 306
White Chili, 53
White Fish Baked in Orange Sauce, 218-219
White Fish with Lemon Stuffing, 224
White Sauce, 380

## Y

Yeast bread(s), See Bread(s), yeast
Yogurt
    Brandied Yogurt, 328
    Creamy Yogurt Sauce, 368
    Creme de Cassis-Yogurt Dip, 6
    Cucumber-Yogurt Soup, 58
    Fruit and Yogurt Cup, 331
Yogurt a l'Orange, 342
Yogurt a l'Orange, 342

## Z

Zucchini-Balsamic Vinegar, 316
Zucchini-Barley Mexicali, 270-271
Zucchini-Buttermilk Soup, 54
Zucchini-Lemon Bread, 84
Zucchini
    Ann's Zucchini-Macaroni Soup, 55
    Carrot Zucchini Sauté, 282
    Chicken Zucchini Crisp, 148

Scalloped Zucchini, 308
Zucchini-Balsamic Vinegar, 316
Zucchini-Barley Mexicali, 270-271
Zucchini-Buttermilk Soup, 54
Zucchini-Lemon Bread, 84
Zucchini Parmesan, 272-273
Zucchini Sour Cream Bake, 317
Zucchini with Marjoram, 318
Zucchini Parmesan, 272-273
Zucchini Sour Cream Bake, 317
Zucchini with Marjoram, 318